THE EUROPEAN CORPORATION

The European Corporation

Strategy, Structure, and Social Science

RICHARD WHITTINGTON

and

MICHAEL MAYER

OXFORD

UNIVERSITY PRESS

OXFORD

UNIVERSITY PRESS

Great Clarendon Street, Oxford OX2 6DP

Oxford University Press is a department of the University of Oxford.
It furthers the University's objective of excellence in research, scholarship,
and education by publishing worldwide in

Oxford New York

Athens Auckland Bangkok Bogotá Buenos Aires Calcutta
Cape Town Chennai Dar es Salaam Delhi Florence Hong Kong Istanbul
Karachi Kuala Lumpur Madrid Melbourne Mexico City Mumbai
Nairobi Paris São Paulo Shanghai Singapore Taipei Tokyo Toronto Warsaw

with associated companies in Berlin Ibadan

Oxford is a registered trade mark of Oxford University Press
in the UK and in certain other countries

Published in the United States
by Oxford University Press Inc., New York

© Richard Whittington and Michael Mayer, 2000
The moral rights of the author have been asserted

Database right Oxford University Press (maker)

First published 2000

British Library Cataloguing in Publication Data

Data available

Library of Congress Cataloging in Publication Data

Data available

ISBN 0-19-924208-9

1 3 5 7 9 10 8 6 4 2

Typeset by Best-set Typesetter Ltd., Hong Kong
Printed in Great Britain
on acid-free paper by
T.J. International Ltd.,
Padstow, Cornwall

For

Maria, Georgina, and Richard

and

Hildegard and Jean

Acknowledgements

International projects require a lot of support, and we have been fortunate in the very many kinds we have been given.

We received a great deal of useful advice at the outset of the project from four key members of the original Harvard team whose work we are extending —Derek Channon, Gareth Dyas, Richard Rumelt, and Heinz Thanheiser. Francesco Curto worked for a year as research assistant on the project, and continued afterwards to give help in many ways. Than-hà Le provided invaluable research assistance also, filling in data gaps in France. Richard found an excellent base at Groupe HEC for a year, and would like to thank especially Daniel Barraud de Lagérie, Georges Blanc, Laurence Capron, Pierre Dussauge, and Frédéric LeRoy for their help and welcome. Michael would like to thank Karl Morasch, Anton Sigllechner, and Oliver Steinbach for similar support in Germany.

Many other people gave us advice, commented on papers, and generally provided important stimulation as we continued: here we would mention particularly Youssef Cassis, Kirsteen Daly, Marie-Laure Djelic, Moira Fischbacher, Anna Grandori, Leslie Hannah, Neil Kay, Colin Mayer, John McGee, Robert MacIntosh, Donald MacLean, Doug Orton, Arndt Sorge, Ken Starkey, and Howard Thomas. Our ideas were much influenced by participants in the INNFORM project on innovative forms of organizing, notably Evelyn Fenton and Andrew Pettigrew, but also Arie Lewin, Leif Melin, Simon Peck, Carlos Sanchez-Runde, Winfried Ruigrok, and Frans van den Bosch. Richard Whitley provided much of the original inspiration for the project, and the EMOT (European Management and Organizations in Transition) programme of workshops which he organized provided us with a superb frame for developing our ideas as well as an opportunity to learn from many other scholars across Europe. Participants in other workshops, conferences, and seminars at Aston, ESSEC, the London School of Economics, Manchester Business School, the University of Gothenburg, the Science Policy Research Unit, the Academy of Management, the British Academy of Management, the European Group for Organization Studies, and the Strategic Management Society all helped us to sort out our ideas. Ray Loveridge found himself listening to our presentations at these events with remarkable frequency. We would like to thank him for his fortitude and especially for his important comments on the first draft of our manuscript. We remain responsible for remaining errors of fact or judgement.

Essential material support was provided by the Economic and Social Research Council (r000221420), the Nuffield Foundation, and Warwick Business School. We would like to acknowledge the library resources and staff at the

Bayerische Staatsbibliothek, the Paris Chamber of Commerce, Groupe HEC, Crédit Lyonnais, the Saïd Business School, Templeton College, and the Universities of Augsburg, Oxford, and Warwick. Warwick Business School was our original base and provided Richard with an essential sabbatical year at the outset of the project. The Department of Management at the University of Glasgow and New College at the University of Oxford have since provided us with necessary and congenial infrastructures for completion. David Musson, our editor with the Oxford University Press, has been very patient, as well as feeding in useful references and gentle suggestions at various points.

Our families and friends have been patient and supportive throughout. Richard would like to thank particularly Maria, Georgina, and young Richard (who was not even a twinkle when we started, but is now a strapping 4-year old), and Michael would like to thank his parents, Hildegard and Jean.

Richard Whittington
New College, Oxford

Michael Mayer,
University of Glasgow
February, 2000

Contents

List of Illustrations

List of Figures

List of Tables

1

Change, Context, and the Corporation

INTRODUCTION

This book traces the largest industrial corporations of France, Germany, and the United Kingdom over more than forty years, from post-war recovery to the last decade of the twentieth century. We shall follow these top European firms as they adopt, and sometimes abandon, new corporate strategies and as they develop new organizational structures to cope with these strategies. With this perspective on the post-war period, we shall be able to take the long view on changing management theory and practice in three diverse yet increasingly connected European countries. Over this period, business in each country has undergone major economic, political, and technological transformations, at the same time as having been subject to the lurching fashions of management theory. But underneath these fluctuations, we shall find that Europe's top industrial firms have followed a steady and parallel path in terms of both strategy and structure. Plotting this path can illuminate at least three sets of important questions—questions about economic performance, about international integration, and about the proper scope of the social sciences.

The first set of questions concerns the most effective strategies and structures for large industrial firms in advanced economies. This book will follow the rise of the large diversified corporation as the dominant actor in post-war European industry. Particularly controversial here is the conglomerate diversification strategy that emerged in the 1960s and 1970s, exemplified by companies such as Hanson in Britain and ITT in the United States. These aggressive strategies of diversification into unrelated businesses—for Hanson from bricks to energy, for ITT from manufacturing to hotels—were justified then in terms of growth and financial discipline. Since the 1980s, however, the conglomerate has fallen out of fashion and the Anglo-Saxon propensity for unrelated diversification is even blamed for British and American relative industrial decline. How viable, then, is the conglomerate strategy of unrelated diversification and what, if any, pattern of diversification is appropriate for large industrial firms?

The leading business historian Alfred Chandler (1962) was the first to urge that structure should follow strategy. As European firms became increasingly diversified over the post-war years, so they also adopted the multidivisional structure pioneered by such large American corporations as DuPont and General Motors. We shall examine how great European holding companies—such as Schneider in France and Guttehoffnungshütte in Germany—gradually reformed their tangled webs of subsidiaries into clearly structured divisions, with increased strategic control and tighter operational accountability. Again, though, fashions change. The multidivisional structure is increasingly accused of short-sighted detachment from the realities of value creation, and of being too obsessed with control to adapt to the networked economy of the contemporary world. Once the pinnacle of organizational design, the multidivisional is now in doubt. As we look back on structural trends over more than forty years, we shall be able to consider the long-term performance of the multidivisional structure in the changing conditions of post-war advanced economies.

Our main story of post-war strategic and structural change in Europe sheds light on the two other sets of questions as well. The first is the extent to which principles of corporate strategy and organization are now common in advanced economies. The initial surge of European diversification and divisionalization occurred during the 1950s and 1960s, a time of overwhelming American political and economic hegemony. Diversified strategies and divisional structures were very much 'made in the USA'. At this stage, the diversified, divisionalized model of management was sold to European economic and political élites with little regard for the diverse and complex industrial traditions of each nation. From the 1970s onwards, however, resurgent European and Japanese industries challenged American economic power and Japan replaced the United States as the model for effective management. As the relative position of the United States has waned, to what extent have European nations been able to throw off the American model of management, and even to reassert distinct national traditions of industrial strategy and organization? By mapping strategic and structural change in three quite different European economies over the whole post-war period, we shall shed light on whether early diversification and divisionalization reflected just a transitory American dominance or more enduring principles of corporate management. We shall also find whether European corporations are now marching in step or still clinging to distinct national traditions.

Behind the original surge of diversification and divisionalization in post-war Europe was a new kind of social science, confident in the universality of principles drawn largely from the experience of the United States. Industrial societies were converging. The social scientific celebration of rationality and generalizability, managerialism and decentralization during the 1950s and 1960s supported the notion of the diversified, divisionalized corporation. It provided the intellectual underpinnings to a new industry, the business school industry, accelerated by the foundation of INSEAD in France and the London and Manchester Business Schools in Britain. This was an ambitious intellectual project, and with the end of immediate post-war economic growth, seen widely

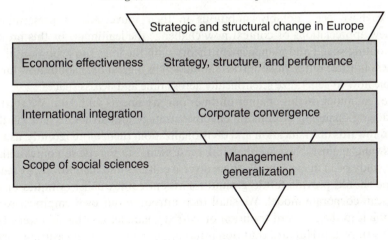

Figure 1.1. *Key Themes*

as naïve. Postmodern relativism asserts itself against the grand narratives of convergence and universality. The possibility of creating a social science capable of prescribing managerial practices over time and across boundaries is now widely rejected (Clegg, 1990). As we trace the strategies and structures of large firms over more than four decades and across three distinct national traditions, we shall be able to judge the enduring and transferable nature of early prescriptions in the face of postmodern relativism, economic transformations, and sustained national differences. At stake here will be the prospects for robust generalization within the management sciences as a whole.

In short, this book is about strategic and structural change among the largest industrial firms in post-war Europe. This is history with purpose. The inverted pyramid of Figure 1.1 illustrates the three main issues we shall be addressing. First, and above all, the careful tracking of strategy and structure over nearly half a century should tell us a good deal about economic effectiveness. We shall see which strategies and which structures succeed over long periods of time, and how far economic advantages are standard across different national contexts. This historical tracking takes us to the second issue, one level deeper. Following the evolution of large European firms over the post-war period allows us to reflect on international economic integration. We shall see the extent to which European corporations are converging on a single model, whether European or American, or rather still following distinct national patterns. Finally, still further down the pyramid, the evolution of big business in Europe gives us a cut into the nature of social scientific knowledge at the turn of the century. The growth of big business has not only taken centre stage in many debates within the established social sciences, but also stimulated a new discipline entirely, the management sciences. As taught in business schools around the world, the management sciences have been notably ambitious in their universalizing prescriptions. But new appreciations of context now challenge the legitimacy of this project. Confronting social and management theory with the long-run evolution of big business in three different countries should tell us a great deal about how far we are able now to generalize scientifically across time and across space.

The remainder of this chapter outlines our arguments and data. We start by introducing changing notions of effective strategy and structure, first as they moved towards diversification and divisionalization, then, more recently, as they have swung against. Next, we shall link these swings to the rise of contextualism in the study of management. With its diverse cultures and institutions, post-war Europe should provide fertile ground for recent contextualist critiques of the American corporate model. We shall then introduce our own empirical work, situating it in the Harvard tradition of Alfred Chandler and his followers. One great merit of this Harvard tradition is its common metric for measuring corporate development across time and countries. We shall finish by summarizing our findings and our argument. Briefly, the original model will have to be amended in detail, but broadly European business has moved towards the same pattern of diversified, divisionalized business as pioneered in the United States in the 1920s and endorsed by American business schools in the 1960s. The trend is common across borders and steady in the face of passing fashions and the rise and fall of American hegemony. We shall not claim a final and universal answer to the problem of the corporation, but within our particular sphere the examples of pre-war American business and the prescriptions of post-war American academia have proved remarkably robust. Between the extremes of universalism and contextualism, we conclude for the value of a modestly generalizing social science of management.

1.1. CHANGING STRATEGIES AND STRUCTURES

For Alfred Chandler (1997), the United States' grip on world economic leadership in the last century relied on the success of American businessmen in building and managing the first large-scale industrial enterprises. During the early twentieth century, men like Irénée du Pont at the chemical company DuPont and Alfred Sloan at General Motors created a model of large-scale, multi-business, and rationally organized enterprise that rapidly superseded the small specialized businesses and rambling holding companies that had prevailed before. This was an epochal transformation. As Chandler (1977: 455) says, an American businessman of the 1840s would be more at home in the environment of fifteenth-century Italy than in the business world of the early twentieth century. And this transformation has had enormous effects. The new industrial giants buttressed American economic leadership through their massive economies of scale, their capacity for organizational learning, their stimulus to suppliers and customers, and their huge investments in research and development (Chandler and Hikino, 1997). As first-movers in building large-scale enterprise in a range of industries from automobiles to computers, the United States still accounted for nearly a third—160—of the world's 500 largest industrial enterprises in 1993 (Chandler and Hikino, 1997: 53).

For Chandler (1962), the key strategy by which these great corporations were built was one of diversification. The essential structure by which they were managed was the multidivisional. In his stylized account of the changing corporation of the twentieth century, these two elements are logically linked in a steady ascent through four successive stages—or 'chapters'—of corporate development. These four chapters start with the entrepreneurial stage of initial expansion and accumulation of resources; continue to the rationalization of these resources within centralized functional structures; move next to diversification, the full use of resources through expansion into new products and markets; and then finally cumulate with adoption of the multidivisional structure in order to ensure the efficient exploitation of the corporation's now more diversified resources (Chandler, 1962: 386–96). The diversified, divisionalized corporation is the pinnacle: Chandler has not added a fifth chapter. Yet, as we shall see, the diversified, divisionalized corporation is now under pressure to change again. This section outlines the phenomena of diversification and divisionalization, at the same time as introducing some recent challenges. The underlying theoretical issues will be developed further in Chapters 2 and 3, but here we shall provide enough for hard-pressed readers to pass on directly to the empirical material starting in Chapter 4.

Diversification strategies

It is a remarkable thing to the observer—and a problem for the economist—that the world's largest industrial enterprise (by assets) and America's most admired corporation is a diversified conglomerate with interests stretching from aircraft engines to domestic appliances, life insurance to broadcasting (www.fortune.com: 2 April 1999). General Electric was one of the great first-movers in American industry. Incorporated in 1892 as a power company, it rapidly diversified into chemicals, medical equipment, and domestic appliances during the first decades of the twentieth century (Chandler, 1990: 212–21). For Chandler (1990), General Electric's early diversification strategy was a logical one, exploiting market and technological relationships to its original core business. Domestic appliances used parts and expertise developed in power generation, as well as increasing the market for electricity. Research on vacuum tubes led to the pioneering manufacture of X-ray equipment. Expertise acquired in the insulation of electrical wiring and the moulding of carbon for light bulbs brought General Electric into plastics, new varnishes, lacquers, and adhesives. All these were examples of 'related diversification', making more efficient use of

the firm's existing resources by extending them over a range of adjacent products and markets. By the end of the 1950s, related diversification was the most
prevalent form of strategy among large American corporations (Rumelt, 1974)
and it remained important at least into the 1980s (Markides, 1995).

More problematic for Chandler (1990) is the rise of 'unrelated diversification',
as exemplified by General Electric's more recent moves into quite remote industries, such as broadcasting and life insurance. This kind of move has no place in
Chandler's (1962) original four chapters. Unrelated diversification may bring
growth but the linkages allowing for more efficient use of resources appear
far more tenuous. For Chandler (1990), conglomerate diversification lacks a
convincing economic rationale and the increasing adoption of this strategy in
the United States during the 1960s and 1970s was a substantial contributor
to American relative industrial decline in this period. Related diversification
produced efficiency; unrelated diversification is a step too far.

Chandler's (1990) reaction against the apparent excesses of the conglomerate
is in tune with business thinking more widely over the last decade or so.
Chandler (1990: 627) himself took heart from the wave of divestitures and buy-
outs that swept the United States during the 1980s onwards. Great old conglomerates such as ITT, AT&T, and Westinghouse have been either breaking
themselves up or shrinking to new cores. This new thinking is crystallized by
Prahalad and Hamel's (1990) seminal article on 'The Core Competence of the
Corporation'. Here the model is no longer American, but Japanese. The new
exemplars are companies such as Canon, Honda, and NEC, each diversified yet
still focused on their 'core competences'. These core competences—'the collective learning in the organization' (Prahalad and Hamel, 1990: 82)—are the roots
which nourish all the various business units of the enterprise. The Japanese art is
to consolidate corporate-wide technologies and skills and leverage them fast
into new products and markets. As this insight became formalized into the new
strategic orthodoxy of the 'resource-based view' of the firm, the theoretical case
against the conglomerate has hardened. In the resource-based view, only related
diversification is now allowed economic merit, for the conglomerate is too
diffuse either to possess corporate-wide resources or to deploy them effectively
(Teece, Pisano, and Shuen, 1997: 529).

The multidivisional structure

Diversification—at least the right sort of diversification—may have created the
modern industrial enterprise, but these economic mammoths still have to be
managed. Chandler (1962: 314) classically stated the problem thus: 'Unless
structure follows strategy, inefficiency results.' The diversification of DuPont
and General Motors in the first part of the century nearly brought both firms to
collapse. The problem was organization, not strategy. DuPont was too centralized to cope with diversification; General Motors too decentralized. The solution at both firms was the same. At General Motors in 1920 Alfred Sloan

rationalized the hodgepodge of subsidiaries acquired by entrepreneurial founder William Durant into a set of coherent product divisions organized around such famous names as Cadillac, Olds, Chevrolet, and Buick. The next year at DuPont, Irénée du Pont replaced the old structure centralized on functions such as sales and production with divisions based on product lines such as explosives, dyestuffs, and paints. These multidivisional structures adopted at the beginning of the 1920s remain the basis on which DuPont and General Motors are still organized today (see Figure 1.2 comparing DuPont in 1919, 1921, and 1999). As Chandler (1962) and Rumelt (1974) show, the multidivisional structure spread rapidly throughout American industry.

The strength of the multidivisional structure lies in its capacity to deal with scale and complexity by separating strategy from operations. Operational decisions are decentralized to divisions; strategy and resource allocation are controlled from the centre. Chandler (1962: 309) puts it thus: 'The basic reason for

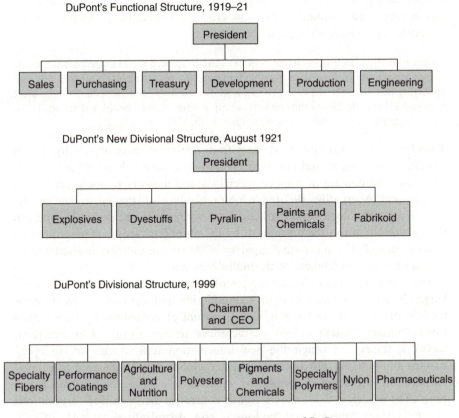

Figure 1.2. *The Changing Structures of DuPont*

Sources: Adapted from Chandler (1962); Data Handbook, DuPont, Wilmington DE (1999); Fortune Magazine, 26, April 1999

its [the multidivisional's] success was simply that it clearly removed the executives responsible for the destiny of the entire enterprise from the more routine operational activities, and so gave them the time, information, and even psychological commitment for long-term planning and appraisal'. It is this decentralization of operations and centralization of strategy that makes the large-scale, diversified corporation possible. Economist Oliver Williamson (1971: 382) acclaimed the multidivisional structure (for him the M-form) as 'American capitalism's most important single innovation of the twentieth century'.

Divisionalization has attracted the same kind of reaction as that against conglomerate diversification and for some similar reasons. The liability of the multidivisional is manifest in its very name: 'divisions divide' (Ghoshal and Bartlett, 1995). For Prahalad and Hamel (1990), the fragmentation of the corporation into discrete, accountable quasi-firms militates against the construction and mobilization of corporate-wide core competences. American business has fallen prey to 'the tyranny of the SBU': the operating businesses in which real value is created are reduced to strategic business units, mere pawns to be moved across the portfolio matrices of the corporate chessboard. As corporations continued to diversify, even Chandler (1990) saw cracks emerging in the multidivisional structure. Excessive diversification brought

a separation, that is a breakdown of communication between top management at the corporate office—the executives responsible for coordinating, managing, and planning and allocating resources for the enterprise as a whole—and the middle managers who were responsible for maintaining the competitive capabilities of the operating divisions in the battle for market share and profits. (Chandler, 1990: 623)

Where once the separation of strategy from operations gave objectivity, now it threatens detachment and isolation. The multidivisional head-office becomes too easily the domain of finance specialists and industry-hopping generalists (Hayes and Abernathy, 1980). Uncomprehending of the intricacies of the underlying technologies and markets, the new financial and generalist élite can do no more than run the businesses 'by the numbers'. This is management by remote control. The innovative capacity of American industry is shattered by the fragmenting detachment of the multidivisional.

The multidivisional's old advantages of segmentation are particularly challenged by the changing nature of economic life and the rise of new business models, often Asian. In his magisterial account of contemporary transformations, Manuel Castells (1996) characterizes today's world as an emergent 'network society' in which the new information technologies are sweeping nations and markets into an interconnected global web. Large-scale, integrated corporations are being challenged by what Castells terms the 'network enterprise'. The models now are not the tightly controlled divisionalized corporations of smoke-stack America, but the loosely knit, decentralized networks of subcontractors, joint-ventures, and alliances found in Chinese family business,

Japanese *keiretsus*, and California hi-tech. These kinds of networks have the flexibility to respond quickly to dynamic markets and to co-opt new partners. The multidivisional, with its elevation of strategy and its obsession with control, is too slow to move and too unwilling to share. Castells (1996: 191) concludes that traditional visions of the enterprise 'are outdated and should be replaced by the emergence of international networks of firms as the basic organisational form of the informational/global economy'.

To summarize: one of the twentieth century's greatest achievements was the creation of great industrial corporations capable of massive investments in research and development and the production and marketing of goods and services around the world. These corporations have been critical to American economic power and global reach. The bases for this achievement were diversification and divisionalization. On the Chandlerian model, the corporation gains efficiency from the full use of resources through scale and diversification, and handles the resulting complexity through the operational decentralization of the multidivisional structure. A key task for this book will be to trace the extent to which European business in the post-war period has been able to follow the same kinds of diversification strategies and adopt similar kinds of structures as the great American corporations such as DuPont, General Electric, and General Motors.

But the recipes developed by these great corporations in the first three-quarters of the twentieth century are now under challenge. Diversification led eventually to the apparent excesses of the conglomerate. The objectivity and order of the multidivisional degenerated too often into remote, numbers-driven inflexibility. American business itself is challenging the conglomerate and experimenting with new models. The source of inspiration is no longer unquestioningly American, but often Asian and especially Japanese. How has European business responded to this crisis of the American lodestone and the emergence of new, alternative models? The answers will unfold in the following chapters, as we trace the extent to which Europe may have reversed its conglomerate excesses—if any—and renewed its traditional corporate structures.

1.2. THE CORPORATION IN CONTEXT

The rise of Japan and the fall of the United States during the 1970s and 1980s did more than challenge the economics of the American diversified, divisionalized corporation. It also helped to change how people thought about big business. To many eyes, Japan succeeded precisely because it ignored the American model of management. American practices suddenly seemed dated. It appeared that success no longer derived from timeless universals, but that fashion and country could define very different ways of working. In thinking about big business, issues of time and territory became important. Theorists of big business began to take context seriously.

Chandler had assumed that the diversified, divisionalized corporation was the natural end-point of some universal march of progress. He confidently predicted 'convergence in the type of enterprise and system of capitalism used by all advanced industrial economies for the production and distribution of goods' (Chandler, 1984: 156). As pioneer of big business, America would be 'the seedbed of managerial capitalism' around the world (Chandler, 1977: 498). Regardless of local cultures and institutions, this managerial capitalism offered irresistible economic gains through the professionalization of management, the scope economies of diversification and the bureaucratic rationality of the multidivisional structure. Countries would resist the logics of managerial capitalism at their peril. In Chandler's (1990) account, it was the stubborn failure of amateurish family managers to invest in the new corporate model that condemned British industry to relative economic decline in the first half of the century. In the meantime, Germany and the United States, despite enormous institutional and cultural differences, had each got on with the common task of building scale, scope, and organization.

But now Chandler is accused of too little respect for context. For Bruce Kogut (1992: 286), the Chandlerian thesis is essentially 'without geography'. For David Teece (1993: 216), it is 'timeless'. As the social sciences have discovered different ways of doing business around the world, and business itself has changed with the passing of time, the original Chandlerian model has become seen as limited and dated. Chandler's original confident universalism has been assailed by the same contextualizing scepticism as has increasingly gripped the whole of the contemporary social sciences.

The contextualist challenge to Chandler in particular comes in two main flavours. There are those who stress territory—particularly national cultures and national institutions. These doubt the universality of Chandler's model. And there are those who stress time—the constant ebb and flow of power or fashion. These theorists allow that the model may once have had some international grip, but doubt its permanence.

The culturalists stress the variety of attitudes to work and organization across the world. National cultures differ, for instance, in their characteristic attitudes towards power, individualism, and the short and the long term (Hofstede, 1991). Each culture, therefore, is likely to have different propensities with regard to strategy and structure. Some countries will be more opportunistic in their typical strategies; some more hierarchical in their typical structures. There will be no single way internationally. National institutionalists agree on international divergence, but take a slightly different tack to get there. For them, nations typically have their own distinctive and entrenched institutions of ownership and finance, education and careers, law and government. These institutions become locked together in integrated national 'business systems', each defining forms of economic activity appropriate in that particular context (Whitley, 1994; 1999). Strategies and structures that work in one system are unlikely to work as well in another, because out of context. Again, that means there may be many different sorts of effective strategy and structure around the world. To the extent that Europe still contains a variety of national business systems, we should expect American-style diversification and divisionalization to have, at best, an uneven welcome.

Theorists of national cultures and institutions are essentially conservative. Cultures are deeply embedded; institutions are locked into self-reinforcing systems. International institutionalists, on the other hand, tend to stress the transitory nature of particular institutional regimes. Moreover, while agreeing with the national institutionalists that it is socially constructed institutional regimes rather than simple principles of efficiency that define appropriate economic activity, their recognition of the cross-national influences makes them a great deal less chary of international convergence.

In the international institutionalist view, then, the Chandlerian corporation is not the natural product of economic progress. The first corporations were created in response to the large investments required for canals and railways, in America typically with the assistance of local federal states (Roy, 1997). However, the creation of these transport corporations stimulated the growth of an international financial infrastructure of stock markets, investment banks, and brokers. These had an interest in driving the basic corporate model into different sectors across both Europe and America: 'the corporate system arose in the context of international finance' (Roy, 1997: 192). European corporations waited for a second wave of international influence before taking on their specifically Chandlerian form. Diversification and divisionalization was widely adopted only under the post-war hegemony of America and with the enthusiastic efforts of American consultancy firms (Djelic, 1998; McKenna, 1997). But the world could not for ever be kept safe for the American model. During the 1980s the Japanese fatally punctured the 'American mystique' of economic power and managerial superiority (Locke, 1996). The international institutional regime that had originally promoted diversification and divisionalization gave way to another one favouring focus and networks. In this view, then, the rise and likely fall of the Chandlerian corporation in Europe was simply the product of transitory historical conditions.

The debate between the Chandlerian view of the corporation and the institutionalists' merely reflects a wider contest between positivist universalism and contextualist relativism within the management sciences (Clegg, 1990; Donaldson, 1996). On the one side are those who assert the possibility of constructing robust rules for managerial action through the steady accumulation of empirical research; on the other there are those whose paradigms deny the possibility of agreement on empirically founded generalizations and prescriptions (Burrell and Morgan, 1979). The 'paradigm wars' (Aldrich, 1988) that divide the management sciences are not, of course, unique. The management sciences are part—an important part—of the social sciences as a whole. As we shall suggest in Chapter 2, management's contests are thus a microcosm of a broader clash between modernist reason and postmodernist scepticism within contemporary social science (Toulmin, 1990). The fate of the diversified, divisionalized corporation in Europe is not important just in itself, therefore. It provides a test case for the kinds of knowledge that are feasible within management and the social sciences much more widely.

1.3. RESEARCHING STRATEGY AND STRUCTURE IN EUROPE

It cannot be said that Chandler or his followers simply assume the relevance of the diversified, divisionalized corporation around the world. Chandler (1990) himself has engaged in extensive international research, particularly comparing Germany, the United Kingdom, and the United States in the late nineteenth and early twentieth centuries. Here, though, we shall be building on an earlier programme in which, from the late 1960s, a group of Harvard doctoral students engaged in systematizing and extending Chandler's (1962) early account of American corporate development around the world. This research on strategy and structure can claim to be the first systematic research programme in the strategic management discipline. In its international scope, its historical perspective, and standardization of national data-bases, it still has few peers.

The programme was led by Bruce Scott at Harvard Business School, with Alfred Chandler himself serving on the doctoral committees. Although Scott (1973) adapted Chandler's 'four chapters' into a 'three-stage' model of corporate evolution, the end-point was the same: stage three was the diversified, divisionalized corporation. Effectively, therefore, the programme's ambition was first to systematize and update what Chandler (1962) had already begun in terms of strategic and structural change in post-war America and then, in the universalistic spirit, to pursue in a similar fashion equivalent changes through the rest of the advanced industrial world. The American work fell to Wrigley (1970) and Rumelt (1974) and has recently been extended by Markides (1995) to the 1980s. Western Europe was divided: Channon (1973) studied progress in the United Kingdom; Dyas and Thanheiser (1976) took on respectively France and Germany; Pavan (1976) did Italy. As we shall be building on and extending the British, French, and German part of the programme, we shall examine the European studies in particular before introducing our own empirical work.

The Harvard programme, 1950–1970

The European Harvard studies examined the progress of both diversification and divisionalization among the largest industrial firms in France, Germany,

Italy, and the United Kingdom, the largest economies in Western Europe. The samples were defined as the top 100 industrial firms by sales in 1970 in each country and the strategic and structural evolution of these firms was traced back from 1970, through 1960, and then to 1950. The primary focus in these samples was domestically owned firms, between two-thirds and three-quarters of the top 100 firms in each country, the rest being mostly American multinationals such as Ford and IBM. The European researchers relied on interviews in a sub-sample of these firms, together with internal and external data. They also used a basically standardized classification scheme of strategy and structure, although there were slight variations that we shall treat in later chapters. The data they collected have proved remarkably perennial, recently being reproduced in studies such as Kogut and Parkinson (1993), Guillén (1994), de Jong (1997), and Djelic (1998).

In terms of strategy, the European studies discovered a steadily rising trend towards the levels of diversification advocated by Chandler (1962) and found in the United States in the parallel study by Rumelt (1974). We shall examine the detailed figures later, but the proportion of large domestically owned industrial firms in France, Germany, and the United Kingdom with diversified strategies had risen steadily from something between one-quarter to 40 per cent of firms in 1950 to between half and two-thirds of firms in 1970 (Channon, 1973; Dyas and Thanheiser, 1976). The European trend in the period to 1970 closely followed the American, except in one respect: American firms were generally more likely to have adopted strategies of unrelated diversification. Rumelt (1974) classified nearly one-fifth of his large American firms as unrelated conglomerates by 1969, and projected (not forecast) that by 1999 these firms would account for nearly 38 per cent of the population. Although in Germany, as we shall see, the proportion of unrelated diversifiers was also high, in general the European researchers were sceptical of the validity of this strategy in the European context (Channon, 1973: 193; Dyas and Thanheiser, 1976: 38).

In terms of structure, the European trends to 1970 appeared also to be in a Chandlerian direction. The divisional organization, which had been practically unknown in Europe in 1950, had been adopted by 40 per cent of large industrial firms in France and Germany at the end of the research period, and three-quarters of firms in the United Kingdom (Dyas and Thanheiser, 1976). Continental Europe was markedly behind the United States, where approaching four-fifths of large firms were divisionalized (Rumelt, 1974). The barrier in Europe seemed to be a strong attachment to loose, decentralized holding company structures. In the United States the holding company had acquired strong pejorative connotations, being associated with the German *Kartels* and Japanese *zaibatsu* that had been central to the Axis war-effort and which had been carefully dismantled after victory (Berghahn, 1977; Fruin, 1992). The holding companies of post-war Europe were very diverse, frequently having distinct national characteristics. Nevertheless, their obscure pyramids of shareholdings, their overlapping subsidiaries, and informal management styles still evoked suspicion among the scholars of the Harvard Business School. The Harvard researchers were confident that the evident superiority of the multidivisional structure would soon drive out obscure and anachronistic alternatives. Scott (1973: 142) drew on the evolutionary metaphor, comparing the impact of the multidivisional on traditional European organizations to the arrival of the weasel in New Zealand: 'once the weasel arrived, birds without wings, such as the kiwi, rapidly declined and are now almost extinct'.

Although in certain respects—particularly conglomerate diversification and adoption of the multidivisional structure—Europe lagged behind the United States, at the mid-1970s the direction of development seemed clear. Europe was conforming more and more closely with the model of the large industrial corporation first developed in the United States fifty years before. In *The Emerging European Enterprise*, Dyas and Thanheiser (1976: 299) recalled Scott's 'three stage' model of development to predict:

more large (European) firms will make the transition to this third stage of corporate development in the coming decade. As long as the impetus continues to be given by technological innovation and competition, and as long as there are market-sensitive, profit-oriented managements to provide the catalyst, the divisional, diversified corporation will increase in importance.

It is exactly this prediction that this book will test.

Extending the Harvard programme to the 1990s

The research we report in this book extends the original Harvard European studies in two directions. In the first place we shall simply continue tracking the strategic and structural evolution of large firms through to 1993. In the second place, we shall explore more systematically the ownership and management of these firms and the relative performance of different strategies and structures.

An essential methodological principle of our research is continuity with the original Harvard studies for 1950–70. By extending these studies to 1993, we gain a longitudinal perspective on strategic and structural change that is consistent across more or less the whole post-war period. By following the same methods as the Harvard studies, we achieve consistency not only between the three European countries, but also between Europe and the United States, where Rumelt (1974) and Markides (1995) have carried out equivalent studies. We have, therefore, a data-base on corporate change utterly unique for its comparability across four major economies and more than four decades.

Our focus will be on France, Germany, and the United Kingdom, the three largest economies in Western Europe. For the purposes of national trends, we concentrate, like Harvard, on the domestically owned members of the Top 100 industrial companies by sales in each country. We compare these top domestic

Table 1.1. *Sectoral Distribution of Domestic Top 100 Industrial Firms by Largest Area of Activity* (%)

	France		Germany		Britain	
	1983	1993	1983	1993	1983	1993
Brick, pottery, glass, and cement	6.8	7.6	3.3	3.2	8.0	9.0
Chemicals and pharmaceuticals	8.1	7.6	23.3	27.0	12.0	16.4
Electrical and instrument engineering	16.2	18.2	15.0	11.1	13.3	9.0
Food, drink, and tobacco	24.3	24.2	6.7	6.3	29.3	25.4
Mechanical engineering and metals	17.6	18.2	21.7	15.9	14.7	14.9
Mining and extraction	1.4	1.5	3.3	3.2	1.3	1.5
Petroleum	2.7	3.0	—	—	2.7	3.0
Printing, paper, and publishing	4.1	1.5	5.0	9.5	5.3	6.0
Rubber and plastics	4.1	6.1	3.3	4.8	1.3	—
Textiles and clothing	5.4	3.0	1.7	—	2.7	1.5
Transportation equipment	8.1	9.1	15.0	12.7	8.0	9.0
Other	1.4	1.5	1.7	6.4	1.3	4.5
Number of firms	74	66	60	63	75	67

companies' strategies and structures at decade points, as Harvard did from 1950 to 1970. Our comparison points of 1983 and 1993 reflect the timing of our field research, conducted in 1994 and 1995. In 1993 the number of domestically owned firms in the British Top 100 was 67; in France the number was 66; in Germany, 63. Appendix 1 lists all the firms and their sectors, but Table 1.1 provides a summary of the sectoral distribution. Apart from Germany's high proportion of chemicals and pharmaceuticals companies, and low proportion of food companies, firms are more or less similarly distributed in each country.

In terms of size, the German firms were on average the largest, with average turnovers in 1993 of DM 14,220 ($8,238m), followed quite closely by the British, with average turnovers of £4,914m ($7,279m), then finally the French with average turnovers of FF 33,538m ($5,629m). Overall, the European firms are comparable to those in parallel American studies. In 1993 our smallest firm by turnover—the French company Taittinger, at $575m—was equivalent in size to the 407th firm in the US Fortune 500, while our largest firm—Royal Dutch/Shell, at $95,134m—would have ranked fourth (Fortune, 18 April 1994; 25 July 1994). There is also considerable continuity with firms from the original Harvard population: 53 per cent of German firms, 41 per cent of British firms, and 39 per cent of French firms survive in recognizable form as domestically owned top industrials through the whole period 1970–93.

Like Harvard, our research method combines documentary sources with interviews in a subset of companies (see Appendix II for details). Documentary sources included annual reports, company histories, teaching cases, business directories, and press reports. We interviewed managers in about one-third of the firms, an equivalent proportion to the original Harvard studies: in France, managers in 28 firms were interviewed; in Germany and the United Kingdom, 25 each. Interviews were generally tape-recorded. As we shall explore further in Chapters 5 and 6, we use the same kinds of measures of strategy and structure as those of the original Harvard studies, particularly focusing on related and unrelated diversification and the multidivisional structure.

We add to the Harvard European studies in two respects. First, we consider more directly the performance issue, measuring it in two ways. Clearly the diffusion of different strategies and structures within the population provides an indirect measure of performance, but we shall be especially interested in the sustainability of particular strategies and structures, in other words the extent to which companies retain them over long periods of time. Also, though more cautiously given the difficulties with accounting data in Europe, we shall pursue the financial performance issues analysed by Rumelt (1974) but left aside by the original European researchers. Our second addition responds to Chandler's (1990) strictures on family managements by examining more systematically than the original Harvard researchers the ownership and management of our firms. These we shall examine more fully in Chapters 4 and 7, considering the implications of different patterns of ownership, control, and managerial backgrounds both from a broad institutionalist point of view and from a more focused corporate political perspective.

Aside from these additions, our basic approach is to test the Harvard programme's predictions on Harvard's own terms. Consistency with the Harvard methods is only fair, as well as bringing great gains in terms of comparability over time and across countries. None the less, this fidelity does introduce some limitations that we should signal at the beginning. First, we have remained true to the focus on large industrial firms. Although many of our firms include service operations—as General Electric does—the relative decline of manufacturing since the 1970s leaves our groups of firms less important in their domestic economies than the equivalent groups researched by Harvard. This may not matter too much if we can still accept these industrial firms as representative of large firms generally in their economies. There are no obvious theoretical reasons why firms in the increasingly important service sector should be less prone to diversify and divisionalize: casual observation of the retail and financial sectors certainly reveals plenty of conglomerates.

Second, we should acknowledge the limits of our corporate focus. Diversification concerns corporate strategy, not business strategy. It is at the level of business units that firms actually produce and sell. However, the corporate level remains critical. The bringing together of different activities across sectors within the confines of a single unit of ownership represents an historically unprecedented achievement, responsible for creating the large firm as one of the distinctive institutions of the twentieth century. These corporations have harnessed enormous economies of scope as well as being the leaders in innovation in many industries (Chandler and Hikino, 1997). The corporate level has a different role to the business unit, but it is certainly important. A third limitation is our focus primarily on issues of formal organizational structure. We may recognize today more clearly than the original Harvard scholars the importance for collective organization of other less-formal instruments such as culture (Ouchi, 1980) and the scope for surface conformity to normative pressures (Meyer and Rowan, 1977). Yet formal structure reflects substantial issues, too. Movement from a functional to a divisional structure involves a transformation of top management positions and systems of accountability; movement from a holding company structure to a divisional structure will typically entail consolidations of ownership involving, even in the smallest of our firms, tens of millions of dollars. Structural change of this kind is not insignificant or superficial. Overall, our account of strategy and structure may not tell the whole story, but it does cover very important parts of it.

1.4. PROGRAMME AND PROPOSAL

This book, then, will follow the changing strategies and structures of large European firms from the 1950s to the 1990s. It will test particularly the prediction of the Harvard group that Europe too would eventually adopt the diversified, divisionalized model that it saw as the final stage of corporate evolution. Efficient American-style weasels should chase quaint kiwis out. This test is a tough one. Our geographical scope encompasses three nations, each with particular traditions and institutions. Our time period extends across nearly half a century, during which management fashions have come and gone, nations have transformed themselves, and the old American hegemony has receded. Since the confident predictions of the mid-1970s, both economic and intellectual climates have radically changed.

   At the practical level, even in America, it is no longer clear that the established diversified multidivisional model is adequate to the demands of the new 'network society' (Castells, 1996). It is too rigid in its boundaries for partnerships; too fragmented across businesses to concentrate and learn. Chandler (1990) himself now wonders whether his model has been stretched too far in the form of the conglomerate. There is, therefore, a clear performance question hanging over the Chandlerian model. It is by no means clear that diversification and divisionalization will have continued their European spread since the original Harvard studies left off in 1970, nor that diversified and divisionalized companies will outperform their rivals any more.

As well as doubts about performance, the original Chandlerian model faces new intellectual challenges. Competition is no longer accepted either as dictating a single recipe for efficiency around the world, or even as the only pressure to which business must conform. Culturalists stress the enduring effects of local history, and national institutionalists point to good economic reasons for local adaptations. International institutionalists accept convergence, but emphasize how international norms are subject to the fluctuating forces of power and fashion.

Our position will be this. In understanding corporate change, believers in international competition, champions of national context, and international institutionalists all make their own distinctive contributions. Each has a role to play. International models will rise and fall; local origins do cast long shadows forward; competition exerts strong pressures towards efficiency. But these three forces are not necessarily equal or constant. The firm is pushed and pulled in different directions, but at some points one force in particular will prevail. In post-war Europe, it has been the forces of competition that have gradually dominated.

Figure 1.3 describes the three forces in terms of an adjustable vice and its inputs. Firms are still the products of their nationally distinctive origins. Their capital, their top management, their critical activities remain disproportionately defined by their home-base (Hu, 1992; Ruigrok and Tulder, 1995). In Figure 1.3, therefore, large firms typically enter from the left-hand side, carrying with them the distinct heritages of their original national cultures and institutions. But these heritages are subjected to two homogenizing pressures. The powers and ideologies of the international institutionalists bear down in one direction. The competitive drives for efficiency press up from another. These two homogenizing forces squeeze inherited business practices closer together, pressing them to converge. The forces for homogeneity may not be complete, however: practices may come to overlap, yet remain distinct. The forces may not be equal: sometimes it will be international institutions that dominate; sometimes competition. There is no necessary teleology either. It is conceivable that the homogenizing forces will relax so that distinct national cultures and institutions may reassert themselves. This, arguably, is what has happened in 1990s Russia, when international norms of bureaucratic efficiency were forgotten and new personalistic business empires emerged in defiance of competitive requirements. The convergence vice is adjustable.

It will be our argument here that it is the stamp of international competition that marks European corporations most strongly today. National cultures and institutions still exert their influence, both as drag on convergence and as resource for local interpretation of international practices. The diversified multi-divisional is not yet wholly triumphant in Europe, nor does it necessarily take

International institutions

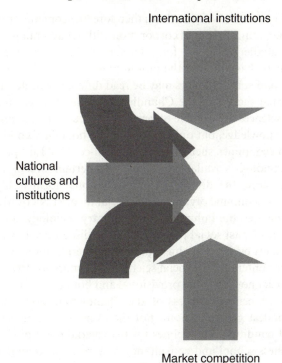

National
cultures and
institutions

Market competition

Figure 1.3. *The Adjustable Vice of Corporate Convergence*

quite the same character in every country. International institutions too have played their role, especially in disseminating the divisional model so fast through Europe in the early post-war period. But more recently in Europe, neither the bleeding of American hegemony nor the lingering pull of national institutions has been able to halt the steady spread of the Chandlerian model. Ultimately, European business has adopted the diversified, divisionalized form because it has shown itself to be more effective than its alternatives, whether national traditions or the latest international fad.

This success of the Chandlerian model in post-war Europe is a conditional one. Chandler and the Harvard group are right, more or less, in this particular instance. This does not allow sweeping generalization. The competitive arena in which the Chandlerian model has succeeded is not a perfect or natural one, but itself a product of the peculiar political and economic conditions of the late twentieth-century world (Strange, 1988; Gray, 1998). In this period, the United States established, and other Western nations entered, a global economic structure that allowed corporations to achieve unprecedented scale and scope with little fear either for their property rights or for their access to international markets for capital, goods, and services. This is a remarkable but by no means entrenched achievement. We can admit, therefore, the contemporary dominance of the diversified, multidivisional corporation without accepting the universalist teleology of Chandler's original 'four chapters of American enterprise'. So far European business has followed the plot in pretty good order, but there will be more chapters, and some chapters may be read differently or not at all.

The conditional success of the Chandlerian model does persuade, therefore, that the social sciences are capable of predicting accurately and providing useful generalizeable knowledge, but only so long as the boundary conditions are well understood. In economies such as late twentieth-century Europe, with particular kinds of technologies available to them and a certain level of social and economic infrastructure, the diversified, multidivisional form is likely to be an effective mode of economic organization. Social theorist Nicos Mouzelis (1995) has recently lamented the failure of contemporary sociology, too dismissive of the achievements of past social theorists and too discouraged by postmodernist extremism to assert even the slightest practical generalization. Mouzelis asserts the need for the contemporary social sciences once more to strive for generality, but this time to acknowledge the provisional and bounded nature of any claims. The late twentieth-century success of the Chandlerian model licenses exactly this kind of modest generalization—not the over-weaning universalism of an earlier age, but conditional guidelines for managerial good practice. There is a future for business school and consultancy prescription, so long as it is forever sensitive to the limits of time and place.

In making this argument for a bounded account of the contemporary corporation, we shall have to make two key theoretical moves. First, we shall distinguish between Chandlerism and the Chandlerian, on the analogy of the distinction between Marxism and Marxian (Parks, 1985). Chandlerism refers to a particular vision of the corporation developed in the specific context of early post-war America, its key elements fixed and universalized at one moment in history. Chandlerism lapses easily into ideology. The Chandlerian perspective, on the other hand, is a broader and more adaptive orientation. As business model, it places value in quite general terms on scale, diversification, and decentralization. As research methodology, it relies on wide-angled, historical, and comparative analyses, combining broad trends with more or less detailed investigations of particular cases. This first move makes possible the second. Once freed of Chandlerism, it becomes possible to develop a more flexible Chandlerian model of the corporation, both comprehensive enough to accommodate the rise of the conglomerate and adaptive enough to accept new initiatives in organization. This Chandlerian model recognizes the kinds of temporal and territorial limits set by the contextualists, but has the kind of pliant resilience that allows it to fit in to different national environments and to stretch over many decades. It is on the basis of this adaptive and renewable Chandlerian model that we shall claim the possibility of bounded generalization, at least within the particular sphere of post-war Western Europe. We can be Chandlerian without being Chandlerist.

The next two chapters concern themselves with extracting and developing the essential Chandlerian core. Chapter 2 is concerned with the original development of Chandlerism as a mode of thought, both situating it within other contemporary movements in the social and management sciences, and confronting it with the challenges of postmodernism broadly and the cultural and institutional critiques more specifically. These challenges help to establish clear limits to Chandlerism, but still leave considerable scope for the development of the Chandlerian model as a boundedly generalizing account of the contemporary corporation. Chapter 3 takes up the Chandlerian corporate model, tackling the awkward rise of the conglomerate and recent strains in the old multidivisional. It argues for the possibility of an extended and renewed Chandlerian corporation, one that is both robust to economic and political change, and adaptive to different national cultures and institutions. Key features of this extended Chandlerian model are the rehabilitation of the conglomerate and the regeneration of the multidivisional. The contemporary rationale for the conglomerate rests on greater recognition of the general but finite skills of top management teams in exploiting corporate relationships. The continued relevance of the multidivisional relies on its incorporation of the opportunities of the network society within the established principles of strategic centralization and operational decentralization.

Chapter 4 turns to the empirical materials and particularly to the national contexts of France, Germany, and the United Kingdom in the 1980s and 1990s. Here we focus on ownership, control, and managerial careers in these three countries, all elements highlighted by national institutionalists as important for corporate strategy and structure. We shall find enduring differences—France and Germany marked by continued personal ownership and control, the United Kingdom by professional managers and financial orientations. Yet, Chapter 5 reveals, these institutional differences seem to matter little to national patterns of strategy adoption or performance. European business has become more diversified and shown little inclination towards aggregate refocusing. Although anomalies persist, corporate strategy conforms better to the predictions of an extended Chandlerian perspective than those of either national or international institutionalists. The conglomerate, moreover, emerges as neither the creature of management abuse nor the creation of financial fashion, but rather as a respectable alternative to the formerly preferred strategy of related diversification. Chapter 6 demonstrates a similar result for corporate structure in contemporary Europe: multidivisionals are overwhelmingly the favoured form by the 1990s. Originally the embodiment of modernist rationality and projected to Europe on the back of American power, the multidivisional shows itself capable of adapting to contemporary critiques of rational segmentalism and the transformations of an emerging network society. Having found that broad institutional accounts largely fail, Chapter 7 goes down to the level of particular firms, examining whether the political interests of specific ownership groups can explain remaining anomalies in strategy and structure. By and large, we shall find that they do not. We are pushed back again to an account of changing strategies and structures in which market drives towards efficiency must have the dominant role.

The path we shall be treading through this book is a delicate one, neither accepting the universalism of the early post-war social sciences nor succumbing to the relativism of the contemporary contextualist challenge. We shall be working in the space between, moulding the essential Chandlerian core to the business and theoretical developments of the contemporary world. Thus we shall rely on Chandler's broad historical and comparative perspective, while setting it within the kind of territorial and temporal limits that theoretical challengers have taught. Likewise, we shall recognize the continuing importance of scale, scope, and decentralization, but renew the model's original core to match the opportunities of changing times. As empirical evidence falls into place within this framework, we shall grow more confident in its value as a basis for provisional and bounded generalization about the corporation. Despite enduring local differences and in the face of substantial economic change, certain fundamental principles of corporate strategy and structure have shown themselves to be of continuing relevance across several countries and over many decades. Our final chapter, therefore, will draw from the post-war experience of Western Europe some tentative implications both for managers concerned with the development of the corporation and for policy-makers concerned with economic reform. As for researchers, the implications are strenuous: the notions of boundedness and provisionality in the social sciences entail a constant, restless probing of the outer limits within which modest generalization and prescription may be both justified and helpful.

2

Chandler and Context

INTRODUCTION

Alfred Chandler has got to be the starting-point for any historical account of the contemporary corporation. After all, Chandlerism is the coming 'new orthodoxy in the development and functioning of modern capitalism' (Alford, 1994: 631). Indeed, 'the tag phrase "Chandlerian" has joined Marxian, Weberian and Schumpeterian as a convenient shorthand for an entire tradition of scholarship' (John, 1997: 158). Chandler dominates the field.

But we shall follow at a certain distance, theoretical and contextual. When Alfred Chandler (1962) first offered to the world the great American corporations as archetype, he was parading just one of many characteristics in which the United States could then feel assured of its superiority. In this immediate postwar period, mainstream Western social sciences—and the emerging management sciences especially—were confident that American practice was the ideal representative of the modern and that the rest of the world only differed in having failed so far to catch up. The social sciences made America the universal pattern.

Not any more. The achievement of postmodern philosophy in the last decades of the twentieth century has been to undermine any such faith in the ideal types of a particular time and place. Postmodernism has created the space for at least three contextualizing themes to emerge in the social sciences of management. Research on national cultures has identified apparently enduring differences in the ways in which different peoples think and go about business around the world. National institutionalists have revealed deeply knit differences in key economic institutions—from educational systems to capital markets—with potentially radical implications for effective business practice in each particular context. International institutionalists have pointed to the ebb and flow of dominant ideologies, leaving the right way of doing business defined precariously according to fashion or power.

These contextualist themes challenge Chandler's American corporate ideal head-on. We acknowledge critiques from contextualism, but wish to hold on to the baby as we throw out the bathwater. Here the distinction we made in the last chapter will be important. Chandlerism expresses a universal and evolutionary perspective that extends too confidently from Chandler's particular experience of corporate capitalism. In the contemporary world, this Chandlerism is out of

place and out of date. The fundamental Chandlerian principles of diversification and decentralization, however, do remain enduring sources of potential
value. It will be our aim in this chapter and the next to extract from Chandlerism
the essential Chandlerian core on which to build a model of the corporation that
is dynamic, profitable, and potentially still relevant to the conditions of contemporary Europe.

We start here by locating Chandlerism within wider universalist accounts of
economy and society, ones that have been particularly influential on the management sciences. We go on to introduce the critiques of universalism offered by
postmodernism and institutionalism. The postmodernists and institutionalists
insist too much, yet their assertion of context does contribute in at least two
ways. First, it helps to understand the cultural and intellectual context in which
Chandlerism developed. We shall highlight this context not so much to undercut
Chandlerism as to see more clearly the kinds of theoretical excess baggage that
Chandler, as a product of his time and place, was almost inescapably obliged to
take on as well. Shorn of this baggage, Chandler still offers a useful core for a
boundedly generalizing theory of the contemporary corporation. Second, contextualism indicates particular kinds of limits to this kind of bounded generalization. Time, place, and the richly complex nature of practice are the critical
boundaries that contextual understanding sets around the management sciences. This chapter, then, will attempt to draw from each of these apparently
opposing modes of thought essential ideas that can be combined into a boundedly predictive and practical theory of the contemporary Western corporation.
We shall conclude by proposing our own way between the poles of universalism
and contextualism. In brief: we shall affirm the continued legitimacy of generalization, but define the scope of legitimate generalization more narrowly than
the universalists and more broadly than the contextualists.

2.1. CONTEXTUALIZING CHANDLERISM

Just as there was a 'young Marx' and an 'old Marx', so with Alfred Chandler:
over more than forty years of active research on the corporation, his thought
has continually evolved. Yet, especially in the three defining books (Chandler,
1962; 1977; 1990), there remains a consistent set of themes that we shall identify
as Chandlerism. This Chandlerism works at two levels (Alford, 1994): on the
one hand, it is a theory of corporate development, proposing steady advance
towards the full maturity of the large diversified, divisionalized corporation; on
the other hand, it is a theory of world development, in which economic progress
more generally depends upon international acceptance of the efficiency, professionalism, and innovativeness of these large corporations. Some misgivings
are expressed by the older Chandler (1990), yet by and large the work is
informed by a strong evolutionary confidence that the economic model discov-

ered in the United States is the necessary and universally relevant end-point for modern societies. In this confidence, Chandlerism is quite typical of the dominant modes of thought within the national and social scientific cultures in which it arose.

Alfred Chandler's own biography is relevant (John, 1997). He is an American, but not just any kind of American. Connected to the business élite—his middle name is DuPont—his youth and education were shaped by the sudden emergence of the United States as the world's pre-eminent superpower. Chandler spent the Second World War in the navy and then entered graduate school in a post-war world which, though still riven by ideological contest, hoped for better things. For John (1997: 156), 'the single most important cultural influence upon Chandler's general outlook was almost certainly the epochal reorientation in intellectual assumptions about the relationship of the United States to the rest of the world brought about by the Second World War'. The experience of war had shown the enormous power of American scale and organization. Victory seemed to endow the United States with a new mission: to ensure the spread of democracy and capitalism around the world. Although this mission broke with traditions of political isolationism, it accorded well with a certain bent to American thinking.

After all, American thought is deeply imbued with a sense of rationalistic progress in which the United States itself was at the vanguard (Carroll and Noble, 1977). Bringing order and reason to the 'wilderness' was long the project of non-native Americans. Nineteenth-century urban planners imposed orderly grids upon Washington, New York, and San Francisco, with scant regard for the natural contours of the land and in conscious contrast to the higgledy-piggledy ancient cities of Europe. The Puritans had stripped religion of the mystical trappings of Old World Catholicism, while the architects of the Constitution embodied an eighteenth-century Enlightenment faith in reason and progress. John Gray (1998: 2) identifies the United States as 'the last great Enlightenment regime'. The Enlightenment culture is starkly universalistic:

The thinkers of the Enlightenment, such as Thomas Jefferson, Tom Paine, John Stuart Mill and Karl Marx, never doubted that the future for every nation in the world was to accept some version of western institutions and values. A diversity of cultures was not a permanent condition of life. It was a stage on the way to a universal civilization (Gray, 1998: 2).

The Enlightenment of Jefferson, Paine, Mill, and Marx was the flowering of a specifically 'modern' system of thought, rooted in the seventeenth century and extending to the early post-war years. In the account of Stephen Toulmin (1990: 30–5), this modernism expressed four key transitions from earlier traditions of thought: from the oral to the written; from the particular to the universal; from the local to the general; and from the timely to the timeless. The move towards the written elevated rational logic above the practical skills of rhetorical argumentation. The abstract laws of rational logic were held to transcend particular instances. Logical principles could be generalized across time and space. Toulmin (1990) contextualizes the decontextualizing: the modernist project was a product of its time and place. In seventeenth-century Europe, it represented a quest for certainty and order at a time of religious and political chaos. During the eighteenth and nineteenth centuries modernism was seized upon by revolutionaries seeking the clean slate of rational social organization—as such, it was particularly attractive to the builders of the American Republic (Toulmin, 1990: 179). Finally, for those alarmed by the fierce ideological contests of the early twentieth century, the extreme rationalism of philosophical and scientific positivism promised an objective, common means of arbitrating between competing truth claims (Toulmin, 1990: 150–4).

The young Chandler was a product of Western modernism in general and the American experience in particular. He was ripe for a view in which American capitalism would be seen as the model of order and reason, with local idiosyncrasies regarded as irrational barriers to world-wide progress. The post-war American social sciences in which he would be immersed certainly did everything to reinforce this view.

Chandlerism and the social sciences

In the years immediately following the Second World War, American social scientists were much preoccupied with where the world was heading. European decadence had been brutally revealed by military defeat and imperial decline. Confrontation with the Soviet Union required a convincing account of capitalism's virtues. Sudden acquisition of global responsibilities obliged the United States to define a vision of political and economic development that it could support around the world. Still gripped by modernism, American social scientists were prone to see the future in progressive and universalistic terms. For mainstream social science, therefore, it turned out that the world was heading for American-style capitalism—vigorous, productive, and powerful. It had worked for the United States so it should work everywhere else.

Talcott Parsons epitomized the triumphant universalism ascendant in postwar American social science. The dominant social theorist of his day and translator of Max Weber, he was also Alfred Chandler's teacher at Harvard. In an influential paper on 'Evolutionary Universals', Parsons (1964) sums up world history in terms of an evolutionary progress through successively more advanced and effective societies. Each stage of this evolution involved the acquisition of additional sets of 'evolutionary universals'. Thus the most primitive societies had only the universals of language, kinship, technology, and religion. More advanced societies acquired such universals as reliable systems of market exchange and the rational administration of Weberian bureaucracy. Key universals for the most advanced societies were democracy and the rule of law. At the pinnacle of development in terms of these evolutionary universals was, of course, the United States.

Parsons (1964) provided the grand sweep, but other social scientists were producing similar visions directly relevant to the business concerns of Alfred Chandler and his colleagues. Kerr, Dunlop, Harbison, and Myers (1960), in their influential *Industrialism and Industrial Man*, defined the large-scale enterprise as the critical actor in global economic development. The standardizing demands of technology, the professionalization of administration, and the 'compulsion of comparisons' as international best-practice became more easily communicated around the world, all combined to produce strong pressures for 'uniformity' across nations. In the name of efficiency and initiative, control would have to be decentralized to some extent, but the large-scale productive enterprise was becoming increasingly characteristic of capitalist world and socialist world alike.

Rostow's (1960) 'stage' theory of economic growth was similar in its avidity to assimilate the socialist experience with capitalist American. The five stages—traditional society, preconditions for take-off, take-off, the drive for maturity, and the age of high mass-consumption—were explicitly offered as an alternative path to that of Karl Marx's troubling vision. Russia's own growth path is shown to be closely parallel to America's—only with a lag. International convergence in the capitalist world was even more striking. According to Rostow (1960: 87): 'All the post-war mature societies of the West and Japan are behaving in a remarkably "American" way'. These mature societies might have been somewhat backward, but they still trod faithfully in the path blazed by America. Rostow (1960: 88) could conclude without embarrassment that by the 1950s 'Western Europe and Japan have . . . entered whole-heartedly into the American 1920s'.

Alfred Chandler did not stand apart from American traditions and social science. Chandler's family was firmly part of the traditional East Coast élite and his colleague, Tom McCraw (1988), identifies as one of Chandler's unusual merits as an historian his immersion in the social sciences. His work, and that of his followers, reflects many of the social scientific preoccupations of the day.

The Chandlerian focus is, of course, the large productive enterprise identified by Kerr et al. (1960) as characteristic of modern industrial society worldwide. Chandler's multidivisional (1962) follows the logic of industrial society in proposing operational decentralization as the solution to the problem of scale. As we shall see in the next chapter, the multidivisional structure also embodies at least two of the critical 'universals' required by Parsons (1964) for advanced societies—the rational administration of Weberian bureaucracy on the one hand, and Williamsonian internal capital markets on the other. Chandler's (1962: 386–96) four chapters of corporate development—from initial enterprise to full-blown divisionalization and diversification—strongly recall the progressive sequences of Rostow's (1960) 'stages of growth' and Parsons's (1966) 'evolutionary universals'.

Chandler was as confident as Kerr, Parsons, or Rostow in the universal relevance of the American experience. His own observations, and those of his students, seemed to confirm it: 'in the post-war years, the governance of European and Japanese groups have become more similar to the American M-form' (Chandler, 1982: 17). As 'the seed-bed of managerial capitalism' (Chandler, 1977: 498), the United States had world-wide relevance. Indeed, Western managerial capitalism was only a particular case of more general processes in industrial societies internationally. As in the Soviet Union, so too in the advanced societies of the West: private capitalist interests were being removed from the direct control of enterprise. Just as Kerr et al. (1960) emphasize the professionalization of administration, Chandler (1962: 38) insists that the great organization-builders of twentieth-century American capitalism were hardly ever the founding entrepreneurs and only rarely members of the original families. All large, decentralized organizations would have to rely on professional managers such as Alfred Sloan. The amateurish, personal capitalism of the pre-war United Kingdom was a catastrophic anachronism (Chandler, 1990).

No less than other social scientists, Chandler and his followers also understood the geopolitical significance of their project. It was not just about management. For Chandler (1990), British reluctance to modernize in the pre-war years had contributed to economic and imperial decline; America's diversification excesses in the 1960s and 1970s jeopardized its standing relative to Japan and Continental Europe. More was at stake even than the fate of particular nations. The Chandlerian corporation was recruited to legitimate and renew late twentieth-century capitalism more widely. Chandler's Harvard collaborator Bruce Scott (1973) deployed the evidence for American and European diversification and divisionalization against the increasing criticism of big business during the 1960s and early 1970s. Large corporations were far from the monopolistic, vertically integrated colossi of J. K. Galbraith's (1967) famous 'technostructure'. According to Scott (1973), the prevailing strategy in advanced economies was not to dominate suppliers and customers through vertical integration but rather to enter new markets by diversifying horizontally. These giants were not governed by omnipotent central planners, but by the internal market disciplines of the decentralized multidivisional.

The political significance of the professional, diversified multidivisional was particularly acute in post-war Europe. Indeed, in an earlier study of France, written as Europe was convulsed by the phenomena of 1968, McArthur and Scott (1969) concluded that the stability of democratic capitalism in Europe depended on the rapid importation of the American management model. Even if the French and others regarded this 'American challenge' with some misgivings, reformist European intellectuals such as Jean-Jacques Servan-Schreiber (1969) broadly agreed. Caught between the power of the Soviet Union on the one hand and American multinationals on the other, the only solution for an economically backward Europe lay in replicating the American combination of scale and decentralization to create a dynamic, independent capitalism of its own.

Thus Chandlerism not only drew its themes from the post-war social sciences, it also provided part of the answer to the social scientific preoccupation with the renewal and extension of American-style capitalism. Issues of enterprise management entered sharply on to the broader agenda of social and political theory. But business was returning the compliment. As we shall explore in the following section, management as a new discipline was simultaneously keen to assimilate the concepts and methods of social science into its own practice.

Chandlerism and the management sciences

Chandler's thinking on the American corporation emerged not just within the context of the broader social sciences but in conjunction with the emergence of a newly scientific approach to management. As Guillén (1994) observes, from around the middle of the century the dominant shapers of management thought ceased to be practical managers and consultants such as Frederick Taylor, Alfred Sloan, and Chester Barnard, but increasingly scientifically trained observers from academia. Elton Mayo, Frederick Herzberg, and Alfred Chandler himself were all academics. This academic turn was not a retreat to the ivory tower; it was pushed by business interests increasingly appreciative of what the social sciences could do for them.

In the post-war period American corporations demanded more and better business education. As two key reports on business education in the United States agreed, business school training in the 1950s had become inadequate to the demands of contemporary large-scale enterprises and to the professional managers who ran them. The future lay in a more scientific approach. For the Ford Foundation, Gordon and Howell (1959: 382) urged:

the development and use of more sophisticated analytical tools, including more utilization of concepts and findings from the various social sciences and greater reliance on the tools of mathematics and statistics, and the systematic collection of detailed and reliable data on the internal workings of different kinds and sizes of business firms.

For the Carnegie Foundation, Pierson and his colleagues (1959: 313) called likewise for more systematic research: there was an urgent need for 'developing analytical findings which can be fitted into a general system of principles and tested in a scientific manner'. In both reports, the underlying scientific model was a particular one, emphasizing objective data, rational analysis, and systematic testing. A 'new paradigm of management' was being constructed, self-consciously scientific and drawing on the rapidly maturing disciplines of economics, engineering and the behavioural sciences (Locke, 1989). Management was finally entering the modernist project.

Published just three years after the Ford and Carnegie reports, Chandler's

(1962) *Strategy and Structure* could hardly have been more timely. Chandler addressed directly the new challenges of scale, scope, and complexity. Moreover, he offered an immense wealth of detailed internal data on which to build and test systematic principles for managing the large firm. Not surprisingly, Chandler's work had enormous impact.

There was an impact on practice, as McKinsey consultants literally carried copies of *Strategy and Structure* into their clients across the United States and Europe (McCraw, 1988). But there was also lasting impact on business schools seeking to upgrade the quality of their teaching and research. Chandler's strictures on strategy and structure were quickly incorporated into the prescriptions of standard business policy courses. While he stayed to teach a highly successful elective on the Harvard MBA, Chandler's doctoral students dispersed to new business schools around the globe (Channon to Manchester, Dyas and Thanheiser to Fontainbleau, Rumelt to Tehran). The Harvard strategy and structure programme also became a general model for business school research in strategy. Rumelt et al. (1994) trace the foundation of strategic management as a modern and independent research field back to the publication of *Strategy and Structure*, and note that its clear constructs and propositions provided a useful guide as the discipline began to advance in the direction of 'positive science' in the late 1960s. Indeed, Jason Spender (1992: 43) suggests that the first generation of doctoral students engaged on the Harvard strategy and structure research programme in the 1960s and early 1970s effectively built what was to become the strategy field. The strategic management discipline was established as an American export industry, transferring and sometimes testing concepts and ideas developed in the United States all around the world.

Chandler was not alone, of course. Guillén (1994) describes the immediate post-war period as the heyday of the structural approach to organizations. The industrial relations problems of the shopfloor had been largely solved—at least in the United States—and the new demands of large-scale, international organization had become salient. Researchers were eager to fill the gap. During the 1960s and early 1970s academics such as Joan Woodward (1965), the Aston group (Pugh and Hinings, 1976), and Lawrence and Lorsch (1967), as well as Alfred Chandler (1962) himself, were all involved in the intellectually novel task of writing the laws of organization design. Together, these researchers constructed a 'structural contingency' theory of organizations, in which strategy joined size, technology, and environment as one of several contingencies related in a predictable fashion to critical features of organizational structure. In this view, rules and hierarchy were not the arbitrary constructions of oppressive managements, but simply the technical conditions for efficient organization. Structural contingency theory was unembarrassed about turning these technical conditions into practical prescriptions (Donaldson, 1995). Specify an organization's size, technology, strategy, and environment and a contingency theorist would be able to prescribe an appropriate organizational structure.

If structural contingency theory was to be useful to the corporations, consulting companies, and business schools spreading around the world, it would be important that its relationships should be 'culture free'. The two main schools of contingency theory, Aston and Harvard, were equally keen to demonstrate the applicability of their views internationally. We saw in Chapter 1 how the Harvard group of doctoral students went out into the world to test their theories; the Aston researchers endeavoured the same. David Hickson et al. (1974) asserted a 'bold hypothesis' of stable relationships between critical contingencies and organizational structure, irrespective of local cultures. Summarizing the Aston school's research on bureaucratization and organizational size in Canada, the United Kingdom, and the United States, they wrote:

Though the *levels* of constituent ingredients of bureaucratization may differ between countries, the pressure exerted by size is the same and in the same direction in every country. Nowhere will traditionalistic custom be adequate for social control once large numbers are gathered. Here is a fragment of a basis in contemporary empirical data from three countries for what Weber (1948) believed so long.

It seemed that Max Weber's notions of bureaucracy, developed in Germany during the early years of the twentieth century, held in the Anglo-Saxon world more than fifty years later. Contingency theory involved timeless universals. In the words of an advocate, 'Structural contingency theory yields generalizations that are valid globally. They are general relationships on which the sun never sets' (Donaldson, 1996: 146).

Of course, the very ambition to create a 'culture-free' science of management is itself culturally loaded. Locke (1989: 46) specifically singles out Chandler and the Harvard group for their exaggerated universalism. But the problem was a general one:

all scientists in the new management studies paradigm are leery of historically-shaped cultural explanations when dealing with managerial behaviour and economic activity. They prefer science to culture. . . . [But] the new management paradigm is itself as much a cultural as a scientific expression. . . . It incorporates the norms and values of the society that gave it birth—primarily America—and builds them into the heart of its scientific analysis. (Locke, 1989: 52–3).

The management sciences were not so much culture free as culture blind. As the times changed, and the American model declined, the new paradigm appeared ill equipped to absorb the implications of Japanese success (Locke, 1989).

Thus Chandlerism as a mode of thought epitomized the American Enlightenment spirit in general and the post-war social sciences in particular. The thinking was universal—its adoption was even urgently vital to the future of European capitalism. The prescriptions were timeless—in the evolution of enterprise, Chandler (1962) envisaged no 'fifth chapter' after the multidivisional. In all this, Chandler and his followers were not particularly unique. Chandler's universalism fitted well with the emergent management sciences of the 1960s, especially structural contingency theory. But as the Enlightenment spirit became subverted by postmodernism and American capitalism was challenged by Asia, this kind of confidence has come under increasing criticism.

2.2. POSTMODERNISM AND CONTEXT

For many contemporary social and philosophical theorists, the years in which Chandlerism first evolved are the fag-end of 'modernism' (Toulmin, 1990). In the last decades of the twentieth century, the political, economic, and philosophical conditions for modernist rationalism appeared to be crumbling away. With increasing damage to the environment, progress no longer seemed unproblematic. After Hiroshima, the claims of science to detached, rational value freedom could hardly be sustained. Democracy and colonial liberation were revealing a plurality of interests and world-views irreducible to a single instrumental rationality. By the 1960s Toulmin (1990: 162) writes, the reaction against the excesses of modernist rationalism was a 'revolution *waiting to happen*' (italics in original).

The 1960s revolution emerged in the sceptical, relativist form of postmodernism. For Jean-Francois Lyotard (1984: xxiv), the postmodern is defined fundamentally as an 'incredulity towards metanarratives'. The grand Enlightenment narratives of universal progress—of Marx, of Parsons, or of Chandler—had been irresistibly undermined by the proliferation of scientific activity and the spirit of enquiry that were the Enlightenment's own products. As the modernistic social sciences piled on nuance, detail, and controversy to initial ideas, so they squeezed out the very possibility of such grand theories. These theories of universal progress failed particularly because of their propensity for unwarranted generalization, especially from the experience of North America (Bauman, 1991). Modernist social scientists had discovered a good deal about particular societies, but in vaunting the experience of these particular societies as universal they trapped themselves into what was in fact a very perilous form of knowledge:

they informed of *contingency* while believing themselves to narrate *necessity*, of particular *locality* while believing themselves to narrate *universality*, of tradition-bound interpretation while believing in themselves to narrate the extraterritorial and extratemporal truth, of undecidability while believing themselves to narrate transparency, of the provisionality of the human condition while believing themselves to narrate the certainty of the world, of the *ambivalence* of man-made design while believing themselves to narrate the *order* of nature. (Bauman, 1991: 232–3) (emphases in the original).

As social scientists discovered the variety of capitalisms around the world, and the uncertain paths they followed, it became harder and harder to represent the post-war American experience as the single, necessary end-point of all human development. Social science would have to learn tolerance and modesty.

In place of metanarratives, therefore, Lyotard (1984) reasserts the value of 'petits récits' (little stories). Here knowledge is captured and passed on in the stories of local communities rather than the law-like generalizations of science. Stories emphasize tradition and the particular—not an abstract, generalized 'savoir', but a practical and contextualized 'savoir-faire' (Lyotard, 1984: 21). In the postmodern condition, it is the practical competence of *savoir-faire* that matters. Practical competence involves not blind confidence in scientific laws, but sensitivity to context and appreciation of the tacit. Getting on in the post-modern world requires a different kind of knowledge, a return to the pragmatic humanism of the sixteenth century (Toulmin, 1990). In this view, the practical skills of rhetoric are again valued above the formal logic of rationality; local contexts, not universal rules, define appropriate conduct; the particular offers insights inaccessible to the general; the exigencies of practice demand timeliness as against timelessness. In short, modernism's pursuit of neat abstractions and theoretical simplifications should be abandoned in favour of direct confrontation with the unavoidable complexities of concrete human experience. In confronting these complexities, the great nation states of modernism—and especially the United States, founded upon Enlightenment notions of progress and reason—are unlikely to be in the vanguard (Toulmin, 1990).

There is real appeal in this postmodern assertion of contextualized *savoir-faire*. After all, managers love to insist on the uniqueness of their problems. Ironically, too, Chandler's own Harvard Business School distinctively relies on individual case studies in its teaching. We must acknowledge, therefore, the practical wisdom embodied in postmodernism's appreciation of the particular and its suspicion of Whiggish metanarratives of inevitability. Context matters: the question is how much?

Some are hard-line. Postmodernism has challenged all the modernist certainties of traditional management and organization theory. The instrumental rationality of contingency theory, its aspiration towards generalization, and even its essential categories are now particularly doubted (Chia, 1995, 1997; Kilduff and Mehra, 1997). The three contextualist critiques of Chandlerism that we shall introduce here take advantage of this collapse of faith in metanarratives of universal reason, but are less radical in their epistemological scepticism. They are not so much postmodern as 'after modernism'. Culturalists such as Hofstede (1980) assert the enduring plurality of national cultures; national institutionalists such as Whitley (1994) and Hollingsworth and Boyer (1997) stress the relationship of business practice with national institutions; while international institutionalists such as Guillén (1994), Locke (1996), and Djelic (1998) take a wider view, emphasizing the ebb and flow of dominant economic and managerial ideologies through the world. All define strict limits to the scope for generalization in the science of management.

National cultures

The culturalists claim enduring differences in business practice between nations based on long-standing cultural characteristics. In a particularly influential formulation, Hofstede (1980; 1991) describes culture as the 'collective programming of the mind'. Acquired through educational and family experience in youth, these programs project certain behaviours into business life. Thus acquired cultural orientations towards the long and the short term will influence typical approaches to strategy; cultural attitudes towards power will indicate characteristic approaches towards organization.

National cultures need not be homogeneous, of course, and the nation is just one of several possible cultural influences on people's behaviour. One way or another, however, these cultural effects are remarkably persistent. For instance, the contrasting cultures of the Romance and Germanic nations in Europe are traceable back to their positions within or outside the Roman Empire two thousand years ago (Hofstede, 1991: 42). The centralized power of Rome and the traditional autonomy of the Germanic tribes still cast their shadows on characteristic attitudes to organization in contemporary Europe. French hierarchies and Nordic egalitarianism are enduring consequences of history. Hofstede (1991: 238) finds little evidence for cultural convergence in more recent years—indeed, the recent upsurge in ethnic disputes may indicate quite the reverse.

The culturalists attribute a particular importance to American culture. The United States is as particular as any other culture. In an international comparative study, Hampden-Turner and Trompenaars (1993) find that American managers are the most strongly attached to general and impersonal codes of behaviour. American managers place high value on universal principles and analytical decision-making. Citing Henry Ford and McDonald's, Hampden-Turner and Trompenaars (1993: 20) conclude: 'The American ideal is of the Universal Product, reducible to parts (analysis) and infinitely replicable'. Again they trace this back in history, to the rational principles of the American Constitution and the deliberate fusion of the Melting Pot.

The special importance of the American culture, however, is that this particular way of thinking has been incorporated into American business schools and consultancies and then preached to the rest of the world as a universal model. In this view, the analytical, rational approach to strategy that originated at Harvard Business School, for instance, is a typical product of American culture (Hampden-Turner and Trompenaars, 1993: 27). Non-Americans should swallow Harvard orthodoxies with caution. Hofstede (1980: 252) quotes Pascal: 'There are truths this side of the Pyrenees which are falsehoods on the other'. He continues:

Organization and management theorists have rarely taken Pascal's wisdom to heart. In the management literature there are numerous unquestioning extrapolations of organizational solutions beyond the border of the country in which they were developed. This is especially true for the exportation of management theories from the United States . . . 'Management' itself is very much an American concept, just as earlier the entire discipline of economics was very much an Anglo-Saxon discipline. However, the empirical basis for American management theories is American organizations; and we should not assume without proof that they apply elsewhere (Hofstede, 1980: 252)

Hofstede is a declared cultural relativist. What works in one country will not necessarily work in another. In designing organizations internationally, Hofstede (1991: 22) confronts Chandler head-on, declaring that 'structure should follow culture'. The Atlantic is an even greater barrier than the Pyrenees.

National institutions

Recent theorizing of the effects of national institutions has much in common with the cultural tradition. There is an equal insistence on national distinctiveness and at least as strong a repudiation of trends towards convergence: Whitley's (1999) title is *Divergent Capitalisms*. The institutionalists differ, however, in putting the emphasis more on the effects of contemporary institutions than the mental programming of youth.

Distinctive modes of business practice in these approaches tend to be described in terms of 'systems'—'social systems of production' in Hollingsworth and Boyer's (1996) formulation or 'business systems' in Whitley's (1994; 1999). The systems notion is intended to underline cohesion. Hollingsworth and Boyer (1997) talk in terms of integrated 'social configurations'. Whitley (1994: 175–6) describes his business systems thus:

Business systems are . . . relatively cohesive and stable ways of ordering firm-market relationships that develop interdependently with dominant social institutions. They become established in market economies where these institutions are sufficiently integrated and mutually reinforcing to generate and help to reproduce distinctive patterns of economic organization . . . They become interdependent with these institutions.

Business and institutions are configured together in a tight system of interdependence.

The kinds of national institution that might be important are wide ranging. Whitley (1991; 1994) tends to emphasize family structures, national systems of finance, and the role of the state, while others put more emphasis on systems of education and training (Hollingsworth and Boyer, 1997; Sorge, 1991). These institutional characteristics vary from Anglo-Saxon capital markets to Germanic credit-based finance, from the familial traditions of Chinese family business to the technocratic élitism of France. However they are constituted, these institutions can stamp their mark on critical dimensions of local business practice. The range of business practice shaped by national institutions includes reliance on external alliances and networks, approaches to product innovation and differentiation, and strategies for employee inclusion and commitment (Hollingsworth and Boyer, 1997; Sorge, 1991). Whitley (1996) steps directly on Chandler's toes by including as institutionally variable the extent of diversification, the degree of structural centralization and the professionalization of management. All these business practices are moulded not by universalistic principles of efficiency but by distinctive national institutions. Whitley (1994) insists that 'efficiency' is institutionally constructed on the basis of local configurations, so that there can be no one best way of responding to particular technical and economic demands.

National institutionalists are sceptical of convergence. Here the systems notion plays a key role, with distinctive practices and institutions reinforcing each other through homeostatic feedback loops. National practices work because of national institutions; the success of these practices reinforces the institutions. So long as the circuit of reinforcement is unbroken, the system can remain effective. Incentives for change are weak, because piecemeal reforms will not work if out of sync with system-wide logics. The risks of change are large, because beyond a critical point equilibrium will be broken and the whole system will begin to unravel. In evolutionary terms, the systems notion implies 'punctuated equilibria' (Romanelli and Tushman, 1994) for national business practice—periods of system-reinforcing conservatism interrupted by episodes of system-wide collapse and transformation.

Theorists of national institutions extend the culturalist perspective in a number of directions. Culture is still there, incorporated especially through traditional institutions such as the family, religion, and education. But space is made for the introduction of new elements, such as finance and the modern state. Moreover, institutions are granted a degree of cultural autonomy and exercise their own effects. National comparisons can become more discriminating. Thus Taiwan and South Korea, for instance, may share a Confucian cultural legacy, but their different state institutions have promoted very distinct models of business (Hamilton and Feenstra, 1995). The introduction of semi-autonomous institutional effects also frees managerial action from dependence on the routines of cultural programs. Instead of being mere 'cultural dopes', managers may adapt to national institutions through deliberate choice. In all these senses, the theorists of national institutions are potentially more comprehensive, more discriminating, and less deterministic. The problems, we shall argue, lie in being both too hermetic and too homeostatic.

International institutions

The international institutionalists add to national institutionalists both a wider vision and a stronger sense of change (Djelic, 1998; Guillén, 1994). In this view, management practices in particular countries are increasingly subject to international and fluctuating ideologies. There are two critical moments in this kind of account. First, the Second World War, from which the United States emerged not only with economic supremacy but also with a social scientific *élan* capable of turning local experience into universal ideology. Second, the late 1970s and early 1980s, when the Japanese challenge and epistemological crisis combined to puncture what Locke (1996) has called the 'American mystique'.

By the late 1940s the West presented a disconcerting asymmetry: on the one hand, there was the United States, powerful and prosperous; on the other, there was a periphery of more or less client states, mostly impoverished and precarious. In the front line of the struggle against Soviet Communism, post-war Europe especially needed urgent support. In Djelic's (1998) account, the American response was the launch in 1948 of the Marshall Plan, or 'European Recovery Programme'. The Marshall Plan not only involved a massive transfer of financial aid; it also provided extensive 'technical' advice. Here the Americans had a mission. As Djelic (1998: 114) describes it: 'the ultimate objective of Marshall planners was to bring about a radical structural transformation of European economies and industries and to redefine trade patterns on the old continent using the American economic space as the model of reference'. Paul Hoffman, head of the plan, summed the strategy up as opposing the 'American assembly line' to the 'Communist party line' (Djelic, 1998: 78). As well as advice on economic and legal structures, the United States poured in new management thinking through extensive programmes of training and study tours for European managers.

As we have seen, Marshall Planners could draw on an increasingly articulate and developed social science base. Guillén (1994) describes the crystallization in the immediate post-war years of a new structural paradigm of organization centred on an 'invisible college' of sociologists led by Talcott Parsons. This soon fed into the structural contingency work of Paul Lawrence, Jay Lorsch, James Thompson, and Charles Perrow, not to mention Alfred Chandler. By the 1960s the American business schools had defined for themselves an increasingly comprehensive, mathematical, and individualistic paradigm of management capable of export to the new European business schools of INSEAD, London, and Manchester (Locke, 1988). The business schools, management consultancies, and expanding American multinationals now took over from the Marshall Plan the role of proselytizing the American way of business. McKinsey & Co. opened its first European office in London in 1959. Within a decade, McKinsey had six offices across Europe, A. T. Kearney five, Arthur D. Little four, and Booz Allen two (Kipping, 1999).

From the perspective of international institutionalists, the spread of the American model of management in the post-war period is not simply on account of its technical efficiency but is at least as much to do with the ideological and economic hegemony of the United States. Comments Guillén (1994: 283): 'Generally the ideological and technical components of the paradigm reinforce each other, but the absence of either does not seem to prevent the adoption of the other'. There was resistance and modification, but in Germany, France, and the United Kingdom at least, also willing adoption.

The hegemony of the American paradigm was short lived, however. Djelic (1998: 271) observes: 'the fate of the peculiar American system of industrial production was closely linked, throughout the twentieth century, to the fate of the USA as a country'. Political, economic, and, above all, managerial influence peaked in the 1960s. As the head of the London McKinsey office recalled: 'Somewhere about 1970 the phone stopped ringing' (McKenna, 1997: 230). European resurgence and Japanese success together dislodged the pre-eminence of the American model. The decline of American self-confidence is captured in the proportion of articles published on Japan in the American general management journal, the *California Management Review*. Between 1978 and 1982 there was only one article on Japanese management; in 1982–3, there were three; in 1983–4 there were eight; by 1984–5, eighteen out of the total of forty-five published articles were on Japan (Locke, 1996: 172). At the onset of the 1990s even the *Harvard Business Review* was promoting Japanese-style competence-based strategy and loose *keiretsu* holding companies (Ferguson, 1990; Prahalad and Hamel, 1990). The 1980s had seen, in Locke's (1996) terms, the 'collapse of the American management mystique'.

Thus the international institutionalists agree with theorists of national cultures and institutions that prevailing models of strategy and structure are unlikely to be adopted according to some universal principle of managerial efficiency: American models of management came to Europe on the back of American hegemony. However, the international institutionalists both open up national systems to international influences and sharpen sensitivity to economic, political, and ideological fluctuations over time: the dominance of American ideas was a temporary one. While national culturalists and national institutionalists are likely to warn management theorists of territorial limitations, international institutionalists underline the temporal. But in either case, all these theorists are united in emphasizing context.

This kind of contextualization is profoundly threatening to many management theorists. The characterization of rules for managerial effectiveness as local and temporary jeopardizes the modernistic ideal of social science as a collective endeavour directed at the steady accumulation of tried and tested knowledge. The epistemological uncertainty undermines the legitimacy of business schools and consultancies world-wide. Lex Donaldson (1996) and Jeffrey Pfeffer (1997) warn passionately against the implications of contextualism. The management disciplines become too fragmented to exercise influence in the world of affairs; the flight from practicality leads to a pernicious anti-managerialism insulting to those who are the discipline's ultimate clients.

For Donaldson (1996), therefore, a return to the sort of generalizable management science epitomized by the Harvard programme of the 1960s and 1970s is a precondition for developing a body of knowledge with the leverage and respect required to help its managerial clientele. He is appealing for a science of management that is both positivist, in the sense of providing testable, general

Table 2.1. *Theoretical Perspectives on Corporate Development*

	Mechanism	Key factors	Prediction
Economic universalists	Competition	Efficiency	Convergence
National institutionalists	Configuration	Locality	Diversity
International institutionalists	Conformity	Time	Flux

propositions, and positive, in the sense of offering managers helpful guidelines for their everyday practice. It is part of the purpose of this book to examine just how far the kind of social science of management represented by the Harvard programme really can still help—more than thirty years after its genesis on the other side of the Atlantic.

To summarize so far, three broad perspectives can be outlined on the future of the American model of strategy and structure. Table 2.1 distinguishes them according to the key mechanisms that drive corporate development, the factors that these mechanisms privilege, and the predictions they make for the future of the corporation. Chandlerism here joins structural contingency theory and much of the 'new paradigm of management studies' (Locke, 1988) as a theory of economic universals. These universalists see competitive pressures as driving out the inefficient, and predict international convergence on models of economic organization valid across time and country. This modernist teleology is challenged from at least two directions. The national institutionalists take up and extend the insights of the culturalists to insist on the importance of locality. Local institutions and cultures can form integrated, self-reinforcing configurations quite capable of opposing the homogenizing pressures of international competition. Their prediction is continued diversity in national forms of economic organization. The spread of the diversified multidivisional would be resisted. International institutionalists are less conservative, emphasizing the importance of conformity to changing norms of appropriate organization. In the early post-war years, the prevailing model was indeed the American diversified multidivisional. But all such international models are provisional, dependent upon the hegemony of particular ideas and states. International institutionalists expect flux, dominant models of organization ebbing and flowing across the world in parallel. As American influence declined and Japanese rose, they would expect to see the diversified multidivisional in retreat.

As Clegg (1990: 75, 105) observes, the fate of the Chandlerian diversified, divisionalized corporation makes a good test for competing views. It is true that these corporations, as large-scale multi-business organizations, occupy a particular level of the economic system, somewhat detached from the everyday activities of small firms and actual business units. These corporations are operating at the meso-economic level, in between the micro-economy of business units and the wider macro-economy and society (Holland, 1976: 50–1). They may not be entirely representative of their local environments. However, Chandlerian corporations are typically the dominant economic actors within their environments, with an influence extending down to their own particular business units and out to the business units of their suppliers, partners, and customers. They may be just one segment of the holistic systems insisted upon by national institutionalists (Whitley, 1994), but they are a very important one. Moreover, if these crucial meso-actors can change faster or slower than other elements of their systems, then the whole circular self-reinforcing motion of national configurations must be in doubt. There is a practical advantage as well. The Harvard group has developed an unusually effective set of metrics and laid down the substantial beginnings of a long-run, internationally comparative data-base. The terms they helped establish are now widely understood and used by the corporate level with which we are dealing. We can build, therefore, on existing work and, in the cosmopolitan and sophisticated world of contemporary European top management, be confident that the conceptual language is a native one (cf. Taylor, 1985). It is not surprising, then, both that structural contingency theorists should have made corporate strategy and structure one of its touchstones of validity (Donaldson, 1996: 143–5), or that international institutionalists should have seized on Harvard data in analysing the spread of American influence (Djelic, 1998; Guillén, 1994). In this debate, the Harvard metrics are used by contextualists and universalists alike.

2.3. BETWEEN CHANDLERISM AND CONTEXTUALISM

At one level, then, the argument over Chandlerism is a classic one—between the timeless and universal on the one hand, and the temporary and local on the other. But this argument need not be seen only in terms of stark choices. Certainly, Chandlerism and the early management sciences more widely were marked by their origins in the American social sciences of the immediate postwar period. In terms of their faith in progress and reason, they carry with them an awkward modernist legacy. To admit this influence of original context does not, however, define them utterly. Rather it helps to identify what is extraneous to these early theories and what is core. After modernism, we can drop the universalistic teleology, just retaining a limited core of good sense about corporate strategy and structure. What is at issue is where the limits of this good sense must be drawn. National institutionalists draw tight limits of territory; international institutionalists tight limits of time. We shall be more relaxed.

Thus, while we are interested in comparing corporate outcomes in Europe with the divergent predictions of Chandlerism, national institutionalists, and international institutionalists, that is not the whole game. After all, empirically our focus is a particular one: corporate strategy and structure in just three European countries over a finite period. At best, our findings will allow us to say only whether the claims of one side hold better than others' in these specific circumstances. Success for the Chandlerian model of the corporation across post-war Europe would be no more than that, circumscribed and provisional. Contextualist defeat for the Chandlerian model would not rule out eventual success in some European future. We shall be neither endorsing Harvard's universals wholeheartedly nor collapsing into out-and-out contextualism.

The issue is not whether context matters, but how much. Toulmin (1990: 179) has argued that we must make the best of the conceptual ideas we have got. Rather than accepting or abandoning them absolutely, we should work with them in a reflective and improving spirit in order to determine the limits of their scope. In this sense, instead of arguing about whether we can generalize or not in absolute terms, we are concerned with the bounds within which generalization might be a reasonable thing to do. Our purpose is to map out a sphere in which a bounded management science might be possible.

Figure 2.1 lays out two dimensions according to which the contextualists have insisted on strict limits to generalization about the Chandlerian model of the

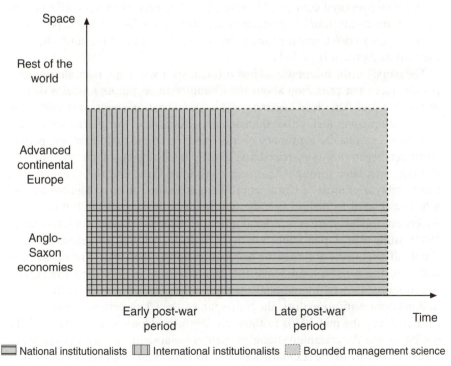

Figure 2.1. *Scope for Generalization of the Chandlerian Corporate Model*

diversified, divisonalized corporation. The vertical axis charts the extent of reasonable generalization across space, distinguishing between Anglo-Saxon
economies—of which the United States and the United Kingdom are exemplars—the advanced Continental European economies, and the rest of the
world. The horizontal axis concerns validity over time, distinguishing between
the early post-war period of American hegemony, and the later post-war period
marked (initially at least) by Japanese success. The patterned areas contrast in
stylized terms the very different claims for the scope of legitimate generalization
made by the national and international institutionalists.

From this perspective, the scope for generalization proposed by national institutionalists is long and narrow. National institutionalists underline the specificity of the institutional configuration necessary to supporting the diversified,
divisionalized firm. In the first place, this configuration emerged in the United
States, but, as we shall see in the following chapters, many of these features have
been reproduced in other Anglo-Saxon economies such as the United Kingdom
where the logics of the capital markets also dominate. At a stretch, then,
national institutionalists might generalize about diversification and divisionalization within the Anglo-Saxon economies (Whitley, 1996), but they would
hesitate to go further. To the extent that efficiency is socially constructed on the
basis of local conditions, performance relationships would inescapably alter in
different institutional contexts. However, as self-reinforcing system effects typically ensure institutional stability, national institutionalists would expect these
relationships to hold over the long term. There should be little change between
the early and post-war periods.

The scope for the international institutionalists is wider spatially, shorter temporally. Here generalization about the Chandlerian corporate model is defined
by the extent of American hegemony. This generalization concerns the diffusion
of the American model, rather than actual performance: the international institutionalists emphasize legitimacy over economics. In the early post-war period,
American hegemony as exercised first directly by the agents of the post-war set-
tlement, then later through American consulting firms and the like, extended
comfortably over most of Continental Western Europe at least. The borders are
a little awkward to define, as Italy and Spain both escaped the full effects of
American modernization for local political reasons (Djelic, 1998; Guillén,
1994), while even Japan might briefly be included within this sphere before it
shook off the effects of American occupation during the 1950s (Fruin, 1992). In
any case, the geographical scope for generalization goes beyond the Anglo-
Saxon limits allowed by national institutionalists. On the other hand, for the
international institutionalists, the time-span of the Chandlerian model is much
shorter. From the mid-1970s to the early 1990s the Japanese challenge and the
decline of the 'American mystique' brought a collapse in its international legitimacy. According to the standard account, the American corporate model lost its
dominance not only in Europe but—such was the self-critical obsession with

Japan—in the United States and the other Anglo-Saxon economies as well (Locke, 1996). In the late post-war period, then, international institutionalists would expect older claims on behalf of the diversified, divisionalized corporation no longer to hold.

Thus the two institutionalist positions are demarcated by quite limited, but contrasting, portions of Figure 2.1. Against these are the ambitious claims of economic universalism, such as those of structural contingency theory and raw Chandlerism. Recalling Donaldson's (1996) strong words, theirs are propositions that are universally valid, and on which the sun never sets. In this view, as the world economy advanced, so more and more nations would irreversibly converge on the rational logic of the Chandlerian corporate model. If not already, then sooner or later, the economic universalists would effectively lay claim to the whole of Figure 2.1.

We are caught here between theoretical extremes familiar throughout the social sciences (Giddens, 1979; Reed, 1986; Mouzelis, 1995). The universalists appeal because of the breadth of their scope and their avowed practical engagement with the problems of the world. They alienate by the imperialism of their generalizations and the unacknowledged simplifications of their prescriptions. The contextualists counsel caution and point to the real complexities of practice. They exasperate because of their disabling relativism, their refusal to offer any general guidelines. We need both the leverage of generalization and the checks of contextualism.

The 'conceptual pragmatism' of Nicos Mouzelis (1995) is attractive here. Generalizations should not take on the universal and foundationalist character of modernism, but simply be admitted as potentially helpful tools in empirical work and theoretical debate. In the kind of modest, tactical social science he proposes, the focus should be on 'tentative, flexible, open-ended, transitional frameworks useful for the empirical, comparative investigation of specific sociological problems' (Mouzelis, 1995: 152). These general frameworks are necessary both for the digging of data and the channelling of knowledge between communities. The essential thing here, however, is always to be reflective and adaptable about which tools work best, where and when. The boundaries of any general framework need constantly to be probed and tested.

Our ambition, then, is to recast Chandler's model in the modest, adaptable mode of Mouzelis (1995). Instead of positing it in the universal and teleological terms of its origins in the modernist, post-war American social sciences, the Chandlerian model should be offered as merely a tentative hypothesis and exploratory tool. Here we are dealing with a 'bounded' notion of the management sciences, in which the scope for generalization is limited and provisional. Returning to Figure 2.1, with the empirical materials we have, we can define a sphere for legitimate generalization about the corporation roughly as follows. Spatially, we may be able to claim robust relationships broadly across the advanced economies of both Continental Europe (with the possibility of the same kinds of exceptions as already identified for Italy and Spain) and the Anglo-Saxon world (if the United Kingdom is accepted as a proxy). Temporally, we may be able to project the same across more or less the whole post-war period, but to go further would be just to speculate.

In the tactical mode of Mouzelis (1995), therefore, the basic proposition would be this, and no more than this: that the diversified, divisionalized model of the corporation has been able to offer real economic advantages that extend across Anglo-Saxon and Western European economies alike and which endure over many decades. National institutional arrangements have not been sufficiently different to block the adoption of this model, even though they might have introduced delays or local interpretations. The economic benefits have been sufficiently substantial and transferable to pull across quite contrasting business systems. In the same way, the rise and fall of different models of good management—first American, then Japanese—has not substantially altered the pattern of diffusion. American hegemony in the early post-war years may have speeded adoption of the Chandlerian model, but American decline has not reversed it. The kinds of real economic advantages to diversification and divisionalization hold across this particular configuration of time and space.

This 'bounded' view of the corporation thus extends beyond the limits drawn by the institutional contextualists. Boundaries are still drawn, of course: the Chandlerian corporation's economic advantages depend upon the conditions of largely free competition that have pertained in Western Europe and the Anglo-Saxon economies through the post-war period. There are very good reasons for thinking that the radically different product, labour, and financial markets of emerging economies, and even of some developed Asian economies, will fundamentally disqualify a model developed for the advanced West (Khanna and Palepu, 1999). With our data, we cannot tell. Nevertheless, as indicated by the contrast of dotted lines with continuous lines, we draw our boundaries less definitely than the contextualists. So long as the present conditions hold for advanced economies, and as these conditions expand their geographical scope, so the reach of the Chandlerian model of the diversified, divisionalized corporation is likely to widen. There is no necessity to this, nor any irreversibility, but the world could continue in its present development towards a more universal condition. Chandler would not be absolutely right, but becoming more right all the time.

We should admit one important limitation to the greater scope for generalization claimed by this bounded management science. Figure 2.1. is noticeably two dimensional. There is no obvious depth to the kinds of generalization that might be made. In fact, this describes the limitations of generalization quite well. The postmodern emphasis on practical competence—on *savoir-faire* rather than simple *savoir*—requires an appreciation of the deep complexity of everyday practice that is absent from our kind of generalization. These generalizations skate over the practical exigencies discovered in local context. It is useful to know broadly which strategies and structures fit the large corporation, but ultimately this kind of knowledge is 'thin'. Generalizations about strategy and structure can tell us something about what to do in general, little about how to do it in particular cases. Fully practical knowledge requires the combination of *savoir* with *savoir-faire*. The postmodern notion of contextualized practice is, therefore, at least as practical as structural contingency theory's laws of organizational design. Contrary to Donaldson (1996), the two forms of knowledge are not in opposition, but in complementarity.

In the empirical materials that follow, however, we shall be concentrating on the broad principles of strategy and structure, *savoir* more than *savoir-faire*. This is a methodological device, a focus on what is most accessible and most pertinent in the comparison of different models of corporate development. Such 'methodological bracketing' (Giddens, 1979: 80) does not deny the importance of contextualized practices; it merely puts them on hold for our principal purpose here. The format of our empirical chapters will acknowledge this bracketed form of knowledge: while relying on statistics to establish general trends and relationships, we shall also detail particular cases in order to recall something of the complex individuality underneath. To this extent at least, the cautionary wisdom of Lyotard's (1984) 'little stories' will run alongside our claims for broad principles.

2.4. SUMMARY

It would be easy to dismiss the Chandlerian model of the diversified, divisionalized corporation as merely the product of its time and place. The contextualist critique would run as follows. Following the national institutionalists, the Chandlerian corporation was well adapted to the type of business system that emerged in the mid-twentieth-century United States and which has since spread to other Anglo-Saxon economies such as the United Kingdom. It took from its birthplace in American culture a very particular faith in universal principles and analytical decision-making. It was stamped with the evolutionary modernism of the mainstream social sciences of its time. It was only certain cultural, intellectual, and political accidents that led to the Chandlerian corporation being projected so enthusiastically further afield. The model was imposed on the world as a by-product of the extraordinary but passing hegemony of the United States in the immediate post-war years. The waning of American power and prestige in recent decades now leaves the Chandlerian model exposed as the over-rational, over-generalizing, and over-confident ideal typical of its origins.

We do not wish to go that far. Our aim, rather, is to rescue Chandler from Chandlerism. As a mode of thought, Chandlerism was incautious. Product of its time and place, it participated in a modernistic vision of rational, universal progress which conceded few limits. This kind of modernist confidence should now be seen as passé. After modernism, there is today a stronger appreciation both of the limits of time and place and of the attenuated nature of the knowledge found in positivist prescriptions. Postmodernism has vaunted *savoir-faire*; institutionalists have underlined temporal and territorial context.

Just how tightly these temporal and territorial limits should be drawn is, however, an empirical question. Institutionalism should be put to the test alongside Chandlerism. This chapter has developed the widely different presumptions of Chandlerism and institutionalism concerning the fate of the diversified, divisionalized corporation in contemporary Europe. As part of a wider tradition of economic universalism, Chandlerism predicts continued, even overwhelming, progress for this model discovered eighty years ago on the other side of the Atlantic. National institutionalists doubt this progress, especially in Continental Europe, outside the Anglo-Saxon sphere. International institutionalists, on the other hand, have challenged the degree to which the Chandlerian model might have entrenched itself, suggesting dependence on an American hegemony that is now long past. As we track the evolution of large corporations in France, Germany, and the United Kingdom, we shall be able to judge whose version comes closest to unfolding empirical reality.

But the objective is not simply to adjudicate between universalist and contextualist approaches. More, it will be to establish a sphere within which we can generalize about the corporation with some confidence. The management sciences need to offer certain kinds of general prescriptions, but they need also to be constantly probing the scope within which these generalizations might hold. The contextualists give us dimensions along which this scope might be defined; they also warn that relationships should adapt over time and place. As we track the strategies and structures of large industrial corporations in Western Europe, therefore, we shall not only be testing the extent to which American principles still fit within the evolving and diverse contours of contemporary Europe. We shall also be demarcating a zone for effective generalization within the management sciences.

As the next chapter will show, diversification and divisionalization are thorny topics for the management and social sciences. It will be no small task to extract from contradictory theories and data broad principles robust across countries and renewable over time. That, however, should be the central objective in developing a bounded science of the contemporary corporation. We shall argue, moreover, that the Chandlerian model still offers an essential core for such an endeavour.

3

Scale, Scope, and Structure

INTRODUCTION

If the Chandlerian model is to be at the heart of a boundedly generalizing science of the corporation, it will have a lot to cope with. After all, a good deal of time has passed since its first formulation. Business has continued to develop; America's influence has waned; other parts of the world, and their social scientists, now assert their particularity. Nevertheless, the project of a bounded management science demands some such general model, one both adequate to the changing conditions of business and comprehensive enough to embrace the varied environments of post-war Europe. The Chandlerian model will have to be both robust and flexible.

All three elements of the original Chandlerian model are now disputed. Chandler's (1990) faith in the large-scale corporation itself is challenged by proponents of a new economic paradigm based on enterprise and networks. Big business is accused of anachronism. Diversification too is in dispute. On the one hand, there are claims for a radical wave of 'downscoping'. On the other hand, the conglomerate is a late-arriving but stubbornly persistent element on the corporate scene. We shall need to find a plausible economic rationale for the conglomerate if we are not to concede to sceptical sociological accounts, putting it down either to managerial abuse or to nationally specific social institutions. Finally, there is the modernist multidivisional structure, where again sociology presses sceptically against protagonists of economic efficiency. International institutionalists attribute the spread of the multidivisional to the short-lived hegemony of the United States. National institutionalists doubt whether the multidivisional ever did make a substantial impact on local traditions of organizing. Even American business schools are now proclaiming the death of the M-form.

This chapter starts by introducing the large industrial corporation—for some, a crowning achievement of twentieth-century capitalism, for others now just a redundant remnant. It will go on to examine the debates surrounding the strategies by which the large corporation grew and the structures by which it was managed. On diversification, we begin by considering the patchy evidence on diversification trends and performance in the United States and Europe, particularly in the light of arguments concerning a general downscoping of contemporary business. We then pitch economic arguments principally from the market-power perspective and the resource-based view of the firm against more sociological arguments pointing to managerial interests and hubris and the changing role of financial markets. The challenge for a bounded management science will be to assemble from these conflicting theories some sort of rationale for the confusing patterns of diversification that emerge in empirical practice. Rather than conceding to sociology, we stretch the Chandlerian model to accommodate the conglomerate, principally by adding the notion of corporate relationships to the operational relationships traditionally stressed by Harvard and the resource-based view.

From diversification, we shall move to consider the place of the multi-divisional. We shall first examine its idealization as the embodiment of modern bureaucratic rationality, superior to its centralized functional and chaotic holding company alternatives. Then we shall develop further the two institution-alist critiques introduced in the last chapter: first international critiques, that see the multidivisional as merely the projection of American power; second, national critiques that again underline the multidivisional's specific origins, but are more sanguine about countries' abilities to resist such alien imports. Here we shall particularly focus on expectations drawn from Whitley's (1994) national institutionalist perspective about the relative propensity of France, Germany, and the United Kingdom to adopt the diversified strategies and decentralized structures advocated by Harvard in the 1970s. As for diversification, however, even in the United States faith in the multidivisional structure is no longer what it was two or three decades ago. We shall also consider, therefore, the argument that business is now going 'beyond the M-form' (Bartlett and Ghoshal, 1993), towards something more in line with a putative postmodern or network economy. The queries here are whether a generalizeable notion of corporate organization is still possible and whether anything can be rescued from the old model of the multidivisional. Part of the answer here is again to extend the Chandlerian model, this time by seeing recent experiments with the 'network multidivisional' as part of a continuous pattern of structural evolution ever since DuPont's pioneering transformation in the 1920s.

3.1. SCALE

Peter Drucker, 1930s *emigré* from a much-reduced Austria, was greatly impressed by the scale of American industry. Drawing on his experience working for great organization-builder Alfred Sloan at General Motors, he wrote:

The emergence of Big Business, i.e., the large integrated industrial unit, as a social reality during the past fifty years is the most important event in the recent social history of the Western World. It is even possible that to future generations the world wars of our time will seem to have been an incident in the rise of big-business society, just as to many his-

torians the Napoleonic wars have come to appear incidental to the Industrial Revolution
. . . the problem of the political, social, and economic organization of Big Business is not
unique to one country but common to the entire Western world (Drucker, 1946: 21)

At the middle of the twentieth century, the construction of American big business seemed not only a supreme achievement of the century; it could also teach
substantial lessons world-wide.

That was then. For many now the American big business of Drucker and
Chandler is a damaging anachronism. For Piore and Sabel (1984), the large corporation was the product of the 'first industrial divide', the superseding of craft
production by mass production at the end of the nineteenth century and the
beginning of the twentieth. But now the large corporation itself is threatened
with redundancy, as a 'second industrial divide' emerges, replacing scale and
standardization with flexibility and specialization. The model moves from the
large American corporation to the networks of small subcontractors in North
Italy and the medium-sized firms of Germany's Mittelstand. Teece's (1993)
argument is similar, only more favourable to the United States. For him,
Chandler's exemplars are the products of the second industrial revolution,
industries like chemicals and automobiles requiring huge scale. The models for
contemporary business are companies like Sun and Dell, products of the third
industrial revolution, based on information. Here it is not integration within
large-scale corporations like DuPont or General Motors that matters, but the
ability to move fast and mobilize extended networks of subcontractors. Again,
flexibility matters more than size.

Rumours of the death of old-style big business are greatly exaggerated. In
Fortune's 1999 Global 500 listing, six of the world's ten largest corporations by
revenue had foundation dates in the nineteenth century or earlier: Daimler
Chrysler in 1883, Mitsui in 1673, Itochu in 1858, Mitsubishi in 1870, Exxon in
1882, and General Electric in 1892 (www.fortune.com, 2000; Derdack, 1988).
The newest company in the top ten was Wal-Mart, founded in 1962. Microsoft
ranked at 284. Hannah (1998) works from the other end, tracing the histories of
big business at the start of the twentieth century forward to the 1990s. Remarkably, twenty of the world's hundred largest industrial corporations in 1912 were
still in the Top 100 in 1995—including European companies in our sample such
as BASF, Bayer, BP (Anglo-Persian), Guinness, RTZ, and Unilever (Lever
Brothers). These big old businesses have great staying-power.

Big business has also held on to a good share of economic activity. Certainly,
the immediate post-war period was a time of spectacular growth for the large
corporation. But even in recent times big business has grown only marginally
less fast than the rest of the economy and at the end of the century was still substantially more important than fifty years before. In the United States, the share
of manufacturing net output accounted for by the Top 100 enterprises stayed
steadily at around 20 per cent between 1909 and 1949, before accelerating to

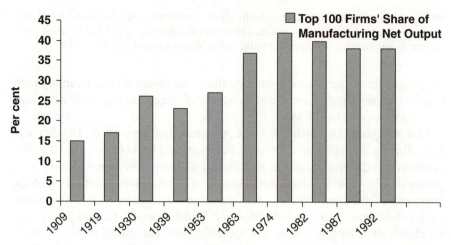

Figure 3.1. *Top 100 Manufacturing Firms' Share of Net Output in the United Kingdom*
Note: Discontinuities over time, for instance due to privatization in the 1980s
Sources: Hannah (1976); Shutt and Whittington (1987); Davies et al., (1999)

reach a good third in the 1970s and 1980s (Supple, 1992; Chandler and Hikino, 1997). In the United Kingdom, big business at the start of the century was quite limited: six out of the seven largest employers in 1907 were railway companies (Supple, 1992). As Figure 3.1 indicates, again it was the post-war period when big business saw its largest gains, with the largest 100 enterprises' share of manufacturing net output rising from 27 per cent in the early 1950s to over 40 per cent in the 1970s. Despite a slight reversal in the 1980s (Shutt and Whittington, 1987), the Top 100 firms still accounted for 38 per cent of net manufacturing output in the early 1990s (Davies et al., 1999). In Germany, the Top 100 firms accounted for 34 per cent of net manufacturing output in 1993 (Davies et al., 1999). The proportion of French, German, and United Kingdom firms among the largest Western industrial companies in the world climbed from 25 per cent to just over 30 per cent between 1962 and 1993 (Chandler and Hikino, 1997). The four or five decades over which this book will range have been years of successful growth for the large European enterprise. Moreover, whatever the contemporary fashion for networks and the small, big business is still big in Europe.

Large firms are not only big in themselves but have disproportionate effects on their economies. Chandler and Hikino (1997) document how it is large firms that have been able to make the necessary investments in the scale and knowledge-intensive industries that have been central to twentieth-century growth. In chemicals, automobiles, aerospace, telecommunications, and computers, large firms have generally dominated both production and research and development. The influence of these large firms radiates beyond their own boundaries via the networks of suppliers and customers that surround them. Large firms are disproportionately active in international trade and link their smaller suppliers into the global economy through the products they export.

As we follow the evolution of large European firms in post-war Europe, therefore, we shall be observing some of the key motors in their respective economies. Size matters. In an oligopolistic world, large firms' decisions can make a critical difference to the development of whole sectors of national production. As Chandler, Amatori, and Hikino (1997: 3) propose: 'How such firms emerged and evolved in various economic, political, and social settings constitutes a significant part of the modern development of international and national economies'. It will be important to supply the large corporation with some sort of general rationale.

3.2. SCOPE

Growth by diversification is the essential basis for the contemporary large-scale corporation. Today's business giants did not grow simply in pursuit of scale economies in their original business. Rumelt (1974) shows that already by 1949 only one in three American Fortune 500 firms was still concentrated in the undiversified 'single' business category; by 1969, the proportion was 6.2 per cent. Nor did they grow just by internationalization. The United Nations' study of the world's largest multinationals showed that as late as the mid-1990s such companies as General Electric and Toyota still had more than four-fifths of their employees in their home countries, while Ford and General Motors had more than two-thirds of their sales and two-thirds of their assets still in the United States (UNCTAD, 1996).[1] Exceptions there are, but the following is true enough: the large corporation is large because it is diversified.

Yet during the 1980s corporate fashion turned against this widening of scope. In their runaway success *In Search of Excellence*, Peters and Waterman (1982: 293–4) warned fiercely against excessive diversification:

both the qualitative guiding value . . . and the hands-on approach are at war with diversification . . . Organizations that do break out . . . but stick very close to their knitting outperform the others. The most successful of all these are diversified around a single skill . . . the second group, in descending order, comprises those companies that branch out into related fields . . . least successful are those companies that diversify into a wide variety of fields.

---

[1] Consistent and comprehensive long-run metrics of internationalization are not available for our corporations. For the British domestic Top 100 industrials, average overseas turnover as a proportion as a whole seems to have increased from about 36 per cent (excluding three highly international oil companies) in 1970, to 42.9 per cent in 1983, to 54.5 per cent in 1993 (Channon, 1973: 82–3; Datastream). Average export sales of domestic Top 100 industrials in France rose from 44.4 per cent of total sales in 1983 to 53.8 per cent in 1993 (*Expansion*, December 1984; 21 November 1994).

Peters and Waterman's (1982) stress on the social against the rational, and the qualitative against the quantitative, challenges the financial definition of the corporation as simply a bundle of liquid assets. Excellent companies have strong cultures, coherent value systems incompatible with the precarious portfolios of conglomerate-style management. Again, there is an issue of national style. Japanese companies are described as managing 'portfolios of competencies', the Americans as just 'portfolios of businesses' (Prahalad and Hamel, 1990). While the Americans put no value on coherence, the Japanese conceive of the corporation as a large tree: 'the trunk and major limbs are core products, the smaller branches are business units; the leaves, flowers and fruit are end products. The root system that provides nourishment, sustenance and stability is the core competence' (Prahalad and Hamel, 1990: 82). Anglo-Saxon conglomerates are bad; diversification deeply rooted in core competence could still be good.

Even in the United States, therefore, diversification and especially unrelated diversification have been coming under attack. American business was typically 'over-diversified', lacking sufficient focus to invest in innovation and the long term (Hoskisson and Hitt, 1994; cf. Markides, 1995). Just as the conglomerate strategy lost its institutional legitimacy in popular management theory, new conglomerate-busting techniques such as the leveraged buy-out were becoming available and a more relaxed antitrust regime allowed businesses to grow in their core markets (Davies et al., 1994). 'Downscoping'—refocusing on core businesses—became the slogan (Hoskisson and Hitt, 1994). Yet the evidence for a widespread return to specialization in the recent period, and especially for the eclipse of the conglomerate, remains quite limited, even in the United States.

Two broad approaches exist for examining diversification trends in the 1980s and early 1990s. On the one hand, many have looked at particular groups of restructuring firms. Two widely quoted studies of restructuring in the United States seem to confirm the instability of unrelated businesses at the firm level in recent years. Williams et al.'s (1988) historical analysis of companies classified as conglomerates in the 1984 Forbes list shows that over the preceding ten years their managers tended to sell off peripheral activities, with restructuring concentrated in the later period. However, as this simply traced existing conglomerates backwards, Williams et al. (1988) do not actually show a decline in conglomerates, just increased coherence within them. Likewise, Bhagat et al.'s (1990) study of hostile takeovers in the mid-1980s seems to indicate that conglomerates were a particular target, and that many of their assets went to related acquirers. Again, however, this study concentrates on one side of the equation, only tangentially reflecting entries into the conglomerate category. A bust-up of one conglomerate could actually lead to an increase in the number of conglomerates if just two of all the various pieces went to unrelated buyers. Hoskisson and Johnson's (1992) more comprehensive study of all kinds of American restructurers in the 1980s found that unrelated diversifiers were actually slightly more likely to stick to their conglomerate strategies than related companies to theirs.

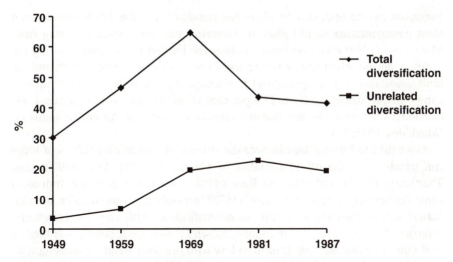

Figure 3.2. *Diversification Trends of American Fortune 500 Industrial Firms, 1949–87*
Sources: Rumelt (1974); Markides (1995)

Similarly, Bergh and Holbein's (1997) study of restructuring Fortune 500 firms in the mid-1980s found that, once time effects are included, there is no significant relationship between degree of diversification and extent of divestment of assets.

Following particular groups of restructuring firms has generally been inconclusive, therefore. Our own approach in Europe will be to trace broad populations of firms, in our case Top 100 industrial firms. However, the picture so far from the analysis of such populations is contradictory as well. Lichtenberg's (1992) study of American firms between 1985 and 1989 finds an overall decrease in the average number of industries in which firms participated. This may reflect de-diversification, but does not discriminate between conglomerates and related diversifiers. On the other hand, Hatfield et al.'s (1996) similar analysis over the longer period of 1981–9 suggests that industry specialization for the average American firm (measured by the concentration of employees by industry) actually decreased slightly.

A particularly relevant population study here is Markides's (1995) examination of American Fortune 500 firms between 1981 and 1987. Because Markides (1995) uses the same categorical approach as we shall be using, i.e. Rumelt's (1974), his findings should provide a particularly good base-line for comparison with trends in Europe. Effectively, he extends the continuous coverage from 1949 to 1974 achieved by Rumelt (1974; 1982) through 1981 to 1987, using comparable samples and the same classification methods. The diversification data from the United States for the whole post-war period to 1987 are summarized in Figure 3.2. We should note the possibility of some discontinuity between Rumelt's (1974) original data and Markides's (1995) data for the 1980s, as suggested by the apparent break in the trends during the 1970s, earlier than most commentators would place it. However, the most striking finding from Markides's (1995) own continuous data is the limited restructuring during the 1980s, a period when restructuring was expected to be greatest. Although he finds some recovery in specialized businesses, there is only limited decline in conglomerate strategies, from 22.4 per cent of his sample to 19.0 per cent. He concludes that there is 'no massive refocusing trend in American industry' (Markides, 1995: 55).

As we turn to Europe, we can note the absence of systematic analysis of long-run trends since the original studies of Channon (1973), Dyas (1972), and Thanheiser (1972). Luffman and Reed's (1982) study of top British industrial firms deliberately extends Channon (1973) but only takes us to 1979: for that period at least they report continued diversification, with very few companies reversing their strategies. From France, Batsch's (1993) study covers only the late 1980s and in a manner that is hard to link with previous trends: confusingly, he finds very slightly more large companies increasing the number of industries in which they participate than companies reducing them. Batsch (1993) also reports financially based groups and firms in declining industries to be particularly active in conglomerate strategies. From Germany, there are only cross-sectional studies on non-comparable bases (Bühner, 1987; Schmitz, 1989; Rondi et al., 1996). For a strategy with such allegedly important consequences for firm and national performance, it is striking how little systematic data we have on recent European trends.

If the picture regarding trends is confused, so too is that for relative performance. The dominant approach here has been to compare the average accounting profit returns of various kinds of diversification, typically using the Harvard related and unrelated categories. Here, orthodoxy predicts advantages to related diversification over unrelated, but no clear pattern emerges. Rumelt (1974) was the first in this tradition, and did find superior performance for his American related diversifiers. Since then, however, a good number of studies have queried this result, with several, particularly from the United Kingdom, finding the advantage of related diversifiers over unrelated to be either small, unstable over time, or even inverted (e.g. Luffman and Reed, 1982; Hill, 1988; Grant and Jammine, 1988; Grant, Jammine, and Thomas, 1988). The capacity to generalize performance differences across time and space is severely in doubt. Reviewing the results of American and European studies more broadly, Markides and Williamson (1996: 341) have observed in some exasperation that 'after so many years of academic research on the relationship between diversification and performance, there is still uncertainty and confusion regarding the nature of this relationship'.

In sum, the model of diversification promoted in the 1960s and 1970s seems to be in trouble, but it is hard to say how much. The data from the United States and Europe on recent trends are ambiguous, but by and large not suggestive of major refocusing. Conglomerates are under fire, but not extinguished. No clear performance advantage emerges to particular patterns of diversification. Diversification is clearly still important, but the picture theory must grapple with is a complex and elusive one.

3.3. EXPLAINING SCOPE

If diversification accounts for the large corporation, it is hard to account for diversification. As Montgomery (1994: 163) observes, most theoretical models offered to introductory and even intermediate students of economics prefer simply to portray the firm as homogenous producers of single products. But it does not seem as if diversification is going to go away. The large diversified corporation deserves a proper theoretical account, one moreover that can accommodate even the awkward persistence of the unloved conglomerate.

Dominant existing theories of diversification fall broadly into two camps: economic approaches that manage to account for part of the phenomenon, but probably not all; and sceptical approaches from economics and sociology that account for the rise of the phenomenon, but not for its persistence. If we are to find some sort of generalizeable managerial rationale for the diversification phenomena that we shall observe in Europe, we shall need to improve on the theoretical accounts currently available.

Economic rationales for diversification

There are two broad economic rationales for diversification in the existing literature. One, the market power explanation, is undesirable and increasingly unlikely. The other, the resource-based view, is fashionable but presently inadequate. This section introduces the market-power and the resource-based perspectives, while touching on other less mainstream approaches. Finding that none of the currently dominant explanations is entirely satisfactory, this section concludes by extending the resource-based view to tackle the thorny but persistent problem of the conglomerate.

Suspicious minds attribute the rise of the diversified corporation to the pursuit of market power. Industrial economics as a discipline founded on the problem of antitrust was quick to seize on the competitive problems raised by diversification. Thus, Corwin Edwards (1955: 334) early expressed this view:

A concern that produced many products and operates across many markets need not regard a particular market as a separate unit for determining business policy and need not attempt to maximize its profits in the sale of each of its products, as has been presupposed in our traditional scheme. . . . It may possess power in a particular market not only by virtue of its place in the organization of that market but also by virtue of the scope and character of its activities elsewhere. It may be able to exploit, extend or defend its power by tactics other than those that are traditionally associated with the idea of the monopoly.

Diversification, then, is essentially about market power. Diversified firms can use the profits drawn from one product market to subsidize a price war in another. In facing particular competitors in multiple markets, they can practice mutual forbearance, explicitly or tacitly agreeing not to compete too hard. They can exploit reciprocal buying arrangements, using interrelationships with other large diversified firms to squeeze smaller competitors out of markets. In all these ways, diversified firms have real economic advantages over undiversified firms, and may be expected gradually to drive them out.

The exploitation of market power remains a potent explanation for individual strategies of diversification. The unfair linkage of its internet search engine to other computer packages is precisely the nature of the 1999 complaint against Microsoft (*The Economist*, 13 November 1999). Yet it is hard to link the steady rise of diversification to simple pursuit of monopolistic power. This would require us to believe in an equally steady increase in opportunities for anti-competitive exploitation of diversification over the course of the century, not just in the United States but also in Europe. It is hard to accept that antitrust mechanisms have followed a smooth path of degradation through most of the twentieth century. Indeed, Davies et al. (1994) show that the severity of anti-trust regulation in the United States has regularly fluctuated. The fashionable explanation now, therefore, is drawn from the resource-based view of the firm.

The resource-based view originates in Edith Penrose's (1959) *Theory of the Growth of the Firm*. Here diversification is driven by the desire to use the services of under-utilized resources, especially managerial time and skills:

Unused productive services are, for the enterprising firm, at the same time a challenge to innovate, an incentive to expand, and a source of competitive advantage . . . The point of origin for the plans of any firm is circumscribed by the firm's resources and the services they can render (Penrose, 1959: 85–6)

In other words, it is the existence of surplus resources that stimulates diversification, and it is the nature of these existing resources that determine the direction in which this diversification goes. Although at the time apparently unaware of Penrose's logic (Chandler, 1962: 453), Chandler's own thinking on diversification was similarly driven by resources. Chandler's (1962: 384–5) 'third chapter' of corporate development emphasized 'the expansion into new markets and lines to help assure the continuing full use of resources'. In his more recent focus on 'organizational capabilities', Chandler (1990: 634) explicitly acknowledges his Penrosian affinities.

The resource-based view turns attention away from the drive to dominate external markets towards the efficient use of internal resources—a much more beneficent motive. Some resources are subject to economies of scope, so that their full and efficient employment requires that they be turned to additional uses to those originally envisaged. Other surplus resources ready for alternative uses are acquired either because they come in awkward lumps larger than strictly required or because they emerge as experience and learning improve the efficiency with which they are used in their original application. In any case, it seems that there are always surplus resources about and that the best way to use them is in diversification.

From the point of view of the resource-based view, therefore, diversification is perfectly natural—so long as it builds on existing resources. However, it is important to recognize a certain slippage in the nature of resources typically emphasized. Penrose (1959) saw the importance of managerial and entre- preneurial resources as drivers to growth and diversification: these have a natural tendency to surplus because experience constantly increases the efficiency with which they are used in their existing activities. Within the contemporary stra- tegic management discipline, on the other hand, the emphasis is typically on less general resources. In his pioneering statement of the resource-based view within strategic management, Birger Wernerfelt (1984) emphasizes operational resources such as machine capacity, customer base, production experience, and technological leads. Similarly, Teece, Pisano, and Shuen (1997: 516), in their recent extension in the direction of dynamic capabilities, give as examples such operational resources as trade secrets, specialized production facilities, and engineering experience. These kinds of resources gain value because they are unique, hard to imitate, and not easily transferred through ordinary markets.

The consequence for strategy of this emphasis on operational resources is that the only approved diversification strategy is related diversification (in the Harvard sense of Chapter 1). Wernerfelt (1984) discusses diversification just in regard to mergers and acquisitions, but here recommends related strategies aimed at acquiring resources that either supplement or complement those already within the firm. It is because these acquired resources will be combined with existing resources that they may gain a value in excess of their likely market price. Teece et al. (1997: 529) are broader and still more categorical: 'Related diversification—that is, diversification that builds upon or extends existing capabilities—is about the only form of diversification that a resources/ capabilities framework is likely to view as meritorious.'

This resource-based perspective relies on a rather asymmetrical view of differ- ent kinds of markets. On the one hand, it asserts that profit can be had from monopoly power over certain resources—the euphemism is 'unique'. On the other hand, it is confident that financial markets work sufficiently well both to exclude under-priced companies for profitable conglomerate acquisition and to ensure that product markets are too dynamic for effective long-run domination. In the absence of bargains or of market power, there is no point to conglomer- ate diversification.

There is the rub. The orthodox resource-based view might account well for the related diversifier, but struggles with the conglomerate. The up-side for the conglomerate is low, with seemingly little opportunity to combine or transfer resources between unrelated businesses in an economically productive way. The down-side is clear, as conglomerate structures lumber otherwise potentially free-standing businesses with the expense and constraints of a corporate head office. In this resource-based view, therefore, conglomerates are non-sustainable, soon eliminated in tightening selection environments such as during recession (Dosi et al., 1992). As in biology, where new mutations emerge all the time, conglomerates are 'hopeful monsters', occasionally thrown up by evolutionary chance:

Nothing in the laws of biological evolution precludes the appearance of such types; on the other hand, one does not expect to see the fossil record strewn with examples because natural selection promptly eliminates all but a tiny fraction of them. On average, there is not much hope per monster. The same may be true of large conglomerates (Dosi et al., 1992: 206)

Essentially the conglomerate is a freak of nature, too unprofitable to survive.

The hostility of this resource-based view does not square well with the empirical evidence for the persistence of the conglomerate. There are, though, some more positive accounts. We shall consider three. Williamson (1970) emphasizes information; Kay (1997) relies on risk and lock-in; Grant (1988) extends the notion of relatedness. We shall argue that Grant's (1988) frame provides the best general rationale for both the conglomerate and the related diversifier. As it happens, this frame can be considered as simply an extension of the resource-based view, one which has the merit of bringing the monstrous conglomerate back within the Chandlerian pale.

Oliver Williamson's (1970: 143–5) early defence of the conglomerate stresses information advantages. Because of its access to reliable internal accounting and reporting information, the corporate headquarters is better informed about its portfolio of businesses than any external investors possibly could hope to be. Even across unrelated businesses, headquarters can therefore allocate and monitor investments better than external markets. In other words, the conglomerate serves as a well-informed internal capital market. However, this argument allows the conglomerate some potential advantages over imperfectly informed external capital markets, but does not provide any over related diversified firms. As Neil Kay (1997: 60) characterizes Williamson's (1970) argument, it suffers from the problem of 'limited comparators'. The related diversified firm has even greater informational advantages than the conglomerate, because of its superior capabilities in accessing and processing information on a relatively limited range of products and markets. On the information argument alone, conglomerates might have advantages over external capital markets, but related diversified companies should have advantages over conglomerates. It is hard to explain the continued survival of conglomerates when the related diversification strategy remains a well-advertised and accessible alternative.

Neil Kay (1997) turns the conglomerate's very unrelatedness to advantage. In a world of uncontrollable and unforeseeable risks, it is positively useful to have a portfolio with few interdependencies: any business catastrophe can be isolated in one part of the business with limited knock-on effects for the rest. By comparison with their less-diversified or more interrelated competitors, conglomerates should be more robust over time. This robustness is reinforced, in Kay's (1997) view, because conglomerate strategies are hard to reverse. Movement from conglomerate to related diversification is an extended process, requiring new managerial skills and systems and the knitting together of new relationships. The point between well-managed conglomerate diversification and well-managed related diversification is a long moment of vulnerability, with incoherence in both management and portfolio. Conglomerates get locked-in. Kay (1997) thus provides two good grounds for the survival of conglomerates, but unfortunately deals less well with why they are created in the first place. At the early stage, as the number of unrelated businesses starts at two or three, it would be easier for investors to spread their risks in a wider portfolio of stocks. Lock-in explains conglomerate irreversibility, but not initial construction. As it turns out, we shall find that it is generally easier to construct conglomerates in Europe than to maintain them.

If an economic rationale is to be proposed for the pattern of conglomerate diversification that we shall report across Europe, it must be able to cope with simultaneous growth in total numbers and a relatively high turnover of particular firms. One promising way forward is both to extend the notion of resources suggested by the orthodox resource-based view and to introduce a stronger and more discriminating sense of headquarter costs than in the Williamsonian perspective. Robert Grant's (1988) neglected research note points us in these directions. First, he proposes a notion of corporate relatedness distinct from the operational relatedness of the original Harvard perspective and currently dominant in the resource-based view. Corporate relatedness might come in the form of similarities between otherwise different businesses in terms of risk, time-span and scale of investments, life-cycle positions, and so on. Where these corporate similarities exist, there is a common 'logic' to decision-making, in terms of the types of information required, the decisions to be taken, and the demands of implementation (cf. Prahalad and Bettis, 1986). It becomes possible for managers to develop skills in strategy and control that are valid across businesses even in the absence of operational relatedness. Conglomerates find a rationale through being good at managing similar types of businesses, regardless of market or technological linkages. In one sense, Grant (1988) is amplifying the rather sparse information advantage of Williamson's (1970) corporate managements; in another sense, he is recalling Penrose's (1959) original interest in managerial and entrepreneurial resources, but stressing the resources of corporate management in particular. In any case, he maintains that the value potential of corporate relatedness can be at least equal to the value of operational relatedness.

Having extended the nature of valuable resources to the corporate level, Grant (1988) then introduces the implications for headquarter costs of different types of relatedness. Operational relatedness is expensive, requiring considerable vertical co-ordination and horizontal interaction to realize its benefits. By contrast, corporate relatedness is exercised relatively cheaply through the skills and knowledge that reside within the brains of the top management team itself. Relying just on the few individuals making up the top team, conglomerate headquarters can be lean and detached. Thus, Grant (1988: 642) remarks, 'unrelated diversifiers may achieve high levels of corporate relatedness while avoiding the co-ordination costs imposed by operational relatedness'. With lower costs and potential benefits at least equal to those from operational relatedness, a conglomerate with the right top management team could out-perform a traditional related diversifier.

Grant's (1988) notion of corporate relatedness provides the economic rationale for the continued attraction of conglomerate strategies, but does not directly predict high turnover. This is, in fact, a small additional step. In the conglomerate, the exploitation of corporate relatedness depends upon the collective cognitive skills of the small group of individuals who make up the lean headquarters team (Prahalad and Bettis, 1986). Such teams are, of course, fragile: retirements, deaths, disputes, and career moves easily break them up. Although corporate relatedness itself may endure, the managerial resources necessary to exploit it are likely to have a much shorter term. The life-cycle of a conglomerate is effectively defined by the life-span of its original top management team. Related diversifiers, on the other hand, are likely to be more robust. The very fact that headquarters develop substantial co-ordinating departments, and that operating divisions are densely intertwined, ensures that the skills and knowledge required to manage the interrelationships are ample and diffuse. Though costly, these investments in co-ordination develop the next generation of corporate management. The operationally related corporation can perpetuate itself beyond the life-span of a particular top team. Contrary to Kay (1997), therefore, the conglomerate unwinds before the related diversifier.

The main propositions stemming from this distinction between corporate and operational relatedness are brought together in the matrix of Figure 3.3. Here diversified firms are distinguished according to whether they enjoy corporate relationships only, operational relationships only, a combination of the two, or neither at all. Because the orthodox Harvard definition of relatedness is just one-dimensional, it is important to see how the two fit together. Firms in the two right-hand boxes would be 'related diversifiers' in the orthodox Harvard sense; firms in the two left-hand boxes would be 'unrelated diversifiers' or conglomerates in the Harvard sense (even though those in the top left-hand box do possess corporate relationships).[2] The varying implications for both financial

---

[2] Because we are using the Harvard categories in our research, the terms related and unrelated diversified will always be used in the Harvard operational sense, unless otherwise qualified.

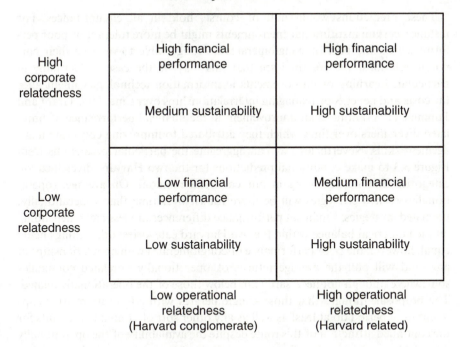

Figure 3.3. *Diversification Types, Sustainability and Performance*

performance and sustainability over time are summarized in each box. In the top right-hand box, where diversified firms enjoy both corporate and operational relationships, we can predict that firms on average should extract high financial returns and, from the interactions developed in operational relationships, have sufficient top managerial depth as to ensure continuity over time. In the box to the left, where diversified firms possess only corporate relationships, firms on average should still be able to make high financial returns, the absence of operational relationships being compensated for by cheaper head offices and the lack of possible conflicts between operational and corporate relationships. However, these firms with only corporate relationships will generally be too reliant on a particular top team to sustain their strategy successfully over very long periods of time. Probably less successful financially, but more robust over time, will be those firms with only operational relationships. There will be resource advantages, but these come with greater head-office co-ordination costs. This same co-ordination effort does, though, help to develop the successive generations of management necessary for sustaining the corporation over the long run. Least successful financially, and with no claim on long-term survival, will be those firms in the bottom left-hand box, having neither corporate nor operational relationships.

These predictions would not, of course, hold in all circumstances. For instance, certain institutional environments might be more tolerant of poor performance on the part of conglomerates no longer able to manage their corporate relationships. We shall see that this may be the case in Germany in particular. Learning or improvements in information technologies might alter the costs and benefits of managing interrelationships over time. Thus Grant and Jammine (1988) noticed an improvement in the financial performance of unrelated diversifiers over time, which they attributed to improving corporate management skills. Nevertheless, we can aggregate the particular predictions from Figure 3.3 to make conditional predictions for the two Harvard diversification categories that we are using in our empirical material. On average, (operationally) related strategies will be more robust over time than (operationally) unrelated strategies. Financial performance differences are less clear, depending on the numerical balance within the two Harvard categories: other things being equal, however, the poor performance of conglomerates with no relationships of any kind will pull the average returns of operationally unrelated companies somewhere, though not necessarily far, below those of the operationally related. The proposal, though, that those conglomerates with corporate relationships might for a period do at least as well as any other sort of company accounts for the continued attraction of this route despite the availability of the operationally related alternative. It also gives some grounds for conglomerate hopefulness: corporate relationships will keep them afloat longer than allowed in the severest interpretations of resource-based orthodoxy, though less than in accounts emphasizing risk and lock-in. Improving corporate management skills might even be shifting the odds in favour of the conglomerate.

The notion that corporate management can exercise skills across diverse businesses will alarm contextualists. It sounds too much like a return to the generalization and abstraction of modernism. But again we can draw some boundaries: the conglomerate recognizes its incompetence in depth, detaching itself absolutely from the detailed practice of operations. It is by holding on to the key Chandlerian idea of decentralization that the Chandlerian model can be extended to the post-Chandlerian conglomerate.

We propose, then, that the original Chandlerian model can be stretched to cover the rise of the conglomerate. The approach developed here, building on Grant's (1988) distinction between operating and corporate relationships, is more generous to conglomerates than the strict resource-based view, more sceptical than that of Kay (1997). It both affords the conglomerate enough profits to provide incentive and constrains its life-span sufficiently to ensure eventual restructuring. It will certainly be important to the prospects of a boundedly generalizing management science that some such comprehensive economic rationale for diversification in Europe is constructed. Otherwise, it will be the sceptics who have all the best lines.

Sceptical accounts of diversification

The sceptical accounts of the diversification phenomenon come in two main groups. On the one hand, there are those which, like Chandler (1977), latch on to the simultaneous rise of diversification and the emergence of a new professional managerial class. While Chandler (1977) sees managerialism as a necessary correlate of diversification, these sceptics view it as a suspicious coincidence. On the other hand, there are those sceptics who largely absolve professional managers, putting the blame on external institutions such as state policy and changing conceptions of the corporation. Both these perspectives, however, place the emphasis not on principles of economic advantage but on potentially shifting and variable sociological characteristics of business and management.

The managerial revolution is a prime suspect in sceptical accounts of diversification. Berle and Means (1932) identified the emergence of a new managerial class at much the same time as DuPont, General Motors, and other large American corporations were first experimenting with diversification and divisionalization. By 1930 only 11 per cent of the Top 200 American companies were wholly or majority owned by a single individual or compact group of shareholders. In about 44 per cent of these Top 200, no group of shareholders owned more than 5 per cent of the shares. As shareholders became more and more dispersed, so their interest and capacity to intervene in the management of these corporations diminished. In Berle and Means's (1932) contention, 'ownership' and 'control' were increasingly separated: American capitalism was succumbing to 'managerial control'.

The emergence of managerial control might give two kinds of impetus to diversification: one self-interested; the other self-deluded. In the self-interested version, diversification serves managers not shareholders. Thus, according to Berle and Means (1932/1967: 114), the interests of the managers now running large corporations are not simply the profits of the shareholder but 'prestige, power or the gratification of professional zeal'. Growth in particular is associated with prestige, power, and, often, salary and security (Baumol, 1962; Marris, 1964). And, for most large established firms, growth is most easily obtained by corporate diversification and acquisition. Conglomerate diversification is particularly suspected of simply being a manifestation of managerial empire-building, with little return to shareholders. Morck et al. (1990) compare the share-price reactions for related and unrelated acquisitions during the 1980s. Bidders' share-prices suffered on average a 4 per cent drop in the case of unrelated acquisitions, against a 3 per cent premium for related acquisitions. Bidders' values also suffered when they bought rapidly growing firms. Morck et al. (1990) conclude that managers were buying new businesses and new growth opportunities in order to defend or expand their personal empires—even when, on average, these were damaging shareholders' wealth. Conglomerate diversification in this view is driven by managerial self-interest.

A more innocent, if not more reassuring, view of the managerial motive in diversification derives from the 'managerial hubris' hypothesis (Roll, 1986). Here managers are again driven towards growth by diversification and acquisition, but this time not out of self-interest but a self-deluding over-estimate of their own capacity to manage new businesses. Evidence for the role of hubris in acquisitions comes from Hayward and Hambrick's (1997) study of large American acquisitions between 1989 and 1991. Here the premium on pre-takeover price paid for acquired companies was positively associated with the chief executive's hubris, as measured by the amount of recent positive press coverage and salary relative to other board members. These highly praised and highly remunerated chief executives not only paid more for their acquisitions, but were completely unjustified in their self-confidence: the more hubristic the chief executives were, the worse their acquisitions performed. The degree of relatedness or unrelatedness of these acquisitions made no difference. On this account, diversification is driven by delusion. Managers are foolish rather than selfish.

As well as internal shift in the control of corporations, there has been change in the social and economic context. In Fligstein's (1990) account of the rise of diversification among large American corporations during the twentieth century, the emphasis is first on the effects of the 1930s Depression, then on the impact of the antitrust 1951 Celler–Kefauver Act. The depressed markets of the 1930s had first spurred diversification into closely related areas in order to maintain volumes. The Celler–Kefauver Act, however, had given the diversification movement real momentum by effectively banning vertical and horizontal mergers in existing product markets. From the 1950s onwards, diversification was increasingly by acquisition into unrelated markets. As acquisitive conglomerates began to emerge as the new dynamic force in American capitalism, the concept of the corporation became redefined in financial terms: 'Rather than conceiving of the corporation primarily as an entity that generates profits by producing goods or services, the more abstract conception of the firm as a bundle of liquid assets permitted a much wider range of possibilities for profit' (Espeland and Hirsch, 1990: 78–9). The logics of finance prevailed over those of production or marketing. The route to top management was increasingly through finance rather than manufacturing, sales, or marketing backgrounds: by 1979 32 per cent of large American corporations had presidents with predominantly financial backgrounds (Fligstein, 1990: 285). These top managers were financial engineers, not designers, producers, or marketers. Diversification, especially conglomerate diversification, became the accepted way of doing business in the United States of the 1960s.

A striking advantage of these sceptical accounts over much orthodox economic thinking is their capacity to explain the rise of the conglomerate, at least in the United States. Instead of being an anomaly, the conglomerate is an essential part of the plot. The sceptics can also provide consistent rationales for recent pressures for downscoping. Managerial selfishness and foolishness have come under control with changes in terms of corporate governance and managerial incentives (Hadlock and Lumer, 1997). Imperialistic or mistaken diversification initiatives can now be curtailed and reversed as managerial incentives are aligned more closely with shareholders' interests and surveillance mechanisms are strengthened. Another important institutional change was President Reagan's relaxation of the post-Celler–Kefauver antitrust regime (Davis et al., 1994). The legal regime for closely related acquisitions became more permissive just as financial theory and new financial techniques such as the leveraged buy-out turned against the conglomerate. It became possible to measure under-valuation in conglomerates and mavericks such as Michael Milken, Sir James Goldsmith, and T. Boone Pickens were only too eager to release the value by breaking them up (Stearns and Allan, 1996). As the institutional environment became more severe, and the managerial revolution came in check, the sceptics would therefore predict a clear reversal of the diversification trends of the early post-war period. Davis et al. (1994) indeed suggest a significant wave of de-diversification in corporate America during the 1980s as monopoly became more attainable and conglomerates became less fashionable. Instead of diversification being part of the steady march of progress, in this sceptical account it is part of the ebb and flow of social and political change.

The sceptics' focus is typically American, but their emphasis on sociological factors in diversification potentially offers considerable theoretical leverage in the diverse and evolving institutional contexts of Europe over the last half century. Chandler (1990) himself has already highlighted the implications for diversification within Europe of different degrees of managerialism and dependence on financial markets. Given continued variation in institutional arrangements across Europe, we might expect enduring differences in patterns of diversification. This argument will be taken up further as we go on to discuss national institutionalists' accounts of structure as well as strategy. In the meantime, we can note that these more sociological perspectives on diversification would broadly suggest continued cross-national differences and non-teleological change.

3.4. DIVISIONALIZATION AND BEYOND

For many, the divisional structure embodies modernistic practice as much as Chandlerism expressed modernistic science. The divisional structure appears to resolve the complexity of the large, diversified corporation by quite literally dividing it into analysable and manageable chunks. The procedure is characteristic of its age. As Taylorism fragmented the tasks of ordinary workers in the first part of the century, so did divisionalization partition the roles of management. In the last analysis, the corporation is just another 'division of labour problem' (Williamson, 1970: 134). Hardly surprisingly, this rebarbative model does not find universal favour. Some propose strong contextual limits to its effectiveness; others proclaim its redundancy in a new network age. The continued relevance of the multidivisional will take some proving.

The divisional idea

The divisional form of organization embodies most of the virtues of the Weberian ideal type of bureaucracy, only with a bit of internal markets mixed in (Clegg, 1990). In a volume translated by Chandler's teacher, Talcott Parsons, Weber (1947: 328) identifies three types of legitimate authority in human organizations: traditional, charismatic, and legal. Traditional authority is that of the chief, the clan elders or the family patriarch. Charismatic authority is that of extraordinary individuals, heroic warriors, or religious leaders. Neither traditional nor charismatic authority is reliably consistent with economic success, the one too conservative, the other too idiosyncratic. Legal authority, however, is that associated with the notion of rational bureaucracy. Here administration is undertaken by professional officials—bureaucrats. These officials are separated from the rights of ownership, appointed on the grounds of competence, given defined spheres of responsibility, operate within a hierarchy and are regulated by a consistent system of abstract and intentional rules. For Weber (1947: 337) the legal authority of the bureaucracy is the universal paradigm of efficiency:

Experience tends universally to show that the purely bureaucratic type of administrative organization . . . is, from a purely technical point of view, capable of attaining the highest degree of efficiency and is in this sense formally the most rational known means of carrying out imperative control over human beings. It is superior to any other form in precision, in stability, in the stringency of its discipline and in its reliability. It thus makes possible a particularly high degree of calculability of results for the heads of the organization and for those acting in relation to it. It is finally superior both in intensive efficiency and in the scope of its operations, and is formally capable of application to all kinds of administrative tasks.

It is exactly this affirmation of rationality, of universality, of calculability, of precision, and of discipline that we find asserted in recent accounts of the multidivisional.

The emphasis on rationality needs underlining, for this has become a characteristic of not only the multidivisional but is central to the emerging management sciences of the mid-twentieth century. The advantage of bureaucracy over other forms of authority lay for Weber (1947: 337–9) in knowledge: 'The primary source of the superiority of bureaucratic administration lies in the role of technical knowledge. . . . Bureaucratic administration means fundamentally the exercise of control on the basis of knowledge. This is the feature which makes it specifically rational.' Though writing originally in the period of the First World War, Weber (1947) anticipated theorists of industrial society (Kerr et al., 1960) when he argued that the evolution of modern technology and large-scale production made the principles of bureaucratic organization indispensable, whether in socialist or capitalist societies. Bureaucracy is the universal, efficient, meritocratic, and rational condition of contemporary existence.

As Weber was writing during the early years of the twentieth century, American industry as a whole was gripped by an equivalent drive to system and rationalization. The replacement of craft production by rational production of standardized, interchangeable parts became known world-wide as the 'American system of production' (Shenhav, 1999). The most evident example of this rationalizing drive towards efficiency was Taylorism, or 'scientific management'. Harry Braverman (1974: 86) claims: 'It is impossible to overestimate the importance of the scientific management school in the shaping of the modern corporation and indeed all institutions of capitalist society which carry on labor processes'. Developed by Frederick Winslow Taylor in the new large-scale production units of the United States, scientific management was concerned with the control and efficiency of workers on the shopfloor. The moving spirit was self-consciously 'scientific'. Work was reorganized only after careful observation and experimentation, what became known as 'work study'. The essential techniques were the separation of task conception from execution and the division of tasks into minute and programmable steps. Professionals would prescribe the most efficient means of working, not labour itself. The aspiration was universal. Scientific management was promoted by business people, academics, and consultants around the world (Littler, 1982; Kipping, 1999). Lenin himself declared the relevance of Taylorism for post-revolutionary Russia (Wood and Kelly, 1982). In all these ways, scientific management exemplified the modernizing spirit.

The principles of scientific management need not be confined to the shopfloor. For Jelinek (1979: 43), the divisionalization of DuPont and General Motors was simply a matter of taking Taylorism to the corporate level. In the rationalization of General Motors under Alfred Sloan, Jelinek (1979: 43) describes the key as 'a method—generalized knowledge about the task, rather than task specifics . . . By decentralizing and delegating, this generalized method tended to restrict top management attention to higher levels of abstraction, to the relationships among the data and refinements of the method.' At the heart of Sloan's reforms was the value placed on general, abstract knowledge. The separation of strategy and operations established in the Chandlerian divisional firm was the analogue of Taylor's own separation of conception from execution on the shopfloor. Divisionalization was the scientific management of the corporation.

Chandler (1962) himself notes that the pioneers of the divisional organization in American industry tended to share disproportionately the same engineering training as Frederick Winslow Taylor. Unlike the industrial leaders of previous generations, the great organization-builders of DuPont and General Motors were typically highly educated, studying science or engineering at such élite institutions as MIT, Harvard, Columbia, and Princeton. Chandler (1962: 318) does not argue that the influence of Taylor on divisionalization was direct, but rather that Taylor and these organization-builders came from a common intellectual culture, sharing as a consequence 'the same rational, self-conscious approach to the management of men'. For DuPont, the connection was even closer, the family having directly employed Taylor during the 1890s (Chandler, 1977: 438).

This élitist rationality is captured by Williamson in his formalization of Chandler's (1962) multidivisional model as the 'M-form'. The characteristics and advantages of the M-form are as follows (Williamson, 1970: 120–1):

1. The responsibility for operating decisions is assigned to (essentially self-contained) operating divisions.
2. The élite staff attached to the general office performs both advisory and auditing functions. Both activities have the effect of securing greater control over operating division behaviour.
3. The general office is principally concerned with strategic decisions involving planning, appraisal, and control, including the allocation of resources among the (competing) operating divisions.
4. The separation of the general office from operations provides general office executives with the psychological commitment to be concerned with the overall performance of the organization rather than to become absorbed in the affairs of the functional parts.
5. The resulting structure displays both rationality and synergy: the whole is greater (more effective, more efficient) than the sum of the parts.

Here the multidivisional form is encapsulated. In its achievement of synergy, it resolves the puzzle of the diversified firm. In its concern for efficiency and control, and its partitioning of responsibilities, it extends the logic of Taylorism to the corporate whole. In its conception of the head office as a general office, aloof from operations, it expresses the modernist faith in abstract, generalizable knowledge—*savoir* against *savoir-faire*. Finally, in its emphasis on rationality and its confidence in staff élites, it embodies the disciplined, professional, knowledge-based principles of the Weberian bureaucracy.

To all this, Williamson's (1970) M-form adds an essential dash of markets. Operating divisions compete among each other for the allocation of central resources, constituted effectively as 'quasi-firms'. Especially in its conglomerate form, the multidivisional thus amounts to something like a miniature internal capital market (Williamson, 1970: 143). Cash flows are no longer the property of the individual divisions, but are assigned objectively by the head office between the competing investment opportunities represented by the businesses. This investor role is central: 'in many respects, this assignment of cash flows to high yield uses is the most fundamental attribute of the M-form enterprise . . .' (Williamson, 1975: 148). Objectivity must be upheld above all. For operational managers to get involved in the assignment of funds represents an usurpation; for head-office managers to compromise their independence by meddling in the usage of funds amounts to 'corruption' (Williamson, 1975). The purism of the M-form had a distinct moral tone.

We can recognize in the M-form's early formalizations the same modernistic confidence in reason and objectivity that we attributed in the last chapter to the contemporary social sciences much more broadly. The postmodern challenge has taught us to be more cautious about timeless types and easy assumptions of superiority. Nevertheless, we shall see that in its time the original multidivisional had marked advantages over its rivals. Since then, moreover, it has learned an adaptability that allows it to introduce the flexibility and integration of contemporary networks while keeping its essential principles intact.

The multidivisional advantage

For its proponents, the multidivisional represented a substantial step beyond the various forms that preceded it. The essential differences can be summarized in Figure 3.4, which compares the different corporate forms according to degrees and types of centralization. As we have seen, the essence of the multidivisional is its capacity to decentralize operations at the same time as keeping strategy firmly in the hands of the centre. Equally centralized strategically, but centralized operationally too, is the functional (or U-form) organization, in the top-left hand corner of the figure. This was DuPont's basic form of organization before its divisionalization (see Figure 1.2). The third formal type is the holding (H-form) organization, highly decentralized strategically and operationally. This form of organization is epitomized by the chaotic, entrepreneurial General Motors of William Durant, whose hasty acquisitions were left to run as autonomous subsidiaries, never integrated into a coherent corporation. The multidivisional, functional, and holding forms are the ideal types, but Figure 3.4 also allows for the functional-holding somewhere in between. The functional-holding is typically constituted with a large core business centralized along functional lines, surrounded by a periphery of more or less independent subsidiaries. These are the four basic organizational forms with which we shall be concerned, but it is the multidivisional that is claimed as superior to them all.

The functional form is not all bad. Specialization by functions permits economies of scale in process and a division of labour for clarity and learning (Williamson, 1975: 133). With its hierarchy and specification of responsibilities,

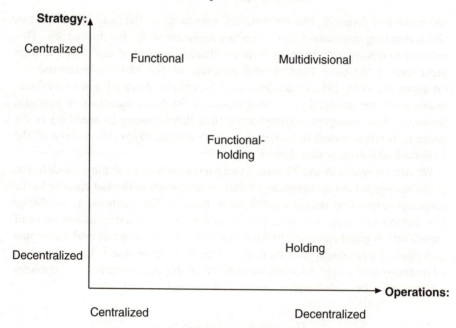

Figure 3.4. *The Harvard Types of Organizational Structure*

it is capable of attaining all the desirable features of Weberian bureaucracy. The functional organization fails the modern corporation only as increasing size and diversity make it too complex. Critical here is the confusion of operations with strategy.

In the functional ('U') form, top management is constituted by functional chiefs—of production, of sales, of engineering, and so on. These functional chiefs are naturally absorbed by the technical details of their functions and ill equipped to take the global view necessary in the large, multi-product firm. The multidivisional's advantage is to extract from operations a layer of general managers, free of functional responsibilities and charged with strategic overview. In the functional form, too, control is elusive, because there is no common metric against which to measure the performance of different units. Comparison of one function (say marketing) against another (say production) is like comparing apples and oranges (Williamson, 1970: 132). Here again the multidivisional has the advantage, for its sub-units are quasi-firms, divisional businesses whose bottom-line performance can always be compared however different the markets they serve. The multidivisional does not override the virtues of the functional form: being smaller and more focused, its own divisions are typically best organized on functional lines. What it adds, though, is the holistic oversight and operating decentralization that allows for strategic initiative and overall control. Williamson's (1970: 134) well-known M-form hypothesis sums up theoretical expectations with regard to relative performance: 'the organization and operation of the large enterprise along the lines of the M-form favours goal pursuit and least-cost behaviour more nearly associated with the neo-classical profit maximization hypothesis than does the U-form organizational alternative'.

The holding company is anathema to modernistic organization theory. As economic theorist, Williamson (1970) passes over it in three lines, not even deigning to compare its performance formally with the M-form. But to Chandler, as historian and student of comparative business internationally, the holding company represents a more substantial problem. The holding defies the logic of Weberian bureaucracy. On the one hand, the chaotic holdings created by entrepreneurs such as William Durant recall too closely the unstable constructions of charismatic authority. On the other, the characteristic holdings of European family business tend dangerously towards the conservatism of traditional patriarchy. In either case, the holding company lacks proper strategic control from the centre. Although this does not preclude excellence at the subsidiary level, the lack of objective, systematic central control over subsidiaries is a critical problem.

In the accounts of Chandler himself, and also of his European students, top management in the holding form is stigmatized as blind, weak, confused, or partisan (Chandler, 1990; Channon, 1973; Dyas, 1972: 153–5; Thanheiser, 1972: 7, 48–54). Top management is blind because lacking either the systematic financial reporting systems or the necessary headquarters' staffs to monitor and intervene. It is weak because confronted by entrenched, baronial business managers or inhibited by significant external shareholdings at subsidiary level. It is confused because unable to rationalize hosts of historically acquired subsidiaries into coherent strategic business units capable of comparison and synergistic combination. Finally, top management in the holding is partisan, because either constituted of privileged shareholding cliques or dominated by the subsidiary managers themselves, bargaining between their own sectional interests. The superiority of the multidivisional lies clearly in its panoptical purview, the clear ownership of its divisions, its rational combination of business units, and the professional detachment of strategy from operations.

The functional-holding may be less egregious than the pure holding, but still is at a disadvantage to the multidivisional. A functional core may be logical on its own, if size does not overwhelm it. But the periphery of historically defined subsidiaries is hard to control. It is impossible to compare the performance, or allocate capital, in a commensurate way between the large, functional business at the core and the profit-accountable subsidiaries that operate alongside. Better usually is to reorganize both core and subsidiaries into discrete, directly comparable business units.

For Williamson and the Harvard scholars alike, the superiority of the multidivisional was evident and its world-wide diffusion merely a matter of time. Williamson (1970) indeed urged the transfer of divisionally experienced American general managers to Europe in order to speed the process. Williamson and Harvard did tend to diverge in detail: Williamson stressing the relationship between size and divisionalization; Harvard that between diversification and divisionalization (Donaldson, 1982; Child, 1982). Since size and diversification reveal themselves as tightly correlated in any case (Donaldson, 1982), this difference is not substantial. For large firms, therefore, multidivisional organization would be associated with superior financial performance to all other forms; among the population of large firms, the multidivisional would gradually emerge as the predominant form of organization, driving out all others.

In the face of these expectations, it was a source of real concern to Scott's and Chandler's European students that as late as 1970 between a third and a quarter of British, French, and German top industrial firms were still clinging to such irrational and anachronistic forms of organization as the holding and the functional holding (Channon, 1973; Dyas and Thanheiser, 1976). After all, at the same point in America, less than one in forty firms still had pure holding forms of organization, less than one in ten the functional holding (Rumelt, 1974). It was vital to Europe's industrial performance that these unprofessional anachronisms should be reformed. Top management in Europe would have to disentangle itself from operations; managerial professionalism should replace patronage and politics; management information should become systematic and comprehensive; clusters of partly owned subsidiaries should be rationalized into coherent divisions. In short, European managers had to get 'modern'.

Institutionalist critiques of the multidivisional

For Chandler or Williamson, the economic superiority of the multidivisional is all that is necessary to explain its diffusion. More sociological perspectives doubt this simple economism. There are crowd effects on the one hand; there are country effects on the other.

Institutional sociologists do not see the progress towards bureaucratically rational organization as a simple response to the efficiency demands of market economies. In an influential article on 'Formal Structure as Myth and Ceremony', Meyer and Rowan (1977) identify a parallel driver towards bureaucratization. The very advance of modernization promulgates 'myths' of rational organization that come to dominate within modern societies: 'once institutionalized, rationality becomes a myth with explosive organizing potential . . .' (Meyer and Rowan, 1977: 346). After a point, there is a sort of crowd effect, in which the myth of rationality becomes sufficiently powerful that all must rush to conform regardless. The consequence within modern societies is that organizational structure takes on a 'ceremonial' role, adopted for reasons of legitimacy as much as efficiency. The pressure is towards 'institutional isomorphism', the homogenization of organizations towards socially accepted modes of behaviour (DiMaggio and Powell, 1983). Institutional pressures for isomorphism are sometimes coercive, driven by legislation or state regulations, for instance; sometimes simply mimetic, imitative behaviour in the face of uncertainty; sometimes normative, where professional norms, educational orthodoxy, or consulting mantras all conspire in the same direction. In all cases, the dominant influence on organizational structure is sociological rather than economic.

Neil Fligstein's (1985; 1987; 1990) historical account of the rise of the diversified multidivisional in the United States can be read exactly in the terms of coercion, normative pressure, and imitation. First, the coercive pressures of the post-war American antitrust regime pushed business in the directions of conglomerates, best managed by extreme decentralization. Then the spectacular mergers and takeovers of the post-war conglomerates established finance as the most prized skill in corporate boardrooms and business schools around the United States. This normative endorsement of finance led to a shift in corporate leadership towards financiers who opted for hands-off management by profit centres and the rigours of internal capital markets. Fligstein (1987) shows that corporate presidents with financial backgrounds were significantly more likely to adopt multidivisional structures than presidents from other backgrounds, even controlling for corporate strategy and size. Once critical mass had been achieved, mimetic effects took over. Fligstein (1985) also shows that once a significant proportion of firms within an industry had adopted the multidivisional structure, the rest were likely to follow, again regardless of strategy or size. In matters of organization, managers like to follow the crowd.

It is the claim of the international institutionalists that equivalent institutional forces were at play in Europe too. Djelic (1998) attributes the adoption of American models of management—including the multidivisional—to the extraordinary relative power of the post-war United States and the eagerness with which European élites tied themselves to international, especially transatlantic, policy networks. Institutional effects were sometimes coercive, as in the forced deconcentration and decentralization of German industry by the American occupation authorities in the immediate post-war period. Sometimes they were more mimetic, as a small group of self-conscious 'modernizers' in France participated in the wave of 'productivity missions' to the United States, bringing back with them the new model of large-scale, bureaucratically rational mass production. In both cases, American managerial influence did not simply follow the construction of the economic and technological conditions for multidivisionalization in these countries. In a period of European weakness and American pre-eminence, American advisers and European protegés were able to introduce the new models of management even in advance of the conditions in which they were theoretically appropriate. As Djelic (1998: 273) sums up: 'a large-scale process of structural transformation had already been in progress in the 1950s in Western Europe, well before the economic and technological environment had started to change in that part of the world'.

The extraordinary political–economic hegemony of the United States over Europe relaxed by the 1960s. At this stage, more normative institutional influences took over. McKenna (1997) emphasizes the strong transatlantic influence of American managerial techniques, especially as promoted by leading consulting firms such as McKinsey & Co., Booz Allen & Hamilton, and Arthur D. Little. Servan-Schreiber (1969), in his alarmist *The American Challenge*, reported that these three firms had doubled their European staffs every year for the previous five years. The most prominent of these firms was the great proselytizer for decentralization, McKinsey. McKinsey had already divisionalized such prestigious American multinationals as Ford and Chrysler when the Anglo-Dutch giant Shell became its first European client in 1957 (McKenna, 1997). McKinsey's client list soon included such leading companies as ICI, Dunlop, Pechiney, Rhône-Poulenc, Air France, Volkswagen, Deutsche Bank, and BASF. McKinsey introduced the divisional structure to twenty-two of the United Kingdom's Top 100 industrial companies during the 1960s; in Germany, the figure was at least a dozen (McKenna, 1997). McKenna (1997: 228) quotes the German academic Fiedler-Winter on the trend towards multidivisionalization: 'the main driving force in Germany, as elsewhere, has been provided by the American management consultants McKinsey'. Unfortunately, the appetite for divisionalization waned in the 1970s and McKinsey's European business turned badly down. McKenna (1997: 230) underscores the short-lived but remarkable influence of the company thus: 'McKinsey & Co. never again had quite the same influence or reputation as it did during the 1960s, when it dominated the European market for top-level organizational studies'.

Thus the international institutionalists emphasize the historical specificity of organizational phenomena. The spread of the multidivisional structure was due to the incidence of American political, economic, and military hegemony at a particular point in time. As the fate of McKinsey in Europe exemplifies, this hegemony had crumbled by the 1970s. Europe itself was resurgent; Japan appeared increasingly to offer the more dynamic model. As a consequence, the logic of international institutionalism would lead one to expect at least a slackening of the momentum behind the multidivisional in recent decades, if not reversal. Figure 3.5 summarizes the implications of the international institutionalist perspective in stylized terms: first, rapid diffusion of the American corporate model through Europe in the 1950s and 1960s; then, probable decline, under the impact of Japan.

However, these international institutionalists also admit national-specific institutional influences upon the rates of change. Not a single large Spanish firm had adopted the multidivisional structure by the 1980s, in part because of McKinsey's refusal to establish a local office earlier (Guillén, 1994; McKenna, 1997). The Italians were significantly less prone to divisionalize during the 1950s

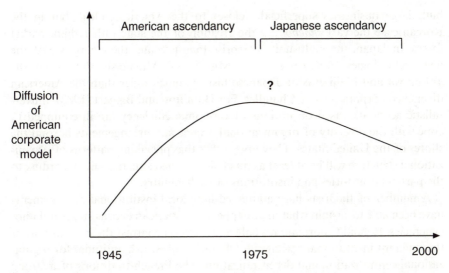

Figure 3.5. *International Institutions and the Expected Diffusion of the American Corporate Model in Europe*

and 1960s because of the Americans' forced alliance with highly conservative Christian Democratic governments and the absence of major crisis in the post-war years (Djelic, 1998: 7, 88–9). Although an international institutionalist, Djelic (1998) still insists on the continuing importance of national institutions for shaping the adoption of American managerial ideas in Western Europe. The importance of country effects is, of course, a theme that is developed further by the national institutionalists themselves.

The national institutionalists emphasize the territorial specificity of organizational phenomena. In a pioneering article, Hamilton and Biggart (1988: S87–8) drew on the contemporary success of the radically different business models of the various East Asian economies to argue:

Economic models predict organizational structure only at the most superficial level . . . The economic theory of the firm may in fact be a theory based on, and only well-suited to, the American firm as it has developed historically in American society.

The targets of this article are the universalistic arguments of Alfred Chandler and Oliver Williamson. Chandler's (1977) account of the origins of the multi-divisional structure in America emphasizes the growth of large-scale, diversified organizations as a product of new production and communications technologies. Japan, South Korea, and Taiwan all have similar technologies, but vary widely in the extent and timing of their adoption of the Chandlerian model. Thus Taiwan is technologically advanced, yet has stuck to loose networks of entrepreneurial businesses, far from the integrated bureaucratic ideal. Korea has built large businesses superficially closer to the American ideal, but in the Korean case the vast *chaebol* are the creation of the state rather than market forces. In Japan, the multi-unit enterprise long predates the emergence of the new technologies: *zaibatsu* such as Mitsui and Mitsubishi date from the Tokugawa and Meiji eras of Japanese history, much older than the American diversified corporations of Chandler. For Hamilton and Biggart (1988), universalistic accounts based on notions of economic efficiency are ill equipped to cope with the diversity of organizational origins and arrangements beyond the shores of the United States. They urge rather that prevailing patterns of organizational structure will be at least as much determined situationally, according to the particular histories and institutions of each country.

A number of theorists have addressed how local institutional arrangements have been able to sustain what might appear to American eyes as structural idiosyncracies. Roland Calori and his colleagues (1997) contrast the implications of the different institutional heritages for French and British aptitudes for organizational centralization and decentralization. The French traditions of a strong centralized state, a rationalistic educational system, and a hierarchical church all incline French organizations towards centralized, or functional, forms of organization. By contrast, British organizations tend towards decentralized modes of organizing on account of the United Kingdom's pragmatic pedagogy and *laissez-faire* politics. Mark Granovetter (1995) takes up the holding company, or business group, demonstrating its robust institutional embeddedness around the world. Business groups come in many forms, from the *keiretsu* of Japan, the *chaebol* of Korea, the business houses of India, or the 'kineconic' groups of Chile to the loose family holdings of Europe. In Granovetter's account, they survive because of the continued resilience of what he terms the 'moral economy' in these countries, adhesion to values other than short-term profit such as loyalty and trust. They are often sustained, moreover, by powerful national institutions, typically banks and the state. Banks supply capital; the state supplies contracts and privileges.

Thus theorists of national institutions have drawn on a range of institutional factors—the state, financial systems, education, as well as 'culture'—to argue for variation between countries in the solution of the structural problems of scale and scope. A good deal of this appears rather *ad hoc*, but the various institutional factors have recently been theorized more coherently in the 'systems' notions developed by Richard Whitley (1994; 1999) and Hollingsworth and Boyer (1997). Here enduring cross-country differences in modes of organizing are possible because of homeostatic feedback loops between local business and national institutions.

Hollingsworth and Boyer (1997: 2) list many of the elements with which we shall be concerned in defining their 'social systems of production' as where:

the following institutions or structures of a country or region are integrated into a social configuration: the industrial relations system; the system of training of workers and managers; the internal structure of corporate firms; the structured relationships between firms . . . the financial markets of a society; the conceptions of fairness and justice . . . the structure of the state and its policies; and a society's idiosyncratic customs and traditions as well as norms, moral principles, rules, laws and recipes for action. All these institutions, organizations and social values tend to cohere with each other

In this kind of social system, every level is linked in a pattern of mutual reinforcement. Firms, states, markets, cultures, and education systems interlock. The national distinctiveness of each element is interdependent with the matching distinctiveness of all others. In particular, internal structures and external relationships between businesses are tied up in a web that includes the training of managers, the structure of the state, and the nature of financial markets. Our empirical data do not extend to every element of this web, but we shall be able to explore exactly how closely national patterns of diversification and divisionalization really are aligned with, particularly, the careers of managerial élites and the ownership and control of firms.

Such a test is due because of the striking conservatism of systems arguments. The point about systems is their cohesion. Cohesion both mitigates forces for change and raises the costs of responding to them. First, the mutual reinforcement implied by cohesion allows institutional peculiarities to remain internationally competitive, rather than historical anachronisms doomed to fade away. Efficiency is institutionally constructed on the basis of local arrangements, so that efficient responses to technical demands can be constituted in a variety of ways (Whitley, 1994: 155). Thus the success of Asian business systems in the recent past is attributed to historic institutions predating industrialization (Whitley, 1991: 24). Second, cohesion imposes large costs on change, on account of its system-wide ramifications. Effective change in any part will require commensurate change in interrelated parts (Whitley, 1994: 176). Interdependence keeps each system element in step with all others: 'The institutional configuration usually exhibits some degree of adaptability to new challenges, but continues to evolve within an existing style . . . these institutional configurations might be exposed to sharp historical limits as to what they may or may not do' (Hollingsworth and Boyer, 1997: 2).

By contrast with the modernizing hopes of Harvard or the transnational ebbs and flows of international institutionalists, national institutionalists tend, therefore, to insist on distinctiveness and stability. For Whitley and Hollingsworth, the hand of institutions is a conservative one. It is extremely unlikely that the dominant patterns of corporate strategy and structure within a country will change without fundamental change at every other level of the system of interdependence.

Whitley (1994) indeed makes specific predictions about the pattern of business organization in Western Europe. He distinguishes several types of coherent 'business system', allocating France to the category of 'state co-ordinated', Germany to the 'collaborative', and the United Kingdom to the 'partitioned'. The mutual reinforcement of the system elements leads to the possibility of sustained differences in strategy and structure. Thus, for instance, Germany forms a coherent system in which the decentralization of economic power (both state and financial) and the continuing involvement of owners in management are seen to link to dominant preferences for relative focus in terms of strategy and decentralization in terms of structure. In the French system, on the other hand, firms are more centralized while similarly diversified; economic power is relatively centralized; owners are also fairly involved. The British partitioned system stands further apart, with firms typically highly diversified and highly decentralized, economic power equally decentralized, and owners quite removed from the management of firms. Whitley (1994) carefully traces the kinds of interdependencies that exist between the various elements in these kinds of systems, making a strong case for their mutual reinforcement. There emerges a kind of hierarchy in terms of expectations concerning strategy and structure in Europe: British firms will be most diversified and decentralized; German firms will be equally decentralized but not so diversified; French firms will be both less diversified and less decentralized than British firms. Figure 3.6 summarizes in broad terms the relative clustering of French, German, and British industrial firms predicted by Whitley's (1994) reasoning. British firms are out on their own in terms of diversification and decentralization.

Whitley, Hollingsworth, and Boyer are arguing for the interrelatedness of strategy, structure, ownership, and control throughout whole systems. As institutional elements coalesce into coherent systems, so they shift the overall balance of viability between different strategies and structures within a particular country. We want to distinguish this system-wide argument from another kind of more micro-political argument that has emerged in the United States and which shares a concern for ownership and managerial effects. However, rather than being concerned for system-wide tendencies, this 'corporate politics' perspective is more modest in focusing on the direct effects of different kinds of owners or managers on strategic and structural choices within particular firms. Thus Palmer et al. (1987; 1993) and Fligstein and Brantley (1992) have examined the effects of personal or bank ownership and managerial career tracks on strategy and structure within the system that is the United States as a whole. Although the findings have not been clear, they presume that the political interests of owners and banks, for instance, might militate against both diversification and divisionalization because of the threats that such growth and decentralization might pose to their control. As we shall be hard-pressed to reconcile our findings on strategic and structural trends in Europe with national systems accounts, it will be worth retaining at least this more limited political perspective. A good part of Chapter 7, therefore, will be concerned with

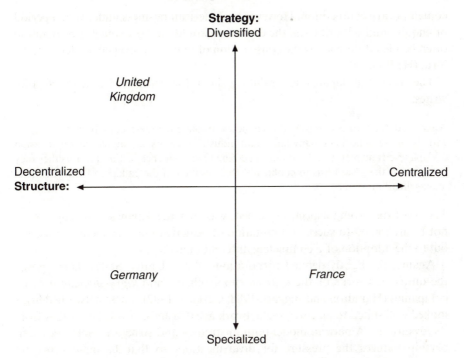

Figure 3.6. *Business Systems Predictions for Characteristic National Patterns of Strategy and Structure*

whether, despite the overall tendencies towards diversification and divisionalization in all three countries, the conservatism of some firms can still be explained in terms of specific ownership effects.

In sum, national institutionalists have radically challenged the global relevance of corporate models 'made-in-America', while international institutionalists have undermined faith in final convergence on an optimally efficient form of business organization. By the 1990s the fate of the Chandlerian model in Europe was certainly moot. But even in the home of its birth, faith in the diversified multidivisional has lately seemed to fade.

Beyond the M-form?

The relativizing enterprise of the institutionalists has been remarkably timely. It coincided with a period when American capitalism appeared soundly beaten by countries that had once been reassuringly backward and dependent. National institutionalists offer an explanation for how different systems could produce different, yet at least equally effective, solutions to the challenges of

contemporary competition. However, as American business underwent a period
of enquiry and self-criticism, the end result would not be so much a recognition
of embedded difference as the construction of another universal model—the N-
form (Hedlund, 1994).

The success of Japan was a salutary shock for America. Locke (1996: 166)
writes:

After 1980 Americans confronted three new economic realities: an inability to compete
with Japanese imports in many important industrial sectors, an unprecedented invasion
of Japanese transplants and a diminished American influence in Europe. Together they
precipitated the great crisis in confidence that resulted in the collapse of the American
management mystique.

The most disturbing aspect, it seemed, was that the Japanese challenge could
not be attributed to successful imitation of American management techniques,
but to the adoption of a completely different model.

Against the tightly defined corporations of the United States, Japan posed
the diffuse networks of the *keiretsu* supply chains and *kigyo-shundan* holding
companies (Hamilton and Biggart, 1988; Gerlach, 1992). These networked firms
looked well suited to an emerging network age (Castells, 1996). They differ from
the traditional American model both in strategy and structure. Network membership reduces the pressure for diversification, so that Japanese firms are
typically less diversified than American corporations and focused on internal
growth rather than conglomerate-style acquisitions (Odagiri, 1992). Being more
specialized, Japanese corporations seem to have less need for the multidivisional
structure. In 1980 large Japanese firms were four times as likely to retain the centralized functional structure as American firms had been in 1969 (Odagiri, 1992:
139). As a consequence, while the American multidivisional makes a virtue of
separating strategy from operations, the Japanese corporation keeps them
closely interlinked (Fruin, 1992: 303; Lazonick, 1991: 45). As the Japanese
showed in a dazzling succession of markets, quality in operations *was* the
strategy.

The rise of Japanese management as the new exemplar directly challenges
the traditional multidivisional. Now the separation of strategy from operations
is seen as a source of weakness through detachment, rather than strength
through objectivity (Freeland, 1996). Even Chandler (1990: 623) is anxious
about a growing breakdown of communications between corporate head offices
and operating divisions. During the 1990s the intellectual climate turned
against the multidivisional. Bettis (1991) condemns the multidivisional simply
as 'organizational fossil'. For Bartlett and Ghoshal (1993), it was high time
to go 'beyond the M-form'. Hedlund followed strict alphabetical order to introduce the 'N-form'—endowed with the fluidity, the synthesis, and pluralism
of heterarchy rather than the rigidity and divisiveness of its hierarchical
predecessor. Hedlund's N-form prototypes are Japanese, of course. The

N-form works best with the Eastern appreciation of the tacit, the embedded, and the ambiguous, rather than the explicit, tightly specified knowledge systems of the West. The modernistic rationality of Weberian bureaucracy is rejected. Volberda (1998), indeed, proclaims a new era of the 'postmodern organization'.

There are valuable insights to be taken from the theories of new organizational forms. We do not think, however, that they justify throwing out all of the old. On the one hand, many of the proponents of N-form, postmodern, or Japanese style management seem to be endorsing features of that supposed anachronism, the holding company (Mowery, 1992: 26). The holding company too lacks clear hierarchy; it too is flexible in its boundaries; it too scorns rational control. The pundits of the network may be going back for their future. On the other hand, it is not so clear that the new models represent such a radical break with the old multidivisional as might sometimes seem. The new experiments can be accommodated within the basic Chandlerian frame. The multidivisional has always been changing and these changes are in principle no different from earlier ones.

Consider the most frequently cited example of the new organization, the European engineering multinational ABB (Handy, 1992; Miles and Snow, 1992; Bartlett and Ghoshal, 1993; Ghoshal and Bartlett, 1998; Barham and Heimer, 1998). The ABB of the early to mid-1990s seems to combine extreme decentralization with new horizontal and vertical processes. In the first place, the company is decentralized into a 'federation' of 1,300 companies, each on average with 200 people. These tiny units have full profit-centre status, with their own balance sheets, the capacity to retain a third of their profits, and their own treasury management. These decentralized units are held together by two key processes, vertical and horizontal. On the horizontal axis, they are integrated through an organizational matrix of products and geography. But it is not just formal structure that assures horizontal integration. The very fact of extreme decentralization into such small units creates interdependence between companies, all of which must rely upon other units for certain functions or resources. Cross-boundary sharing and swapping are requirements for survival. Moreover, in an environment where knowledge has become as important a resource as capital, horizontal processes of networking and learning emerge through functional councils or *ad hoc* task forces exchanging experience between decentralized units. These horizontal processes are encouraged by distinctive vertical processes. Organizational layers have been reduced to just one, so that corporate-level top management becomes more responsive to the needs of operations. Head-office staffs have been reduced to 200, reducing the capacity to meddle unasked. Central functions operate on a customer–contractor principle, the operating businesses clearly in the role of buyer. The ABACUS computerized information system provides financial transparency throughout the whole corporation. At least with the highly visible and charismatic Percy Barnevik, top management engages in constant company visits dedicated to creating and communicating a shared mission and sense of corporate unity. As Bartlett and Ghoshal (1993: 42) sum up, the ABB of this period was

based on a principle of *proliferation and subsequent aggregation* of small independent entrepreneurial units from the bottom up, rather than one of *division and devolution* of resources and responsibilities from the top. . . . In contrast to the classic M-form, where control over most resources is held at the corporate level, in the new model resources are decentralized to the front-line units which operate with limited dependence on the corporate parent for technological, financial or human resources, but with considerable interdependence among themselves (emphases in the original)

Thus was ABB going 'beyond the M-form'.

ABB is different, certainly, but not that much different. There are significant innovations in terms of information technology and horizontal processes, which have their imitators or parallels quite widely in contemporary big business. We shall report a number of our organizations—particularly Rhône-Poulenc (Aventis) and Unilever—to have been experimenting in similar directions. For the moment, however, we shall interpret ABB quite cautiously. After all, ABB retained an effective product divisional axis through all its transformations during the 1990s. Indeed, in its latest transformations in 1998–9, the internal tensions of its matrix were resolved with the triumph of the traditional product-divisional axis (Ruigrok et al., 2000). We prefer, therefore, to represent these experiments less as significant steps beyond the M-form, more as consistent developments within the existing frame. Contra Ghoshal and Bartlett (1998), we find little evidence among large European industrial firms for a contemporary organizational revolution equivalent to that from the functional to the multidivisional in the early years of this century. ABB is refining the M-form, not going beyond it.

We can see the continuities more clearly if the changing multidivisional is presented in three stylized forms, each associated with a particular period of emergence, as in Table 3.1. Here the structure originally described by Alfred Chandler (1962) is just an early type of multidivisional. It was innovation in accounting systems that made safe the separation of strategy and operations achieved by the multidivisional structures developed by DuPont and General Motors before the Second World War. These newly diversified companies needed a reliable way to allocate capital between competing alternatives and then to monitor performance. Their new tool was the famous pyramid of accounting ratios culminating in the Return on Investment criterion developed by DuPont. It became possible to make systematic comparison of commensurable business units. With this innovation, corporations themselves took on something of the shape of the pyramid, with clear hierarchies and top-down allocation, monitoring, and control. However, our schema highlights a second

Table 3.1. *Evolving Types of Multidivisional*

	Investor	Managerial	Network
Origins	1920s–	1960s–	1980s–
Key resource	Capital	Scale and scope	Knowledge
Key technique	Accounting ratios	Planning	Exchange
Key function	Finance and accounting	Corporate planning	Human resources
Structure shape	Pyramid	Pear	Pancake
Examples	DuPont	General Electric	ABB

Source: Adapted with permission from Whittington and Mayer (1997), 'Beyond or Behind the M-form?', in H. Thomas, D. O'Neal, and M. Ghertman, *Strategy, Structure and Style*, Chichester: John Wiley, 1997, 241–58. Copyright John Wiley & Sons Ltd. Reproduced with permission.

generation of multidivisional, the 'managerial', relying on a new technology, corporate planning. Here too, strategy was rigorously separated from operations, but now the focus was on the search for advantages of scale and scope. The model is clearly that of General Electric during the 1960s and 1970s, when its 200 corporate planners were at the lead in creating the technological apparatus of modern planning (Pascale, 1990). To continue the alliteration, companies like General Electric began to adopt rather pear-shaped profiles, their middles swelling as corporate staffs and second- and third-level managers struggled to co-ordinate potential synergies.

Since the 1980s the 'managerial multidivisional' has been widely challenged. General Electric's radical delayerer and down-sizer, 'neutron Jack' Welch, famously denounced old-style formal planning as 'a ticket to the bone-yard' (Pascale, 1990: 215; Tichy and Sherman, 1993). This challenge, we argue, has not resulted in the complete superseding of the basic multidivisional structure, but the emergence of a new flatter, more co-operative version, which we term here the 'network multidivisional' (cf. Hoskisson et al., 1993). This multidivisional is more focused on managing the key resource of knowledge, the fundamental basis of competitive advantage in many contemporary industries (Spender and Grant, 1996). Knowledge shifts the emphasis: from the vertical to the horizontal; from command and control to exchange; from planning to human resources; and from managerialism to networking. If one more summary image is allowed, then it is of the pancake—flat, flexible, and with the emphasis on the circular and horizontal.

With the label 'network multidivisional', we acknowledge proponents of new forms of organization and incorporate key elements of their analysis into our model. But we also stress substantial continuities with the multidivisional on critical organizational dimensions. The recent rejection of planning and the resort to internal network forms of co-ordination do not alter the fundamental centralization of strategy and decentralization of operations. Indeed, the extreme decentralization of ABB in many respects accentuates the divide. The purging of ABB's corporate staffs, as at many other companies, removes even the means by which senior management might get involved in operating decisions. They have neither the staff nor the time to meddle. Moreover, reliance on market mechanisms for the control of remaining central services simply extends the internal market principle so emphasized by Williamson (1975) and other theorists of the multidivisional. At the same time, the rigorous reporting systems (such as ABB's ABACUS) work effectively to increase the transparency of the internal capital market. Even the partial retention of profits allowed to subsidiaries in ABB, although apparently a flagrant contravention of the internal allocative efficiency of the multidivisional, is finally provisional: it has not inhibited the closure and sale of many businesses within the company's extensive empire. The centre retains clear overall control of the corporate portfolio, and, stretched in its newly delayered form, is necessarily even more focused on the strategy and performance of the corporation as a whole. In short, in the 'network multidivisional' accountability for operations is more transparent, and top management more objectively detached, than ever in the older 'managerial' model. Returning to Figure 3.4, the network multidivisional occupies exactly the same place as its predecessors: decentralized operationally; centralized strategically.

This network multidivisional must be offered with the modest conditionality of Mouzelis's (1995) conceptual pragmatism. It is certainly not situated in the kind of progressive series of earlier evolutionary perspectives: the network is likely to exist beside, rather than beyond, other types of multidivisional. Industries vary in the types of organization they require. The network is just the latest comer, and will do best where knowledge is key (Whittington et al., 1999). Equally, the network multidivisional does not claim for itself the universal scope of earlier theories: the experiments on which it builds have been observed in very specific types of economy. At this point, it is likely to be most relevant to the advanced economies of Japan, Europe, and the United States. It is noticeable, though, that the prototypes of this version of the multidivisional are much less narrowly based than those of the original in the 1920s.

Nevertheless, as we consider the structural question more broadly, it is clear that the multidivisional's career is no longer as secure as it once seemed to the Harvard group. Distrusted as alien American export, doubted for its adequacy to contemporary demands, the Chandlerian multidivisional is not the be-all and end-all of yesteryear. There is real uncertainty about whether the multidivisional is still capable both of adapting itself to the varied contours of Europe and of reshaping itself to the new demands of a network economy. The general and enduring advantages of the multidivisional will be tested as we observe the evolving structures of European business in Chapter 6. In the meantime, we assert that recent obituaries for the M-form may be rather overdone.

3.5. SUMMARY

Big business still matters in Europe, but its shape and organization remain surrounded by uncertainty and controversy. We have little long-run comparative data on patterns of diversification; we do have accumulating concerns about the appropriateness of the multidivisional. It would be easy to let the European corporation dissolve into a fog of contextualism and doubt.

We want to do more than this. Given the enormous resources at stake, the search for a coherent economic rationale for the contemporary contours of European business seems a pressing one. What we have to date does not match the case. Orthodoxy's struggle with the conglomerate concedes too much to the sceptics. Fashionable critiques condemn the multidivisional to anachronism. Contextualists define their models very specifically. If we are to find that related and unrelated diversification coexist across Europe, and that multidivisionals still thrive, we will be alarmingly close to having no performance rationale at all. As Kogut and Parkinson (1998: 271) observe, without an economic account of the contemporary corporation, we are driven to a rather bleak view of human action and calculation. We should recognize that economic efficiency has no absolute definition, being context-bound. Nevertheless, the search for some coherent economic rationale for the post-war European corporation seems an apt and important project for the management sciences.

Stripped of its modernist universalism, we shall argue that the Chandlerian model of the corporation still offers the essential core for such a rationale. The model will have to cope with a pattern of diversification that has gone further towards conglomeratization than originally expected. Here, following Grant (1988), we propose to stretch the resource-based view in order to include corporate relationships as well as just operational resources. The model will have to cope too with recent experiments that blur the modernistic trenchancy of the original multidivisional. Here we shall argue that these experiments do not so much go 'beyond the M-form' as extend its fundamental principles. The multidivisional concept is sufficiently adaptive to permit change at the same time as affirming continuities. In the dimensions of both strategy and structure, therefore, the Chandlerian model can be extended and renewed.

We should recognize, though, strong grounds for doubting the continued relevance of any such general model across Europe. The starting point is an American experience that, as the international institutionalists emphasize, has lost the influence of the early post-war period. The national institutionalists warn, moreover, that this experience is likely to be a highly specific one, conditioned by Anglo-Saxon institutions that are remote from those of Continental

Europe, apparently more reliant on personal ownership and control, engineering rather than finance, and banks and the state. Each in their different ways, these contextualist perspectives challenge the possibility of general prescriptions holding across different systems and long periods of time. The next chapter, therefore, turns to the particular contexts of France, Germany, and the United Kingdom in order to consider just how challenging for the prospect of social scientific generalization they really are.

4

Corporate Careers and Control

INTRODUCTION

At the opening of the 1990s Michel Albert (1991), banker and French intellectual, declared the victory of capitalism and the onset of a new struggle. Communism and socialism had clearly failed. But this did not necessarily mean the triumph of American-style capitalism. The contest now was between different kinds of capitalist economy—'*capitalisme contre capitalisme*'. In particular, he counterposed the Rhenish capitalism of central and northern Europe, respectful of long-term relationships between firms, shareholders, and employees, with neo-American capitalism, focused ruthlessly on the cut-and-thrust of competitive markets and short-term profit maximization. Germany, with its technically oriented firms and faithful banks, exemplified the virtues of the Rhenish model; the United Kingdom under Margaret Thatcher and her Conservative followers was Europe's neo-American Trojan Horse. France, with the Rhine on one side and the Atlantic on the other, was caught in between.

Albert (1991) captures, rather dramatically, a wider sense within the social sciences that American capitalism is neither the only nor the most attractive model available. The national institutionalists particularly have been keen to assert the continued viability of alternative national business systems. Typically they contrast the American or Anglo-Saxon style of capitalism exemplified by the United Kingdom, especially since the victory of Margaret Thatcher in 1979, with the more consensual capitalist societies of Continental Europe, of which Germany long appeared the most successful and powerful representative. While the United Kingdom under successive Conservative governments pursued a consistent course towards deregulation and privatization, and Chancellor Helmut Kohl's Germany emphasized continuity, France during the 1980s and early 1990s was a more complicated case. First, there were the sweeping nationalizations of the new socialist President François Mitterand after 1981; then came the partial reversals of the 1986–8 'cohabitation' between conservative Prime Minister Jacques Chirac and the socialist presidency; next the socialists returned to government, ostensibly committed to '*ni-ni*' (neither privatization nor nationalization); and finally came the 1993 election victory of privatizer Edouard Balladur (Schmidt, 1996). On the face of it, the French predicament in these years seemed exactly as Albert (1991) described it, tugged vigorously in opposite directions. Other commentators, however, detect some fundamental continuities, particularly in the French systems of élite production and financial relationships (Morin and Dupuy, 1993; Kadushin, 1995). The 'French exception' remained intact.

It is the contention of the national institutionalists that business systems are indeed characterized by considerable underlying stability, with important and enduring implications for the nature of business and management in particular countries. Thus we have seen how Hollingsworth and Boyer's (1997) conception of the social system of production emphasizes the melding of finance, managerial training, state relationships, corporate scope, and structures into coherent, self-reinforcing, and distinct national configurations. In this chapter, we shall focus on three particular elements of these systems: firm ownership; managerial control; and the careers of managerial élites. We shall draw on other wider data concerning these elements, but also treat our own particular companies as broadly representative of the national systems in which they play such an important part. One feature of our own data is their comparability between countries and over time. As we examine the three central institutional structures of ownership, control, and careers, we shall want to establish both how distinct they are between countries and how stable they are over time. National institutionalists will expect continued divergence and considerable stability. More than that, proponents of national systems will expect these institutions to lock corporate behaviour into character-istic national modes. As the national institutions of ownership, control, and man-agement development do not change at the macro-level, so should countries remain tied to their particular patterns of strategy and structure at the meso-level.

The arguments for the effects of ownership, control, and top management careers on strategy and structure run broadly like this. On the positive side, the original Harvard group associated the spread of diversified, multidivisional firms with the rise of professional management. Family ownership and control was seen as a barrier to optimal economic organization, as most notoriously in Chandler's (1990) account of managerial failure in pre-war Britain. From a more sceptical perspective, national institutionalists suggest that the separation of ownership and control, and the dilution of shareholdings, have created a market for corporate control that facilitates conglomerate takeovers and pro-motes the finance concept of the corporation embodied in the multidivisional. But this market for corporate control is an Anglo-Saxon phenomenon, confined in Europe largely to the United Kingdom. In this view, it is chiefly the British who pursue short-term profits through opportunistic conglomeratization and financially fixated operating divisions. In France and Germany, where families, banks, and even the state can take a longer term view, the diversification and divisionalization imperatives are much less strong.

The United Kingdom is again an outlier in terms of the training and career tracks of its managerial élites, also with implications for strategy and structure. Traditionally British resistance to the logic of divisionalization has been blamed on managers' lack of higher education. Amateurism has held the United

Kingdom back (Channon, 1973; Chandler, 1990). Oddly, national institutionalists now turn the United Kingdom system of élite formation in the opposite direction, seeing the recent predominance of finance and accounting specialists in British boardrooms as exaggerating the role of conglomerate strategies and divisional structures in recent years. While engineers have been excluded from the top of British business, financiers have seized control, just as in the United States. Knowing no other way, these finance professionals manage by the numbers. Related and unrelated acquisitions are all one to the financier, the only relevant points of comparison between competing divisions being their bottom-lines. French and German managers are granted very different orientations due to their characteristic training and career paths. In Germany through high-level apprenticeships and even doctoral training, in France through the élite military engineering school Ecole Polytechnique, Continental managers are early endowed with an appreciation of real technologies. This technological appreciation has kept French and German managers more focused on their core businesses and uncomfortable with the corporate detachment of the pure multidivisional. Again, therefore, French and German firms are expected to be less prone either to diversification—at least conglomerate diversification—or to divisionalization.

We shall examine these arguments in more detail in the course of this chapter, but at this stage we should recognize a continuum regarding the importance of national institutions for strategy and structure. The original Harvard group is at one end, optimistic universalists who recognize institutional factors but see them as ultimately transitory frictions in the triumphant progress of the diversified, professional multidivisional corporation. In between are theorists of corporate politics such as Palmer and his colleagues (1993), who accept the possible enduring impact of ownership or managerial peculiarities in particular cases but are less concerned for systematic effects throughout a whole economy. At the other end are the national institutionalists, who emphasize how the dominant institutional configuration of an economy can transform system-wide the relative effectiveness of different strategies and structures. For these national institutionalists, the concern is with how ownership, control, and management development interlink as parts of an integrated whole. It is therefore the task of this chapter and the two following chapters to consider whether distinctiveness and stability in the three national contexts are still reflected in enduring differences in overall patterns of strategy and structure. Chapter 7 will return to the political question—whether ownership, control, or managerial development matter to the strategies and structures of particular firms.

4.1. FINANCIAL SYSTEMS AND CORPORATE OWNERSHIP

Ownership defines power and provides motive in economic life. It is also something that varies widely between capitalist societies, with implications for corporate behaviour and even national performance. Chandler (1990: 390) identified the dominance of family capitalists, preferring dividend income over investment, as one contributor to the United Kingdom's economic decline: 'in Britain a large and stable income for the family was more of an incentive than the long-term growth of the firm'. As late as the 1960s Channon (1973) found family-owned firms in the United Kingdom less likely to make the kinds of diversification moves that Harvard prescribed for economic effectiveness.

The national institutionalists have also seized on the possible implications of financial systems and corporate ownership for system-wide patterns of economic organization. Thus Whitley (1994) gives a central place within his business systems to the degrees to which capital remains private, public, or owned by the state and to which additional capital is supplied by volatile financial markets or through relatively committed banks. In economies where firms depend greatly on the state for investment co-ordination and access to credit, Whitley (1994) suggests, decision-making is likely to be highly centralized because of the importance of this single contingency for success or failure. Likewise, private ownership, at least if combined with active managerial roles, tends to be associated with centralization. Control remains important to the family firm. By contrast, where ownership is dispersed and governed by the capital markets, firms are obliged to internalize risk management through unrelated diversification and decentralization into discrete units. The nature of ownership has system-wide implications:

High levels of isolation and self-reliance in capital-market based financial systems leads to distinctive business systems which usually have relatively low levels of market organization and of employer-employee commitment. Additionally, the internalization of risk management by industrial firms encourages the diversification of activities, resources and skills, and so low levels of integration and interdependence of sub-units (Whitley, 1994: 171)

In short, national systems dominated by liquid financial markets are likely to promote the construction of conglomerate modes of diversification and highly decentralized and segmental forms of divisionalization. In bank-centred systems, on the other hand, the growth of longer term relationships between firms and banks reduces the need for diversification and allows greater concentration on particular specializations and competences.

Financial systems do seem to differ still, despite certain pressures towards harmonization and integration within the European Union (Fukao, 1995). The most common typology of financial systems distinguishes between market-based and so-called bank-centred systems. In this scheme the United Kingdom is typically lumped with its Anglo-Saxon cousin, the United States, while Germany and France are put more or less closely together (Canals, 1996; Edwards and Fischer, 1994; Zysman, 1983). These are ideal-typical characterizations and the empirical detail of each country introduces more complexity.

Thus, in the case of France, for instance, Zysman (1983) further highlights the role of the state as an influential shareholder. However, the distinction between market-based and bank-centred systems does capture many of the important features of our European economies. Moreover, it intriguingly places the United Kingdom in the same category as the United States, the birthplace of the diversified multidivisional. Market-based systems may plausibly favour the Chandlerian enterprise.

A fundamental characteristic of market-based financial systems is the existence of 'deep and active equity markets' (Coffee, 1996: 113). Here capital is mobilized and distributed through commodity-market like processes (Whitley, 1999: 49). The depth of these markets rests, on the one hand, on the high proportion of companies that are quoted on stock exchanges (Mayer, 1994: 9), and, on the other, on the extent to which shares are traded. High levels of trading activity within such systems mean that relationships between owners and corporations are usually short term and detached (Mayer, 1994: 9; Whitley, 1999: 49).

In contrast to these market-based arrangements, financial systems such as those found in France and Germany are typically characterized as being relatively small in terms of the number of quoted companies and 'thin' in terms of the extent of trading (Coffee, 1996: 113; Berglöf, 1990). Thus, during the mid-to-late 1980s, the stock market in Germany was worth only 14 per cent of Gross National Product, compared to 81 per cent in the United Kingdom (Prowse, 1995). Even among the German stock corporations (*Aktiengesellschaften*), little more than 20 per cent had publicly traded stock during the early 1990s (Fukao, 1995). Ownership stakes in thin financial markets are typically large and hard to trade; in market-based systems stakes are small and liquid. Thus in the United Kingdom 48.6 per cent of shareholders in the largest 500 firms hold less than 5 per cent of shares, whilst in Germany the equivalent figure is 9.5 per cent (Windolf and Beyer, 1995: 7–9). Edwards and Fischer (1994: 194) conclude that 'the structure of share ownership in Germany is markedly different from that in the UK', with 'the vast majority' of German *Aktiengesellschaften* having single shareholders owning more than 25 per cent.

The differences between the types of financial systems go beyond these structural attributes, extending to the way corporate control is exercised. Being geared towards the promotion of market-type, arms'-length relationships the regulation of financial markets in the United Kingdom has traditionally discouraged the development of close relationships between investors and firms (Franks and Mayer, 1990: 214). At the same time there are few restrictions on the transfer of ownership. Owners, therefore, do not exercise their control so much directly through intervention in the governance of their firms as indirectly through the market for corporate control. The sanction on poorly performing firms is takeover or merger, as shareholders vote with their feet by selling to the dearest bidder. Thus in the latter half of the 1980s the value of mergers and acquisitions as a proportion of total stock market capitalization was more than eight times as great in the United Kingdom than in Germany (Prowse, 1995). Allegedly, this liquidity of financial markets has far-reaching effects. On the one hand, the frantic turnover of corporate assets may discourage both the long-term development of particular businesses and their integration into cohesive corporate wholes. On the other, it provides a pool of readily available assets for diversification, with the absence of existing relationships or close familiarity exercising no particular constraints on acquisition.

In bank-centred systems, by contrast, relationships tend to be longer and closer. The archetypal relationship is that between Deutsche Bank and Daimler Benz, dating back to the 1920s and until recently accounting for about a quarter of the automobile company's capital. Banks bring to their firms both the long-term perspective of patient capital and the rich information of their relationship networks (Canals, 1996; Dittus and Prowse, 1996). They have the commitment and the capabilities to make them particularly effective monitors of corporate activity. So much so, indeed, that Cable and Dirrheimer (1983), reflecting on the apparent lack of any multidivisional advantage over holding companies in Germany, suggest that the banks can serve as effective substitutes for multidivisional structures. Organically involved in their network of firms, banks do not need the bare abstractions of divisional financial figures; rather they can bring to bear long and wide experience sensitive to the complexities of business as it has grown over the years.

We shall be studying the proportion of our firms under various types of ownership in 1983 and 1993. These firms are the domestically based members of their respective national Top 100 industrial corporations for each particular year. Firms with no shareholders having 5 per cent or more of the voting stock are classified as under dispersed ownership, as usual practice in the agency and corporate governance literatures (Shleifer and Vishny, 1986) as well as the institutionalist studies (Palmer et al., 1987, 1993). The key owners of firms under

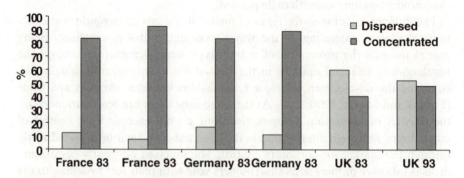

Figure 4.1. *Concentrated and Dispersed Ownership: the United Kingdom, France, and Germany, 1983 and 1993 (Domestic Industrial Top 100)*

more concentrated ownership are identified broadly according to the schema developed in the American institutionalist studies of Palmer et al. (1987, 1993), distinguishing between personal ownership, bank ownership, and ownership by other financial institutions. However, we have also added two categories of owner of particular relevance in the European context, that is the state and other non-financial firms. Personal ownership, for which Palmer et al. (1987, 1993) used the term 'family ownership', covers both firms under entrepreneurial and inherited ownership. A company was considered as entrepreneur-owned if it remained under the ownership of its founder or a person who had altered very substantially both the scale and scope of the enterprise (e.g. Lord Hanson of Hanson plc or Antoine Riboud at BSN/Danone). State ownership included national, regional, or local state institutions, all particularly relevant in the German context. The data for our classifications came from annual reports and business directories such as *Who Owns Whom*, *Liens Financiers*, and the *Schmake* and *Wegweiser durch deutsche Unternehmen* directories.[1] At this point, we shall take these firms as representative of wider national macro-institutional structures as wholes.

As we can see at once from Figure 4.1, the United Kingdom's more competitive market-based financial system is reflected in the very high proportion of firms under dispersed ownership: 60 per cent in 1983 and 52 per cent in 1993. The proportion of firms under dispersed ownership in France and Germany is considerably lower in both time periods. In France we find 12 per cent in 1983 and 7.6 per cent in 1993. For Germany the figures are similar, with 16.7 per cent in 1983 and 11.1 per cent in 1993. These figures for dispersed ownership are clearly in line with generally observed differences in the national financial systems. If anything the figures may under-estimate the differences between the national financial systems. In this period shareholders in Germany were only required to disclose holdings above 25 per cent with the result that stakes of less than 25 per cent are usually under-reported (Edwards and Fischer, 1994: 191; Franks and Mayer, 1998).

Concentration and dispersion does not follow any strong sectoral pattern. In the United Kingdom dispersed ownership even applies to such former family businesses as the food companies Cadbury and United Biscuits, on the one hand, and entrepreneurial electrical companies such as Racal and Thorn-EMI on the other. In France and Germany, where it is dispersed ownership that is exceptional, there is no obvious sectoral pattern either among those few companies that have outgrown particular shareholders. The dispersed German firms range from chemicals company Bayer to engineering company Mannesman. In France, the acquisitive and iconoclastic food company BSN (Danone) had

---

[1] Our French and British sources do not distinguish systematically over this period between nominee and beneficiary holdings. In Germany, proxy votes held by banks are not practically traceable whilst stakes of less than 25 per cent in Germany are usually under-reported (Becht and Boehmer, 1998; Franks and Mayer, 1998).

outgrown its roots in a family glass company. Essilor, a world leader in contact lenses, was unusual in handing over family control to a diverse group of managers and employees.

If ownership is much more concentrated in France and Germany than in Britain, who are the dominant owners? Table 4.1. indicates the key types of owners of large industrial firms in France, Germany, and the United Kingdom. Note that the columns may sum up to more than 100 per cent as some firms have large shareholders of more than one type. The figures for our firms are closely in line with the more generally observed differences between the national financial systems, as well as giving a more longitudinal perspective than prevailing cross-sectional approaches. It is clear again that there are sharp and relatively stable differences between the two Continental countries on the one hand and the United Kingdom on the other.

The prominent role of banks in the ownership of our French and German sample fits the more general characterization of France and Germany as broadly bank-centred systems. However, we should note too the importance of other financial institutions such as insurance companies (see Table 4.1). By comparison, the importance of banks is slight in the United Kingdom. However, by 1993 other financial institutions are becoming more important, though a more detailed look beneath the raw statistics suggests that their role in the United Kingdom is different from that in the Continental companies. We begin our more detailed discussion of financial links with France.

Table 4.1. *Ownership Patterns in the United Kingdom, France, and Germany (Domestic Industrial Top 100)*[a] *(%)*

	France		Germany		UK	
	1983	1993	1983	1993	1983	1993
Dispersed (none)	12.2	7.6	16.7	11.1	60.0	52.2
Personal	44.6	42.4	53.3	46.0	8.0	4.5
Bank	5.4	13.6	18.3	20.6[c]	0	5.9
Other financial	17.5	9.1	16.7	11.1	9.3	22.4
Other firm	20.3	30.3	8.3	14.3	4.0	10.4
State	28.4	24.4	10.0	9.5	6.7	1.5
Other[b]	0	4.5	8.3	12.7	1.3	13.5
Number	74	66	60	63	75	67

[a] Beneficiary and nominee shareholders in France and the United Kingdom; proxy shares excluded for Germany.

[b] Includes: Foreign governments, foreign firms, trusts.

[c] Increase in number of participations at least partially due to more stringent reporting requirements.

French banks and other financial institutions, many of which remained state-owned, were significant shareholders in a fifth to a quarter of French firms, their stakes often being quite large. Over the time period there appears to have been a switch in the relative roles of banks and other financial institutions. By 1993 bank ownership had become more important, often as trusted banks took stakes in privatized corporations. These changes can be seen as consistent with an old tradition of insider capitalism in France, according to which the state, élitist educational institutions, and the great financial and industrial enterprises have long been closely interlinked. The Mitterand nationalizations after 1981, and the subsequent gradual privatizations after 1986, altered the character of French business little. Privatization did not bring about a radical marketization of the French system, on British lines. Rather, privatization was typically accompanied by the construction of '*noyaux durs*' ('hard cores'), interlocking shareholdings between friendly banking and industrial firms pledged to protect each other from hostile attack. These hard core relationships were often long standing, building on pre-existing connections. Two analysts of the French shareholding system concluded: 'a large part of the co-operative relationships or alliances that could be clearly seen before the nationalizations were pretty faithfully reproduced after the privatizations of 1986–88 and continue today' (Morin and Dupuy, 1993: 47). These relationships were reinforced by an essential stability in the closed, incestuous Parisian financial élite, little changed in character by the nationalizations and privatizations of the Mitterand years (Kadushin, 1995). For Vivien Schmidt (1996: 381), the webs of French industrial and financial relationships even recall the Japanese *keiretsu*.

Illustration 4.1. *Matra Hachette: Between Personal and State Control*

Matra Hachette is a peculiar combination of high-tech industry with international publishing. Matra had its origins as an aerospace contractor in 1945; Hachette started as a booksellers in 1826. In the 1960s young engineer Jean-Luc Lagardère took the helm at Matra, developing it rapidly before using his new wealth to take over Hachette in 1981. Matra, of course, was the original designer of the Espace people-carrier. When Matra was nationalized under President Mitterand, Lagardère continued with Hachette, diversifying into television. Upon privatization, Lagardère returned to control of Matra with the aid of major allies such as Crédit Lyonnais, the Banque Nationale de Paris, and his original supporter, Groupe Floirat. Until 1993 Jean-Luc controlled both companies from his own personal holding company the Arjil Groupe. Growing problems at Hachette led to a full merger with Matra, which offered a clean balance sheet, under the new vehicle of the Lagardère Groupe. Control remained very personal: Jean-Luc's son Arnaud was being cultivated for succession as Corporate Director and Special Adviser to the President, his father; old friend Daniel Filipacchi ran the press division, of which he owned 34 per cent.

Principal sources: Interview; Servan-Schreiber, 1992; Nouzille, 1998.

In France, therefore, the same, well-established financial institutions—Suez and Paribas (nationalized by Mitterand), Crédit Lyonnais, Société Générale, and BNP (long state-owned)—dominate throughout this period. Their share-holdings were often large. Thus in the early 1990s Crédit Lyonnais held 20 per cent of aerospace giant Aérospatiale, 20 per cent of steel-maker Usinor Sacilor, and 7 per cent of chemical company Rhône-Poulenc (*Le Monde*, 8 March 1994, 5). State-owned or recently privatized banks often clustered around particular key industrial companies. At Matra Hachette, owner of key space and defence technologies, Crédit Lyonnais, Paribas, and BNP were at the head of a secure group of financial institutions holding around a quarter of the shares in the early 1990s (see Illustration 4.1). Friendly industrial partners such as Daimler Benz, Northern Telecom, and GEC also held another quarter of the voting shares. Another example of a strategic company under friendly banking surveil-lance in the 1990s is provided by Alcatel-Alsthom, formerly the Compagnie Générale d'Électricité (CGE) and the French state's largest industrial supplier through its telecommunications, nuclear power, and railway engineering activi-ties. Privatized during the late 1980s after Mitterand's earlier nationalization, Alcatel Alsthom's largest shareholder, with 9 per cent, was the Société Générale bank, itself recently privatized after forty-two years in the state sector. Family merchant banks and holding companies such as Lazard Frères and Worms fre-quently took substantial stakes in companies too. For instance, the family finan-cial holding group Worms, founded in 1842 but partially nationalized in 1982, re-emerged in the early 1990s as an active shareholder with one-third of the prominent paper and sugar Saint-Louis group as well as near complete owner-ship of the Athena insurance company.

If the role of banks and other financial institutions is notable in France it is even more pronounced in Germany, again in line with expectations. In Germany we are dealing with a universal banking system where banks act as providers of both equity and credit. As we have already mentioned, banks frequently also control significant amounts of proxy votes, votes cast on behalf of other owners. Here however we concentrate on the role of banks as shareholders in their own right. In passing we should mention that research suggests that these proxy votes appear to be highly stable (Nibler, 1998), as stable at least as the bank's own shareholdings to which we now turn. As expected, we find bank ownership to be most significant in Germany where it holds at about 20 per cent in both time periods. For Germany one can differentiate between traditional 'big three' national banks—Deutsche Bank, Commerzbank, and Dresdner Bank—and the regional banks—such as the state-controlled Landesbanken—and the 'private' regional banks (though regional governments can play a role in these as well, as reflected in the shares of the Bavarian State in the Bayerische Vereinsbank). All three types of large banks are represented among the owners of large industrial firms in Germany. Most notable are, of course, the shareholdings of the

Deutsche Bank, which include participations in tyre manufacturer Continental, Klöckner Humboldt Deutz, cement producer Heidelberger Zement and Linde, as well as in Daimler Benz. Although Daimler Benz has since merged with Chrysler to form DaimlerChrysler, the Deutsche Bank still remains one of the three main shareholders of the newly formed company (see Illustration 4.2). Turning to the other national commercial banks, we find the shareholdings of the Dresdner Bank to include a participation in BMW (via GFA, Gesellschaft für Automobilwerte) and Heidelberger Zement, whilst the Commerzbank holds notable participations in Linde and heavy engineering firm MAN. The WestLB, the largest of Germany's state-controlled Landesbanken, holds shares in mechanical engineering firm Deutsche Babcock and Preussag, whilst the Bayerische Hypotheken und Wechselbank (since merged with the Bayerische Vereinsbank) controlled a participation in the paper producer PWA.

Illustration 4.2. *Daimler Benz: Deutsche Bank Client?*

Deutsche Bank had links with both Daimler and Benz since immediately after the First World War, and was heavily involved in the merger of the two firms in 1926. Over the next decade Deutsche Bank supplied the chairmanship of the newly merged company. Relations remained close, in 1975 Deutsche Bank taking over the 29 per cent of Daimler Benz held, directly or indirectly, by the Flick empire. During the mid-1980s the chairman of Daimler Benz's supervisory board was Alfred Herrhausen, chief executive of the Deutsche Bank. It was under Herrhausen, and with the support of McKinsey, that Daimler Benz transformed itself from a relatively focused and centralized automobile company into a diversified and divisionalized industrial corporation.

In 1998 Daimler Benz merged with the American Chrysler corporation to form DaimlerChrysler. The new concern remains a German stock corporation (AG) incorporated under German law. As such the company retains the two-tiered German system of corporate governance with a supervisory board made up of shareholder and employee representatives and a separate management board. Jürgen E. Schrempp, the former Daimler Benz chairman, and Robert J. Eaton were initially co-chairmen and co-chief executives both maintaining offices in the two operational headquarters in Stuttgart, Germany, and Auburn Hills, Michigan. Shares of the company are traded on both the NYSE and the Frankfurt Stock Exchange as well as in nineteen further locations around the world. Shareholder meetings will be held in Germany though financial reporting follows US-GAAP. Ties with the Deutsche Bank remain, however. Although Deutsche Bank's holding was diluted from 22 per cent to 12 per cent by the merger, it remained the largest single shareholder. At the time of writing the chairman of DaimlerChrysler's supervisory board is the chairman of the management board of the Deutsche Bank, Hillmar Kopper.

Principal sources: Gall (1995); www.daimlerchrysler.com; *Wirtschaftswoche*, 30 June 1984; *Wirtschaftswoche* 1 March, 1985; SEC Form 20-F, 31 March, 1999.

Though the role of banks such as the Deutsche Bank in the German economy is frequently highlighted, we should not overlook the role of other financial institutions. The Allianz insurance company is particularly important, with substantial participation in cosmetics company Beiersdorf, as well as in MAN. Here it is joined by the Müncher Rück, a globally leading reinsurance firm which, next to this participation in MAN, also holds shares in energy company RWE. This kind of joint ownership by financial institutions is quite common in Germany. Dresdner and Deutsche Banks, for instance, both hold shares in Heidelberger Zement, whilst the Commerzbank joins the Allianz and the Münchner Rück in controlling a stake in MAN. In this context we also need to mention the notable ties that exist between many of Germany's banks and other financial institutions. Cross shareholdings between these financial institutions are also common, for instance, between Deutsche Bank and the Allianz and between the Allianz and the Münchner Rück (each holds 25 per cent of the other). Dresdner and Deutsche Bank each hold about 10 per cent of the Münchner Rück. The Allianz in turn holds above 20 per cent of the Dresdner Bank, which alongside the Deutsche Bank holds about 10 per cent of the Allianz. As these examples indicate, Germany's financial and industrial sectors are highly distinctive in their reliance on extensive networks of financial and other relationships. Whether these networks still affect strategy and structure is quite another matter, to be pursued in later chapters.

Whilst we have found various forms of network relationships in the financial and industrial sectors of France and Germany, the situation in the United Kingdom is very different. Bank ownership is clearly irrelevant in this country. Only in 1993 do we find some bank ownership and here it is down to the presence of foreign banks. For example, in the early 1990s the Morgan Guaranty Trust of New York held nearly a quarter of the oil company BP as a depository for American Depository Receipts (ADRs). The Kuwaiti Investment Office held a further 10 per cent. The most prominent British financial institution in BP was the Prudential insurance company, holding only 3 per cent of the shares.

This Prudential stake was very typical. By 1990 the insurance companies had grown increasingly important on the British scene. However, these stakes were usually quite small and often did not register at our threshold 5 per cent level. For example, by the early 1990s the Prudential held small stakes in a wide range of Top 100 industrial companies, including RMC, Unigate, Racal, Smith Kline, ICI, Hanson, and BP (Morin and Dupuy, 1993: 70). None the less, only two of the Prudential's industrial stakes exceeded the 5 per cent limit, and then only marginally—those in BICC (5.9%) and RTZ (6.25%). It is clear that British financial institutions do not have the kinds of strategic stakes common in France and Germany.

But it is not just in the role of banks and financial institutions that the Continental countries differ from Britain. The high proportion of firms under personal ownership in both France and Germany is particularly striking. The figures are so substantial that we need to remind ourselves that we are dealing with some of the largest and most successful industrial firms in Europe. In France more than 40 per cent of firms had significant owners who had either inherited their stakes or created their firms themselves. These cover a very broad range of industrial sectors. High-technology firms under personal ownership include Electronique Serge Dassault and Dassault Aviation, both created by the post-war entrepreneur Serge Dassault himself; and Matra Hachette, whose founding entrepreneur, the brilliant Jean-Luc Lagardère, managed to retrieve control after partial nationalization during the 1980s (see Illustration 4.1). Tyre company Michelin and automobile company Peugeot were industrial giants with substantial family stakes despite the demands of their capital and scale-intensive industries. A host of food and drinks companies managed to keep substantial family shareholders into the 1980s and 1990s, including Bel, Besnier, Moët-Hennessy (later part of LVMH), Pernod Ricard, and Rémy-Cointreau. The 1980s also saw the emergence of entrepreneurial acquisitive conglomerates, such as Financière Agache in luxury goods and Fimalac in publishing, precious metals, and finance. Personal ownership was thus well entrenched in France in the last decades of the twentieth century.

The situation in Germany is similar to that in France. In 1983 more than half of all firms had personal owners and though the figure dropped somewhat by 1993 it remained at a substantial 46 per cent. As in France, this includes a number of the country's most prominent companies. Nearly a century and a half after being founded by the engineer Werner von Siemens, developer of the electromagnetic telegraph, the Siemens family still retains a sizeable stake in Germany's largest electrical and electronics firm. Though the family holds only about 5.3 per cent of so-called 'Stammaktien', their control of preferential shares raises their share of the votes in matters of strategic significance to over 14 per cent. The Quandt family's holdings spread widely through German industry, including substantial participations in battery producer VARTA and the pharmaceutical company ALTANA, as well as the luxury car manufacturer BMW. Luxury car company Porsche, too, is under the personal ownership of the related Porsche and Piëch families. In the media and publishing industry, we find all three major players still with major personal shareholders, including Bertelsmann and Springer, which owns Germany's only national tabloid, the *Bildzeitung*, and the less well-known Holtzbrink company, owner of the *Scientific American* and the leading German business daily, the *Handelsblatt*.

The position of firms under personal ownership in Germany is usually quite stable, with firms remaining successful over long periods and families managing to maintain their positions. Nevertheless some owners did lose their personal control during our period, as for example was the case for computer manufacturer Nixdorf, taken over by Siemens, and the athletic footwear and sportsclothing manufacturer Adidas, passing into French ownership. These two cases also illustrate one of the few changes in the ownership pattern of large industrial concerns in Germany: the exit of Germany's post-war entrepreneurs. By 1983 only a few entreprenerial companies remained, meat producer Moksel being one of these. Overall, however, no new generation of entrepreneurs appears to have emerged in Germany, a marked contrast to France. We shall return to recent German entrepreneurial failure in our discussion of management and personal control.

In the United Kingdom, personal ownership is much more limited. Although many other companies in the sector have been long under dispersed ownership, it is striking that three of the personally owned companies are in the food and agriculture business. Associated British Foods is a long-established family foods business, with Canadian roots dating back to the nineteenth century, and firmly under the control of the Weston family (see Illustration 4.3). The Vestey family's Western United Investments also had colonial connections, this time to the Australian sheep industry, but by the 1990s was active in a range of food production and distribution activities. Hillsdown Holdings was more recent and less international, its 1975 founders, Thompson and Solomon, retaining large stakes into the 1980s. Publishing group Pearson is another anomaly on the British scene, with the Cowdray family trust retaining a significant stake into the 1980s. Significantly, the Pearson group is linked into the French system through its stakes in Parisian banking house Lazard Frères and the leading financial paper, *Les Echos*. Pearson's board of directors in 1993 included two prominent French bankers, the influential Michel David-Weill and Jean-Claude Haas.

Illustration 4.3. *Associated British Foods (ABF): Family Survivor*

ABF has its distant origins in George Weston's Toronto bread-delivery route in 1882. This became the base for a successful bakery group, which George's son Garfield internationalized through the acquisition of seven bakeries in the United Kingdom in 1935. These bakeries were the core of Associated British Foods, which rapidly expanded in both baking and retailing throughout the United Kingdom and overseas. The company built a portfolio of strong brands such as Twinings, Ryvita, Allied Bakeries, and Burton's Biscuits. In 1978 Garfield's son Gary became chairman and continued expansion. The last major acquisition was of British Sugar, in 1991. ABF's many subsidiaries are only loosely co-ordinated, except on key issues such as transfer pricing and purchasing. The corporate centre in the early 1990s had just fifty staff, spread over three London sites. The dominant personalities were Gary—on the board since 1948—and Harold Bailey—who had originally worked with Garfield Weston as his junior accountant immediately after the war. Fifteen separate subsidiaries reported directly to Gary Weston; the Australasian businesses were largely left on their own except for annual personal visits by the chairman. There were three Weston sons in the business—Guy as managing director of Ryvita; Garth as site manager at Ryvita; and another Gary as managing director of Westmills.

Principal sources: Interview and *The International Directory of Company Histories*.

Pearson's chairman in 1993, Viscount Michael Blakenham, had worked for Lazard Brothers and was a member of the Cowdray family. These curious aristocratic and banking connections were no obstacle to Pearson being one of the world's leading financial publishers, with the *Financial Times* at its masthead.

One further difference between Continental countries and the United Kingdom is the role of other non-financial firms in the ownership of industrial enterprises. As others have already observed, mutual cross-shareholdings between corporations are both 'permitted and commonplace' in Continental Europe (Franks and Mayer, 1990: 208). Our group only includes independent firms in the sense of the original Harvard studies (Channon, 1973; Dyas and Thanheiser, 1976), and therefore excludes firms with corporate shareholders above 50 per cent. Thus Kraus-Maffei, for instance, is treated as a subsidiary of Mannesmann, which had a 71 per cent stake in 1993. From a traditional business school point of view, however, these non-majority stakes are not easy to understand. Substantial minority shareholdings of one industrial company by another are likely to introduce constraints on selfish profit-maximization. For the owning firm, these stakes can tie up a substantial set of assets without the control obtainable in the case of a wholly or strong majority-owned subsidiary. For the owned firm, the activities of the dominant shareholder may involve conflicts of interest, inhibiting strategies that might be otherwise attractive. Yet the rise of partnerships and joint ventures within contemporary economies is inescapably driving many firms closer together, especially across international boundaries (Mowery, 1992). It is in terms of these pressures and constraints that national differences and trends in industrial firm ownership should be seen.

As we can see from Table 4.1, ownership by other firms is most important in France. In 1983, 20 per cent of firms were already under the partial ownership of other firms; by 1993, this had grown to no less than 30 per cent of French firms. In Germany the role of firms is less pronounced, but again moving in the same direction: just over 8 per cent of firms were under partial ownership in 1983, but over 14 per cent in 1993. The proportion of firms owned by other firms is lowest in the United Kingdom, though again there is a notable increase between 1983 and 1993, from 4 per cent to over 10 per cent.

In France these cross-shareholdings are not simply a construct of the protective *noyaux durs* relationships set up after the privatizations of 1986–8. Clearly, there was a high level of cross-shareholding even in the early 1980s. Besides, most of the *noyaux durs* relationships were between industrial firms and key financial institutions and typically less than our 5 per cent threshold. A quite typical example is Alcatel-Alsthom in the early 1990s, which held 2.5 per cent of the services conglomerate Générale des Eaux and 4.4 per cent of the industrial materials company Saint-Gobain, as well as 4 per cent in its major shareholder, the Société Générale. Less typical, but expressive of where this logic could lead, is the state-controlled oil-company Elf Aquitaine. By 1993 7 per cent of its assets were in the form of financial participations, including stakes in Suez, and the Banco Central Espagnol, and the collapsed textile company Biderman. Personal friendship between chief executives and a desire to save manufacturing jobs were said to have played a role in Elf's Biderman stake (*Les Echos*, 18 October 1993).

Nevertheless, the more substantial stakes among French firms tended to have some industrial logic. For example, the steel company Usinor Sacilor and the water utility and construction company Lyonnaise des Eaux Dumez together owned more than 40 per cent of the leading French tube manufacturer, Vallourec. The dominant family tyre company Michelin held 6 per cent in the leading French family automobile company, PSA Peugeot Citroën. Growing internationalization also played a role, as for example the stakes of ITT in Alcatel-Alsthom, Daimler Benz in Matra Hachette, or, briefly and controversially, Volvo's in automobile manufacturer Renault. In the last two cases at least, these financial participations underpinned real business co-operation.

Although the proportion of financial ties between independent firms is lower in Germany when compared to France, they remain important. However, German ties are typically more introverted, within the German world rather than outside. In some cases, such as white goods manufacturer Bosch-Siemens, they represent long-standing links between key players in the German industry, in this case Bosch and Siemens. In other cases, such as the chemicals company Wacker, they combine personal ownership with the clout of the largest concerns. Wacker is under 50-50 ownership by the Wacker family and Hoechst. At times the links between companies are indirectly associated with the role of personal owners. Personally owned Tchibo, for instance, holds substantial shares in Beiersdorf, whilst the Henkel family had moved its personal holdings in Degussa under the Henkel company umbrella by 1993. Some links are grounded in company history, such as the stake of trading company Klöckner & Co. in manufacturer Klöckner-Werke, both originating in the now dissipated Klöckner empire. Klöckner & Co. is itself owned by the metals to energy company VIAG. Although VIAG has since the time period investigated by this study merged with the Bayernwerk AG, the links between these two firms and the paper producer PWA illustrate the complexity that inter-firm networks can reach (see Illustration 4.4 and Figure 4.2).

In the United Kingdom inter-firm linkages are still rarer than in Germany, but typically more outward looking. The case of precious metals company Johnson Matthey is one of quasi-vertical integration, with the South African mining company Anglo-American controlling a dominant stake via Charter Consolidated through the 1980s and 1990s. In 1990 the internationalization of the paper industry brought French paper company Arjomari-Prioux into a near 40 per cent stake in what became Arjo Wiggins Appleton. Another key French link was that between drinks company Guinness and the drinks and luxury goods conglomerate LVMH, each involving about a quarter of the other's

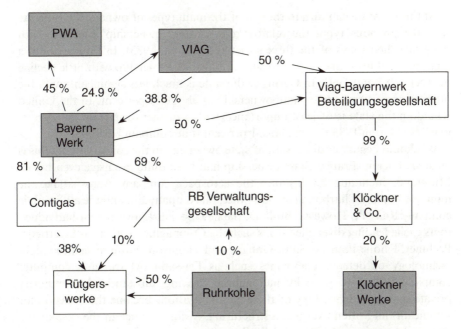

Figure 4.2. *Ownership Linkages between German Industrial Concerns, 1993*
Note: Shaded companies are domestically owned Top 100 industrials

---

Illustration 4.4. *Viag: State-owned Networker*

The VIAG concern was founded in 1923 as a holding for the industrial participations of the German state. In 1939 a participation in the electricity generator Bayernwerk was added to the company's shareholdings thereby confirming a pattern of partial participations which together with a detached management style long characterized the company. By the early 1980s the VIAG was effectively operating as a department of the German government, though privatization was soon to follow, beginning in 1986. Despite this change in ownership, the structure of the company remained highly decentralized with a limited role for the central office. Through to 1993 partial participations included shares in companies such as glass manufacturer Gerresheimer Glas (51 per cent), packaging firm Schmalbach-Lubeca (51 per cent), and the Didier-Werke (51 per cent) manufacturer of fire and heat resistant materials, as well as those indicated in Figure 4.2.

Principal sources: Interviews in VIAG and Bayernwerk; *Wirtschaftswoche* No. 22, 24 May 1991.

---

shares. This Guinness-LVMH financial link underpinned joint international distribution for their various drinks brands. In general, then, British firms appear to have stayed closer to industrial logic in their financial links to other businesses, and also to have been relatively international.

At this point we can turn to the last of the main types of owners, the state. As with the previous types the relative role of state ownership is in line with the established views of the three societies (Zysman, 1983). In France about a quarter of all firms are subject to substantial state ownership with little decline between 1983 and 1993. In Germany the state is much less significant, with the proportion of firms under state ownership at about 10 per cent. In the United Kingdom the state is of least importance, with a further drop from the already low 7 per cent in 1983 to just above 1 per cent (one company) in 1993.

We should begin our discussion of state ownership in the country where this is most significant, France. State ownership had been quite extensive even before Mitterand, including for instance the aerospace company Aérospatiale, the mining company Charbonnages de France, oil company Elf, and the automobile company Renault. However, by 1983, the new Socialist government had added to its cache leading diversified firms such the Compagnie Générale d'Electricité, Pechiney, Rhône-Poulenc, Saint-Gobain, and Thomson. More specialized high-technology or defence companies such as Dassault, Matra, and computer company Bull were partially nationalized, leaving substantial but minority private shareholdings. Many of these nationalizations became the occasion for significant, and often overdue, restructuring, as for instance in the case of the two steel companies Usinor and Sacilor, merged into a single company. Charbonnages de France, Elf, Pechiney, and Rhône-Poulenc swapped around France's major chemicals interests (Woronoff, 1994). The first of our group of large industrial firms to be privatized were Saint-Gobain, Compagnie Générale d'Electricité (Alcatel Alsthom), and Matra, during the first 'cohabitation' between the conservative government of Chirac and the Socialist presidency of Mitterand during 1986–8. However, plans for more extensive privatization were disrupted by the October 1987 financial crash and the Socialists' return to government in 1988. The socialist governments of 1988–93 did, nevertheless, engage in some partial privatizations, often driven by the desire to internationalize French industry. Thus, for example, Pechiney needed private capital to finance its acquisition of American National Can, and the Swedish automobile manufacturer Volvo took a 20 per cent stake of Renault as part of a finally aborted strategic alliance (Schmidt, 1996). Although these diluted ownership, the French state still remained the dominant shareholder. As Table 4.1. indicates, the proportion of French firms with substantial state ownership slipped quite slightly.

State ownership in Germany is both less significant than in France and more plural. Reflecting Germany's federal nature, state shareholdings are found at various levels—federal, regional (the various region states, the Bundesländer), and even municipal. One municipal example is the town of Friedrichshafen, which controls the stake of the Zeppelin-Stiftung in the automotive supplier ZF-Friedrichshafen. Traditionally Friedrichshafen's mayor is also the chairman of the company's supervisory board. Various municipalities also play an important role as partial owners of energy company RWE, which originated as a regional energy supplier. By controlling shares with enhanced voting power, the municipalities effectively hold the majority of RWE's voting rights. Among the regional states, the most notable participation is probably Lower Saxony's in VW which, in 1993, stood at about 20 per cent. We have already noted the Bavarian state's holdings in the Bayernwerk AG (after the VIAG-Bayernwerk merger Bavaria retained a stake of above 25 per cent in the restructured company). There are further important holdings by regional states. In 1993 Saarland retained a 26 per cent stake in the coal-mining company Saarberg-werke, with the German federal state holding the remainder. The Carl Zeiss Stiftung, which in 1993 owned the optics companies Carl Zeiss and Schott, is also effectively under state control. Over most of the post-war era Carl Zeiss was administrated by the regional state of Baden Württemberg. Following the unification between the Federal Republic of Germany and the German Democratic Republic, influence over Zeiss began to be shared with the former East German state of Thüringen.

The United Kingdom, of course, was subject to the prototypical privatization programmes of the various Conservative governments of the 1980s and 1990s. Although such large companies as British Leyland, British Aerospace, British Petroleum, British Shipbuilders, and British Steel still figured in the list of state-owned companies in 1983, a decade later all had arrived in one form or another in the private sector. In 1993 the last large industrial company under state ownership, food company Dairy Crest, was something of an anomaly, being owned by the government's Milk Marketing Board. During 1994 and 1995 the Board was abolished and Dairy Crest was floated on the stock exchange.

To summarize, the ownership patterns of the large industrial firms in the three countries do broadly conform to the opposition of the market-based United Kingdom and bank-centred Continental Europe. The United Kingdom is characterized by a highly dispersed pattern of ownership, with only the activities of financial institutions such as the Prudential leading to a limited amount of ownership concentration. State ownership has crumbled as a result of intense privatization. In France, by contrast, firms typically have large shareholders, whether personal, financial, state, or other firms. Germany is much closer to France than the United Kingdom, again with ownership typically concentrated in the hands of banks or personal owners. Germany differs, however, in the less prominent role of the state, particularly the central state, and in the decline of its entrepreneurial class.

These ownership patterns support the case for enduring differences between the three national systems. According to national institutionalists, these differences should be consequential for corporate strategy and structure as well. In France and Germany, where personal owners may insist on control and where banks can play a substitute monitoring role, they would expect the place of the multidivisional to be relatively limited. In the same vein, the centralized functional form should be flourishing particularly in France, where the state plays such a central role. In the United Kingdom, by contrast, the need to manage risk without the support of stable shareholders would be expected to promote diversification, especially unrelated diversification, and the segmentation of the corporation into discrete divisions. In other words, instead of Chandler's (1990) laggard, the transformation of ownership since the pre-war period should make the United Kingdom the champion of the diversified, multidivisional corporation.

4.2. MANAGERIAL CONTROL

Since Bearle and Means (1932), it is generally assumed that the normal process of modernization would produce a separation of ownership and control among large firms. Even if families do retain large stakes, professional career managers would take over day-to-day control. Families would lack sufficient managerial resource and talent to manage the large complex enterprises of the twentieth century. Failure to hand over control to professional managers would inhibit both growth and the development of organizational structures and capabilities. Chandler (1962: 316) is particularly insistent that the original builders of the diversified, divisionalized corporation at DuPont, General Motors, Sears, and Standard Oil 'closely resembled the professional administrators of today. With the exception of Pierre du Pont, they did not control or even own large blocks of stock in the company that they managed.' Professional rather than family managers are the carriers of modernity in the enterprise. Chandler (1990: 293) is scathing about the tradition of 'personal capitalism' in British industry in the early years of the twentieth century: 'In Britain, sons and other relatives of the founders usually took over control of the enterprise. . . . In the United States, nepotism had a pejorative connotation. In Britain it was an accepted way of life.' The failure of family managers to make the investments in scale, scope, and organizational capability supposedly had tragic and enduring consequences for British industrial performance.

Chandler's (1990) association of personal control with antipathy to diversification and divisionalization is not unusual. Institutionalists with no particular love for the diversified multidivisional corporation imply a similar relationship. Thus, from the corporate political tradition, Palmer et al. (1993) and Mahoney (1992) have both proposed that continued participation of family or entrepreneurial owners in the management of their firms will inhibit the adoption of the multidivisional form, as requiring both a decentralization of power and a transparency of performance likely to curtail personal discretion. From a national institutional perspective, Whitley (1994) reprises this kind of argument to suggest that in business systems characterized by strong owner control there will be a general inclination to centralize decision-making, whereas in systems characterized by professional career managers, firms will be both more ready and more able to decentralize. There is a consensus, therefore, that the prevalence of personal control in an economy is likely to tip the balance against diversification, because of its demands upon managerial capability, and against divisionalization, because of its uncongenial decentralization and accountability.

What is striking by the 1980s, however, is how far the United Kingdom had departed from the Chandlerian caricature of the earlier period. For the United Kingdom Scott (1997) has identified a steady decline of personal ownership and management among large companies since the 1950s. Bauer and Bertin-Mourot's (1996) broader study of European firms found that by 1992 only 16 per cent of chairmen or chief executives of the United Kingdom's largest 200 firms were either entrepreneurs or members of families with significant shareholdings. According to this study, it is now Germany—for Chandler (1990) a pioneer of modern management—and France that represent the strongholds of personal managerial control. In 1985 29 per cent of top managers in the largest French firms came from entrepreneurial or owning-family backgrounds, a figure that even increased to 32 per cent in 1993 (Bauer and Bertin-Mourot, 1996). For Germany the figures were lower but still substantial, with 26 per cent in 1989 and 23 per cent in 1994 (Bauer and Bertin-Mourot, 1996). All this confirms Cassis's (1997: 126) survey of the backgrounds of European business leaders which has shown that during the post-war period French business leaders were much more likely to be inheritors than either in the United Kingdom or Germany.

To capture the extent of personal control among our own firms we followed the corporate political studies of Palmer et al. (1987, 1993) and Fligstein and Brantley (1992) by coding a firm as under personal control if the top manager was either the original entrepreneurial founder of the firm or a member of the founding family, with the entrepreneur or family controlling at least 5 per cent of shares. Again, significant developers of originally small firms were classified as entrepreneurs. The titles of top manager vary from country to country, of course. In the United Kingdom, we classified according to the nature of the chairperson, except where clearly without executive responsibility; otherwise, according to the chief executive officer. In France, we classified according to the 'Président-Directeur Géneral' (PDG), 'Président du Directoire', or 'Gérant', depending on the legal constitution of the company. In Germany, we focused on the 'Vorstandsvorsitzende' (Chair of the Executive Board), the 'Vorsitzende der Geschäftsleitung', or equivalent. We should note that these top management positions do not hold equal power across countries: the French PDG is probably the most powerful of the above positions; the Vorstandsvorsitzende the least (Cassis, 1997). The data were obtained from business publications such as *Who's Who* or its national equivalents (for example, in Germany *Wer ist Wer*), from reports in the business press, and directly from the firms. All our top managers were men.

The figures for management and personal control of the large industrial firms presented in Table 4.2 confirm the more general patterns discussed above, as well as the patterns of ownership introduced earlier. Personal control is most pronounced in France. Here the total percentage of top industrial firms under

Table 4.2. *Firms under Personal Ownership* and *Control: the United Kingdom, France, and Germany, 1983 and 1993 (Domestic Industrial Top 100)* (%)

	France		Germany		UK	
	1983	1993	1983	1993	1983	1993
Personal	21.7	28.8	20.0	15.9	6.7	3.0
Entrepreneur	6.8	13.6	10.0	1.6	1.3	1.5
Inherited	14.9	15.2	10.0	14.3	5.3	1.5
Other	78.3	71.2	80.0	84.1	93.3	97.0
Number	74	66	60	63	75	67

personal control rose from not quite 22 per cent in 1983 to almost 29 per cent in 1993. Several of the French companies still under personal control in 1993 included the kinds of food and drinks companies for which France is famous, such as Besnier, BSN (Danone), Pernod Ricard, and Rémy-Cointreau. But the extent of personal control in France cannot be put down just to the peculiarities of the French food and drinks tradition. Others included such international giants as the world's largest industrial gas company L'Air Liquide, where Edouard de Royère had married into the family, and Michelin, where the founder's grandson François Michelin had presided since 1955 (the great-grandson Edouard Michelin joined as co-gérant in 1995). Other spectacularly long-lived exemplars of personal control in 1993 included the 85-year-old Jacques Durand, who had presided over Verrerie Cristallerie d'Arques since 1927, and Robert Fiévet at Fromageries Bel, who had joined the company in 1936, marrying into the family.

The 1980s did see the end to some old personal firms in France, such as Olida et Caby and Ortiz Miko in the food sector. Nevertheless, the entrepreneurial spirit of that decade more than replenished the supply. Marc Ladreit de Lacharrière had propelled Fimalac, a mini-conglomerate, into the French Top 100 by 1993. Jérôme Seydoux made the old Chargeurs textile company into the vehicle for his own mini-conglomerate. Most spectacular of all was Bernard Arnault's construction of a luxury goods conglomerate under Financière Agache, founded in 1984 but just ten years later among the Top 40 industrial companies by sales in France (*L'Expansion*, 10 November 1993). It is notable, however, that all three of these entrepreneurs were well connected within the traditional French establishment. Ladreit de Lacharrière had passed out twenty-first in his year at the élite ENA postgraduate school and entered the Suez group, with its network of relationships, before moving on to L'Oréal where he began to build his empire on the side (*Les Echos*, 27 January 1992). Seydoux is a member of the wealthy industrial Schlumberger family and had worked as a banker in New York. Arnault came from an established business family, had graduated from

Illustration 4.5. *Bernard Arnault: Entrepreneur of Privilege*

Bernard Arnault is the son of a prominent businessman in Roubaix in the north of France. He entered the Ecole Polytechnique, but departed from the usual royal road of polytechniciens by returning to his family construction business, which he eventually bought out from his father. Partly out of boredom and partly in reaction to the election of the Socialist François Mitterand, Arnault departed for the United States in 1981. There he mixed in financial circles and appreciated at first hand the new corporate raiders of the early 1980s. In 1984 Arnault returned to France to take over the failing Agache-Willot conglomerate from the hands of an embarrassed state. Here the support of Banque Lazard and state-owned oil companies Elf and Total proved critical. Among the pearls of the Agache-Willot group was the fashion company Christian Dior, which would become the seed of the new luxury goods conglomerate Financière Agache. The creation of this new luxury goods conglomerate took an irreversible step forward in 1988 when Arnault launched a successful hostile bid against LVMH, the recently formed partnership between Moët-Hennessy and Louis Vuitton. The bid demanded all the ruthless determination that Arnault had observed in the United States, and was finally successful among much controversy in 1989.

Principal sources: Interviews in Financière Agache and LVMH; Kerdellant, 1992.

the élite Ecole Polytechnique, and also worked in New York (see Illustration 4.5). These French entrepreneurs were not forced into founding their own businesses through lack of alternative opportunity, but rather used privilege to create still more privilege.

In Germany the level of personal control is slightly lower compared to France but still significant with 20 per cent in 1983. By 1993 there is a slight decrease to 16 per cent due to the departure of Germany's post-war entrepreneurs already noted in our discussion of ownership. This appears to be the key difference between France and Germany: over the mid-to-late 1980s to the early 1990s France brought forth a new generation of industrial entrepreneurs whilst Germany did not.

Among the disappearing generation of entrepreneurs we find the industrialist Flick and publisher Axel Springer, both significant and often controversial figures on Germany's post-war industrial and political scene. Whilst some companies such as steel pipes manufacturer Benteler, coffee producers Tchibo, and rubber to textiles manufacturer Freudenberg remained under personal control, others such as FAG-Kugelfischer and Nixdorf succumbed under the impact of serious financial or managerial crises. Although few entrepreneurial firms succeeded in entering the population of largest industrials, it is notable that a number of well-established family-owned and controlled firms did manage to grow fast enough to enter the population of Top 100 industrial firms over the 1980s and early 1990s. Among these fast-growing family enterprises we find the publisher Holtzbrink, white goods manufacturer Miele, and Vorwerk, a company known for the innovative marketing of household goods.

In contrast to both France and Germany, personal ownership and control in the United Kingdom is almost unknown. By 1993 the only established family firm still under personal control was the sprawling food business ABF (see Illustration 4.3). An entrepreneurial exception was Michael Green, chairman and (with his brother) major shareholder at Carlton Communications. Like many of the French entrepreneurs of the 1980s, Green had his privileges: son of a successful businessman and public-school educated, he had married in 1972 the daughter of Lord Wolfson, the immensely wealthy owner of Great Universal Stores (*Management Today*, April 1989). Besides these, there was a handful of British top managers who effectively exercised personal control and held significant shareholdings (though less than 5 per cent): most prominent among these were Arnold Weinstock at GEC and Lord Hanson at Hanson plc. Otherwise, however, it seems that British top management—once pilloried by Chandler (1990) for its amateur personalism—had become much more 'impersonal' than French and German.

Just as with ownership, therefore, the characteristic patterns of management control among our companies generally conform to more widely observed differences between the three countries. Again we find a notable difference between the United Kingdom, on the one hand, and France and Germany, on the other, differences with potential implications for corporate strategy and structure. In the Continental countries, families and entrepreneurs manage to maintain a strong hold on the running of large industrial firms. Such families and entrepreneurs are allegedly hostile to the decentralization and accountability required by the multidivisional form and fearful of the financial and managerial stretch involved in diversification. The United Kingdom, by contrast, is now the home of the professional manager, supposedly well able to take on the demands of diversification and divisionalization. As we shall see in the next section, the United Kingdom's professional managers are likely to be still more favourably disposed towards the Chandlerian model because of the peculiarities of their career development.

4.3. MANAGEMENT DEVELOPMENT

As Alfred Chandler (1962) had recognized, the diversified, multidivisional corporation requires a particular kind of managerial skill both to introduce and then to administer. Chandler's (1962) great organization builders were well-educated men. They were capable of raising themselves from the everyday and of thinking analytically and abstractly. Their successors as administrators of multidivisional firms likewise require an ability to look beyond the operational. Derek Channon (1973: 241) is emphatic that in the multidivisional, 'the role of top management is that of the strategist and the policy maker and not that of the operations manager'. For Channon and his contemporary Harvard researchers, the availability of a pool of appropriately trained managers was critical to ensuring the spread of the new diversified, divisionalized corporate model throughout Europe (Dyas and Thanheiser, 1976: 319–21).

Institutionalists too recognize that the ways in which top managers are trained and developed through their careers can make an important difference to their readiness to diversify and divisionalize. Neil Fligstein (1990: 286–7), in his account of the rise of the American diversified multidivisional through the twentieth century, stresses the varying relevance of different kinds of functional experience acquired on routes to the top. He argues that the highly operational orientation of managers with purely manufacturing backgrounds is likely to be a handicap in the running of a diversified, multidivisional firm. However, sales and marketing backgrounds would be relevant to top management roles, especially for firms diversifying in a related manner. Financial backgrounds, on the other hand, are particularly adapted both to multidivisional organizations, where decision-making is based upon relatively detached financial information, and to strategies of unrelated diversification, typically involving the valuation of acquisitions and little concerned by the operational detail. Fligstein (1990) goes on to show that the movement towards diversified and multidivisional concerns in the United States was driven in part by a shift in the dominant backgrounds of corporate presidents away from manufacturing to areas such as finance, marketing, or general management. By 1979 the most common functional background for large American corporations was finance, accounting for 27.5 per cent. There had grown up in the United States a 'finance conception of the corporation' in which diversification and divisionalization were the orthodoxy and finance experts dominated the élite.

The national institutionalists are sensitive both to the significance of management development for corporate strategy and structure and, of course, to national variations. Whitley (1994), for instance, links market-based systems of skill development, such as the United Kingdom's, to strategies of unrelated diversification, while associating organization-based skill systems, such as Germany's, with organizational integration and the pursuit of synergy. Mobile managers make for disintegrated conglomerates. On the other hand, Lane (1995) highlights the traditional lack of technical and engineering skills among British top managers. The causality is different from Whitley's, but the consequences for strategy and structure go in the same direction. British managers, financial wizards but technical ignoramuses, are likely to incline towards loosely integrated strategies of unrelated diversification. German managers, on the other hand, draw on their technological expertise to drive integrated strategies of related diversification.

Commentators do frequently observe marked differences between the management development systems of France, Germany, and the United Kingdom (Bauer and Bertin-Mourot, 1996; Lane, 1995). France is perhaps most remarkable for its combination of élitism with meritocracy. French top managers, with or without family connections, are typically well educated, products of one of the highly competitive grandes ecoles (Shaw, 1995). Two schools dominate in particular. Pre-eminent still is the Ecole Polytechnique, an élite military engineering school. According to Bauer and Bertin-Mourot (1996), between 1985 and 1993 graduates of the Ecole Polytechnique accounted for a steady quarter of top executives among the 200 largest firms in France. As polytechniciens typically move afterwards through an élite postgraduate engineering school (such as Mines, Ponts et Chaussées, or Télécom) and then into initial engineering or technical posts in industry, this guarantees for French industry a top management cadre well versed in science and technology. A close second in influence is the Ecole Nationale d'Administration (ENA), accounting for around one-fifth of top French managers (Bauer and Bertin-Mourot, 1996). These business graduates of ENA (*énarques*) have typically followed high-flying careers in the French civil service, before transferring to top positions in private-sector or state-owned firms (the practice known as *pantouflage*: literally 'putting on the slippers'). It would seem that, whether on account of their technical orientation or their bureaucratic experience, about half of the top managers in French industry are unlikely to be naturally disposed to the diversification and decentralization associated with the Chandlerian model.

In Germany we do not find any élite system comparable to that in France. One important factor is the federal nature of the German political system in the post-war period. Bonn as a capital was not capable of exercising the same centralizing role in politics, society, or industry as was Paris. With a weak political centre and the isolation of the former capital of Berlin, the headquarters of Germany's largest concerns are dispersed throughout the country, attached to regional centres such as Frankfurt, Munich, or Stuttgart. However, France and Germany are similar in managerial skill systems. Many German top managers train as engineers or scientists, even to doctoral level (Lane, 1989, 1995; Eberwein and Tholen, 1993). Those who do not pursue a university education, and some of those who do, will often follow an engineering-oriented course of vocational training or apprenticeship in a large firm (Lane, 1991). An important characteristic of German industrial managers, therefore, is that their managerial identity is typically not separated from technical proficiency (Whitley, 1999; Stewart, 1994).

Whilst French and German managers have frequently been associated with technical and scientific knowledge, it has long been a complaint that these areas have been shunned by British top managers (Swords-Isherwood, 1980). Indeed, the overall educational level of British managers has traditionally been lower than that of their Continental counterparts (Eberwein and Tholen, 1993). Those top managers that have acquired a university education come disproportionately from the United Kingdom's own élite educational institutions, the Universities of Oxford and Cambridge. There future British top managers will typically have followed a liberal arts type degree in a setting in which the values of industry and technology have low prestige (Wiener, 1981). But if technology and science have been relatively neglected in the British system, accounting and finance have not. In a market-based financial system characterized by a frantic round of mergers and acquisitions, financial skills have a premium. Not surprisingly, then, finance has been identified as the dominant function on British boards (Doyle, 1990; Shaw, 1995). Bauer et al. (1995) found that no less than 15 per cent of the top managers in the largest 200 British enterprises had qualified as chartered accountants. In this respect, the United Kingdom again is close to the United States with its 'finance conception' of the corporation (Fligstein, 1990).

Broadly, therefore, British managers are held to be financially oriented; French and German managers more technically oriented, with the quirk in France being its strong statist tradition. As we look at our own top managers, we shall want to know how far they conform to these general stereotypes and whether their characteristics are changing. Here particularly we shall be interested in these top managers as representatives of wider systems of management development—as the most successful, they presumably reflect the most valued skills and backgrounds of their societies. These systems form part of the general context influencing patterns of strategy and structure in different countries. Later, in Chapter 7, we shall examine the direct effects of these managers' backgrounds on the strategies and structures of particular companies according to the corporate political perspective developed by Palmer and others.

Our top managers here are the same as those in the previous section. Thus in the United Kingdom we focused on the chairperson if he had executive responsibility; otherwise the chief executive officer. In France it was the 'Président-Directeur Général' (or Président du Directoire or Gérant). In Germany it was the 'Vorstandsvorsitzende' or equivalent. As we compare managerial backgrounds internationally, we need to bear in mind problems of equivalence. The French Président-Directeur Général is probably the strongest of these positions; the German Vorstandsvorsitzende the least. Moreover, the engineering training of a French polytechnicien and a German university graduate is not the same by any means; the one élitist and military, the other civil and more vocational. Accountancy is a less clearly defined discipline in Germany than in the United Kingdom, where it is strongly associated with a formal apprenticeship and qualification. We should recognize too that our top managers are not absolutely typical of their respective countries, being the most successful, but nevertheless they are unlikely to be eccentric and furthermore constitute role models for those other managers who would follow them.

The classification process followed Fligstein (1987) and Palmer, Devereaux Jennings, and Zhou (1993), focusing on the manager's dominant track to the top. A top manager was considered as having a 'general management' background if he either entered general management directly or passed through at least two functional positions before taking up a general management position, with no single track dominating (Fligstein, 1987: 51). A manager was assigned to a particular functional category if he spent a minimum of two years in the respective function and did not qualify for a 'general management' category. The main functional categories used in this study are financial/accounting,

Corporate Careers and Control

marketing/sales, and 'technical'. The term 'technical' covers managers from manufacturing, engineering, and scientific backgrounds. Those whose rise is associated with a family connection or entrepreneurship are assigned to a separate 'personal' category. These family or entrepreneurial top managers are less representative of broader national management development systems and their 'political' interests are likely to be different from professionals.

Information on career backgrounds was obtained from business publications such as *Who's Who* or its national equivalents (for example, in Germany *Wer ist Wer*), from reports in the business press, and directly from the firms. It should be noted that the quality of data varied significantly between countries and individuals and that in the absence of full information, especially regarding early careers, we were sometimes obliged to extrapolate from what we had: for example, without information to the contrary, we would assume that a German engineering PhD (Dr. Ing.) or a British chartered accountant continued in engineering or accounting roles until arrival in some more identifiable position. The fullest information was available in France, perhaps because of the credentialist and incestuous nature of its élite (Kadushin, 1995), and in the United Kingdom, probably because of the transparency required by financial markets. Personal information was poorest in Germany, especially in the earlier period (perhaps reflecting a decentralized society and partly developed financial markets). Consequently German management backgrounds will only be reported for 1993, a period for which we have reasonable confidence. As we shall see, the career patterns among our top managers broadly conform to those found by other studies.

Table 4.3 shows the proportions of top managers according to their career

Table **4.3.** *Top Managers' Backgrounds in the United Kingdom, France, and Germany, 1983, 1993 (Domestic Industrial Top 100) (%)*

	France		Germany		UK	
	1983	1993	1983	1993	1983	1993
General management	9.5	4.5	na	27.0	29.3	32.8
Technical	29.7	24.2	na	25.4	21.3	11.9
Finance	4.1	7.6	na	7.9	14.7	19.4
Marketing	2.7	1.5	na	4.8	5.3	9.0
State	12.2	16.7	na	3.2	5.3	—
Personal[a]	28.4	34.9	23.3	17.5	12.0	16.5
Other	1.4	6.0	na	4.8	1.3	—
Not available	12.2	4.5	na	9.5	10.7	10.4
Number	74	66	60	63	75	67

[a] Personal includes founders or inheriting family members who may have less than 5 per cent ownership.
na, Not available.

tracks in each country. As might be expected given the wider systems of management development, technical functions are indeed more important in France and Germany than in the United Kingdom. Though the proportion of British managers with a technical background is possibly surprisingly high in 1983, there is a clear drop by 1993. Again in line with expectations, the financial function is clearly most dominant in the United Kingdom, by 1993 more than doubly important than in the two continental countries. State backgrounds are markedly more important in France than in either Germany or the United Kingdom, and becoming increasingly so. On the other hand, German and British top managers are more likely to have general management backgrounds. We can explore these differences by looking at cases in more detail, starting with different functional backgrounds.

As we have said, the role of the technical function in France is underpinned by the engineering education offered at the élite Ecole Polytechnique. Unsurprisingly, polytechniciens cluster particularly in leading engineering and technology enterprises, often state-owned: thus Eléctricité de France and France Télécom both had more than 200 polytechniciens in their employ in the early 1990s, while SNCF, Elf, Thomson, Aérospatiale, Alcatel, and SNECMA had more than 100 each (*L'Expansion*, 3 March 1994). The PDGs of Alcatel, SNECMA, Total, Dassault, Pechiney, Bull, Saint-Gobain, Framatome, Usinor Sacilor, Saint-Louis, and LVMH were all polytechniciens in 1993. Although several polytechniciens—such as LVMH's Bernard Arnault—had not pursued technical careers, many did. Jean-Claude Leny, PDG of nuclear engineering company Framatome from 1985, had a particularly strong technical bent. After the Ecole Polytechnique, Leny had gone through the Ecole nationale supérieure des Télécommunications to work as an engineer at Radio-Télévision Française, before joining the Commisariat à l'énergie atomique, again as an engineer. Serge Dassault, son of Dassault's founder, was another polytechnicien who, after attending the Ecole nationale supérieure de l'aéronautique, worked in engineering development for the family firm, becoming director of test flights at the age of 30. He became Dassault's PDG in 1986, aged 41.

In Germany, for which we only have sufficient data for 1993, more than a quarter of all top managers come from a technical background. Here we find managers in the chemical and pharmaceutical industries such as Dr F. J. Kohl of Wacker, who began as a research chemist, and Prof. Dr Wolfgang Hilger who had been head of the department of inorganic chemistry at Hoechst. Prof. Dr Hans Joachim Langmann of Merk is a physicist who worked as a researcher at the University of Heidelberg and was a member of the scientific committee of the nuclear research centre in Karlsruhe. Among these managers we also find Dr med. Guiseppe Vita, who is one of the few foreign nationals heading German concerns, in this case an Italian. Dr Vita began his working life at the X-ray institute at the University of Mainz before joining the research department at Schering. Among the 'technical' managers with a more engineering bent we find Bernd Pischetsrieder of BMW, whose technical basis is in manufacturing

Illustration 4.6. *Ferdinand Piëch, Vorstandsvorsitzender, Volkswagen:*
Germanic Engineer

Ferdinand Piëch was born in Vienna, Austria, in 1937. He is a member of the Piëch
family who, together with their relatives of the Porsche family, continue to own the
Porsche AG. Following his studies in engineering at the ETH (Eidgenössiche Tech-
nische Hochschule) in Zurich, Switzerland, Ferdinand Piëch joined Porsche in 1963,
initially in the engine testing section, later becoming the technical director of the
company in 1971. He moved to Volkswagen's Audi division in 1973, where he
became director of engineering in 1975 a post that he held until 1988 when he took
up the position of Vorstandsvorsitzender. Piëch became Vorstandsvorsitzender of
Volkswagen AG in January 1993. Piëch is an accomplished engineer and is credited,
for instance, with the development of the five-cylinder internal combustion engine
and the permanent four-wheel drive. He received an honorary doctorate in engineering from the Technical University of Vienna in 1984.

Principal source: Stiens (1999).

systems, and Dr Bernhard Schmidt, who was head of the development department at Dornier System before joining Diehl as a member of the executive
board with responsibility for research and development. The head of VW,
Ferdinand Piëch, worked on the development of the permanent four-wheel drive
(see Illustration 4.6), whilst Dr Hermann Scholl of Bosch led the development
of fuel injections in the late 1960s. Dr hc. Werner H. Dieter of Mannesman also
worked as a development engineer at Bosch at the start of his career.

Although not uncommon in the early 1980s, the proportion of top managers
with technical backgrounds fell in the United Kingdom to 12 per cent by 1993.
More typical in the higher echelons of British management were those who had
come up predominantly through financial or accounting tracks. Thus, by 1993,
the percentage of accounting and finance types was twice as high in the United
Kingdom than in either France or Germany, confirming the expectations of
orthodoxy. British accountants can reach the top even in heavy industrial and
high-technology firms. Thus Brian Moffat at British Steel trained as a chartered
accountant at Peat Marwick Mitchell (later KPMG), before joining British
Steel's head office as deputy controller, finance (see Illustration 4.7). Pharmaceuticals giant Glaxo was headed by Paul Girolami, a chartered accountant who
ascended to the top first as the company's financial controller and then as its
finance director. Although the proportion of finance and accounting specialists
is not yet as high as Fligstein (1990) found for the United States, with its 'finance
concept' of the corporation, the United Kingdom appears to be heading in the
same direction.

In Germany, by contrast, we find relatively few managers with a purely
financial background. Many of these enjoyed quite mobile careers relative to
most German top managers. The trajectory of Dr Klaus Götte of MAN, for

Illustration 4.7. *Brian Moffat, Chairman and Chief Executive, British Steel:*
British Accountant

Brian Moffat was born in Scotland in 1939. He did not take a degree, but trained as a chartered accountant at the accounting firm of Peat Marwick Mitchell (later to become part of KPMG). He joined British Steel's head office in 1968, one year after nationalization, as deputy controller, finance. Moffat's big break, unusual for an accountant, was his appointment as director of the Port Talbot steel works in South Wales in 1976. There he weathered the bitter national steel strike of 1980 and cut jobs from 13,500 to 4,700. He then moved back to head office in 1986 as managing director, finance, masterminding the privatization of British Steel in 1988. He became chief executive in 1991 and chairman in 1993.

Principal sources: *Management Today*, June 1995; *Who's Who in Britain*.

example, led him to most corners of Germany's business system. He began his working life as a banker with the prestigious private banking house C. G. Trinkhaus (from 1955 until 1968). He then moved to Krupp as director for finance before becoming a member of the board of the Allianz and briefly, between 1980 and 1982, a managing partner at the Flick Industrieverwaltung. Dr Klaus P. Bleyer of ZF-Friedrichshafen was a financial analyst at SEL and later financial director at ITT. Volker Hanneman of GEA began as a bank trainee then worked for an auditing and tax consulting company before taking up management posts in two industrial enterprises, eventually becoming managing director at GEA in 1975.

Marketing is a relatively insignificant basis for top management careers in all countries. Even in the United Kingdom the proportion of marketers was still only 9 per cent in 1993. In the Continental countries the numbers are below 5 per cent. In France the only marketer in the top job was the British chief of L'Oréal, Lindsey Owen-Jones, who had started in cosmetics sales in Normandy after doing his MBA at INSEAD. In Germany one of the few marketers is also one of the few with an MBA, Dr Klaus O. Fleck of sugar and frozen foods producer Südzucker. Before joining Südzucker, Fleck had taken an MBA at Wharton and worked with Procter & Gamble and as a marketing consultant with McKinsey. In the United Kingdom marketing professionals most often reached the top in fast-moving consumer goods companies, such as Michael Jackaman of Allied Lyons, Anthony Greener of Guinness, and Sir Robert Clarke of United Biscuits.

However, for both Germany and the United Kingdom a general rather than specialist career is the most common background for top managers. This is probably not surprising among those who have reached such prominent positions: as Chandler (1962) himself underlined, top management responsibility in the diversified multidivisional requires the acquisition of a general management perspective of some sort. In this sense, too, top managers are only partially representative of wider management development systems. It is the differences in functional backgrounds among the specialists who do reach the top that is most revealing about the wider systems. The French pattern—with few apparent generalists—will require some commentary, but we shall start with the German and British systems.

For Germany, though, the high proportion of general managers reflects the number of 'high flyers' beginning their careers as assistants to general managers, such as Dr Frank Niethammer of the AGIV, and the practice of managers moving through various types of management functions such as Dr Jürgen Strube of BASF (Strube originally joined the finance department at BASF in 1969, before moving on to the logistics department, followed by a stay in Brazil where he carried out logistics and administrative functions). Other generalists reflect the close association between technical and managerial knowledge embodied in the German vocational and higher education systems. This was, for example, the case with Diplom Kaufmann, Diplom Ingenieur Hans-Reiner Biehl of the Saarbergwerke. Mr Biehl studied both business administration and engineering to the equivalent of an Anglo-American masters degree level and joined the Saarbergwerke as a departmental deputy, then becoming a planning engineer and assistant to the executive director for mining and later head of corporate planning.

British top managers too frequently gain a wide range of general experience in their early careers. This is often a result of the wide opportunities and deliberate development offered by large companies to their young career managers. An example here is Denys Henderson, who joined ICI in 1957 in the company secretary's department after two years' National Service in the army's directorate of legal services. From there, Henderson became new ventures manager in one of the divisions, then general manager for catalysts and licensing and then corporate general manager, commercial. He became chairman of the paints division in 1977, reaching ICI's management board in 1980 and the position of chairman and chief executive in 1987. Although he had started with a legal background, his career to the top had not been through success in a specialized function, but through a range of posts demanding general management capabilities.

The lack of French generalists is anomalous at first sight. To a large extent, however, this is explicable by the high proportion of top managers who have had some personal route to the top, whether entrepreneurial or family. Because this includes those without shareholdings above the 5 per cent threshold, this is a still larger proportion than those who exercise personal control. In France, this means that more than one-third of top managers do not owe their positions to a purely 'professional' career track. On top of this, we should add the substantial numbers that have followed state careers. These practitioners of *pantouflage* account for over 12 per cent in 1983 and almost 17 per cent in 1993. The increase was due both to the nationalizations of the early 1980s and to a growing

Illustration 4.8. *Jacques Calvet, Président du Directoire, Peugeot SA;*
Enarque

Jacques Calvet was born in 1931 to become a classic practitioner of the French art of pantouflage. After studying political economy at the famous Institut d'études politiques de Paris, Calvet entered the civil service via the Ecole Nationale d'Administration. After a first job as auditor in the Cours des comptes, he rose finally to become, in 1973, directeur of the Ministry of Finance and Economics. In 1974, he took his first step into commerce and industry, joining the Banque Nationale de Paris, where he became Président in 1979. In 1982, he joined automobile manufacturer Peugeot, becoming Président du Directoire at PSA in 1984. Here he was able to apply his financial skills to rescue the family-owned group from heavy debt and years of underinvestment.

Principal sources: *Dynasteurs*, December 1990; *Figaro Economie*, 20 March 1990.

recognition among high-flying civil servants of the relatively greater rewards available in industry. This is in stark contrast to Germany, where we only have about 3 per cent in 1993, and the United Kingdom, where the figure is 5 per cent for 1983 and none in 1993. If we allow for both those with state backgrounds and those with personal backgrounds, slightly less than half of France's top managers in the last decade of the twentieth century had the sort of 'professional' backgrounds that Alfred Chandler (1977) assumed to be the 'modern' managerial norm.

A few examples can illustrate the extent to which ex-civil servants had colonized the French business world by the 1990s. There were of course the state-owned enterprises such as Aérospatiale, Elf, Charbonnages de France, and the tobacco monopoly Seita, all run by ex-civil servants. Striking, however, is the penetration of such men into prominent firms in the private sector. Jean Dromer, PDG of the conglomerate Financière Agache from 1989, had entered the prestigious Inspection de Finances after ENA, pursuing a series of high-level civil service positions for ten years before entering banking. Jacques Calvet, PDG of the family-controlled Peugeot, followed a high-flying civil service career for more than fifteen years after ENA, before also moving into banking and thence into industry (see Illustration 4.8). Generally, nationalizations and privatization made little difference. In their wider study of the PDGs of the Top 200 French enterprises, Bauer and Bertin-Mourot (1996: 15) found that more than two-thirds of the privatized firms in their group were run by men with strong state backgrounds: 'the men changed, but the conditions of access to the top remained the same'.

It is very likely that these high-flying French civil servants brought to their enterprises some of the general perspective that British and German managers acquired more typically through a multi-functional private sector career. However, in a society still dominated by the state—state-owned banks as well as state-owned enterprises—they also brought influence within one of the key institutions of French business life, the French central state (Zysman, 1994). In Germany the absence of a central state with equivalent powers to the French renders the civil service a much less significant starting point for top managers. Bayernwerk's Dr Otto Majewski, one of the very few German examples of a state background in top management, perfectly reflects the more decentralized nature of the German political economy. Majewski started out briefly as assistant to the legal director to the public Bavarian broadcasting corporation (Bayerischer Rundfunk), before becoming governmental director at the Bavarian Ministry for Regional Development and the Environment. From 1977 until 1988 Majewski was head of the Bavarian state's shareholdings department within the Bavarian Ministry of Finance. In 1988 he joined the executive board of the Bayernwerk and became its chairman in 1990. There was no equivalent to the regional career of Majewski in our group of French companies.

It is clear that the systems of top management development in France, Germany, and the United Kingdom are still highly distinctive through the 1980s and 1990s. In France we find a prevalence of technical and state managers alongside a flourishing group of 'personal' managers. In Germany technical managers and generalists dominate, though 'personal' managers remain important. The United Kingdom is an outlier in terms of the overwhelmingly 'professional' backgrounds of its top managers and the importance of generalist and financial backgrounds in particular. Personal and state backgrounds are nearly irrelevant. In this sense, British top managers correspond most closely to the typical profiles of top managers in the United States, original home of the diversified, divisionalized corporation. From a Chandlerian perspective on managerial competence, it is now France, not the United Kingdom, which appears most anachronistic.

4.4. SUMMARY

Our survey of French, German, and British ownership, control, and management does not show yet the triumph of any single form of 'capitalism'. The Continental countries are still far from the American model of professional managers and dispersed ownership. In France and Germany family ownership endures and personal control is common. Chandler's (1977) managerial revolution is still incomplete. It is only in the United Kingdom that the publicly held and professionally run large, established concerns of Alfred Chandler's (1990) United States dominate. There have been changes in the three countries, but these are not evidently towards convergence. British top managers have become more financially oriented, but French top managers have become more statist. The proportion of firms under dispersed ownership has fallen in all three countries, and France has seen an entrepreneurial revival. Even these changes have been largely of degree. In France and Germany the systems of ownership have been consistently less market-based than in the United Kingdom, control has been more personal and technical backgrounds more important throughout our period. The macro institutional contexts for French, German, and British corporations still differ.

Contrary to the hopes of the Harvard scholars, and consistent with the expectations of national institutionalists, the institutional peculiarities of our three countries have clearly not faded away. Institutionalist wisdom holds that these continued differences should have consequences for national patterns of strategy and structure. If we follow the reasoning of Whitley (1994) or Hollingsworth and Boyer (1997), we should expect the effects to be systemic. In an economy where technical skills are abundant and technical expertise is valued, we may expect narrower strategies of diversification than in one where finance rules the roost. Where the norms of professional management prevail, divisional structures will be both more legitimate and more manageable. But there will be direct effects as well: regardless of context, family owners may resist diversification and decentralization out of their own interest; financiers will plug divisionalized conglomerates because that is all they know how to do. The next two chapters will test the systemic proposition by examining the overall patterns of strategy and structure in France, Germany, and the United Kingdom. Chapter 7 will pick up direct corporate political effects. We shall see, though, that even if the European context still does not conform much to the American ideal, it nevertheless increasingly follows the American practice.

5

Changing Strategies

INTRODUCTION

In the United States at least diversification has been key to the growth of the twentieth-century large firm. But, as we have seen, both the timelessness and the universality of this growth formula are now in doubt. Doubts have hardened particularly in reaction to the apparent excesses of conglomerate diversification in the 1960s and 1970s. The success of the Japanese, supposedly focused on core competencies, undermined confidence not only in the appropriateness of this growth formula across countries, but even about the effectiveness of diversification in its very country of origin. Diversification is no longer the uncontested good it once seemed.

In Europe the case for diversification is even less clear. The Harvard group's original confidence in rapid diffusion predated the Japanese successes and American restructurings of the next decade. International institutional support for diversification—Anglo-Saxon style at any rate—has ebbed away. Europe has recovered in economic strength and confidence, while pundits now pedal the competence-based specialization of the Japanese. The United States has lost its grip on the European corporate imagination. At the same time, national institutional barriers to diversification have proved more persistent in the face of the managerial revolution than the Harvard group might originally have hoped. In Germany and France at least the pitch seems heavily queered against diversification by undeveloped capital markets, continued resistance to professional managerial control, and a chronically low value placed on finance. Thus national and international institutionalists alike raise strong doubts about the attractiveness of diversification without very particular institutional supports.

We, however, do want to hold on to the possibility of a general, economic rationale for the kinds of diversification patterns and performance that we shall observe in Europe. This rationale will have to acknowledge the conditional definition of economic advantage and accommodate the awkwardness of the conglomerate. Our approach, based on Grant (1988), relies on conditions fundamentally equivalent to those of the United States and effectively extends Harvard's original focus on operational relationships to include corporate relationships between similar types of businesses. Given appropriate conditions, we predict continuing and general economic attractions for strategies of diversification, whether operationally related or conglomerate. Even if not utterly optimal, conglomerates will be more profitable and survive longer than severe versions of the resource-based view would allow. In line with the project of bounded generalization, we thus propose an economic model of diversification capable of exerting a steady and common pull across Europe regardless of enduring institutional differences and the decline of the American mystique. Although no longer following his model in detail, European corporations are with Chandler in spirit.

This chapter, then, explores the fate of diversification in the contested terrain of contemporary Europe. In particular, we shall want to see whether European business did step on to the conglomerate bandwagon that American business had pioneered in the 1960s but about which even the Harvard group had misgivings in Europe (Channon, 1973; Thanheiser and Dyas, 1976). If Europe did march up the conglomerate diversification hill, we shall want to know whether it also followed the United States in edging down again. We shall be interested, too, in how far the trends around diversification were underpinned by real performance differences, or rather merely reflected the swings and roundabouts of business fashion. Here we shall consider both financial performance and longevity, particularly that of the conglomerate. Finally, of course, we shall be looking out for the effects of national contexts. We know that systems of ownership, control, and management development were both different and essentially stable in Europe over this period. How far did these enduring national differences undermine any general economic rationale for diversification?

We start next by introducing our measures of strategy and strategic change. We shall go on to examine the historical trends in each of the three countries: first France, with its high levels of personal ownership and control, its technocratic managers, and its interventionist state; next Germany, again both technically oriented and attached to personal capitalism, but also with powerful banks; then finally the United Kingdom, theoretically most inclined to diversification on account of its diffused ownership system and a professional managerial class incompetent technically but fascinated by finance. From there we shall compare the European diversification trends with the American, asking how far our different countries are still in line with the original pioneer of modern business. Finally, we shall look at performance, to see how the various strategies perform over time and in different contexts.

5.1. MEASURING STRATEGY

The Harvard group developed a so-called 'strategic category' approach to diversification, reliant on qualitative judgement of differences in basic strategic orientation rather than simple quantitative and continuous measures. This strategic category approach has its limitations (we describe how we address these in Appendix II). Nevertheless, it is the most widely used approach in strategy

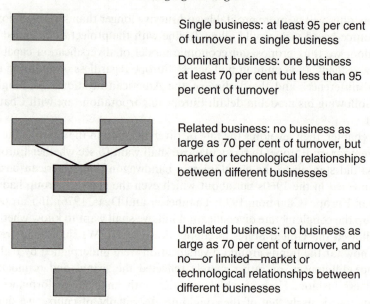

Single business: at least 95 per cent of turnover in a single business

Dominant business: one business at least 70 per cent but less than 95 per cent of turnover

Related business: no business as large as 70 per cent of turnover, but market or technological relationships between different businesses

Unrelated business: no business as large as 70 per cent of turnover, and no—or limited—market or technological relationships between different businesses

Figure 5.1. *Diversification Strategy Categories*

research (Dess et al. 1995) and is a particularly obvious choice for this study. If we wish to test Harvard, then we should do so in Harvard's own terms. Moreover, this approach offers a striking advantage. Thanks to the work of the various Harvard scholars, there exist already extensive and well-tried data-bases for strategy not only in Europe but also in the United States, Japan, Australia, and New Zealand.[1] Our data, therefore, can be directly compared both to the Harvard group's earlier findings in Europe and to findings in other countries, particularly the United States. By using the same measures as the Harvard studies, we are able to offer a long-term view of European corporate development spanning more than forty years, from the immediate post-war era to the 1990s. We are also able to compare long-term trends in Europe with the American trends observed by Rumelt (1974) and Markides (1995) at least into the 1980s. Put together, Harvard-style researchers have accumulated a data-base that is exceptional in terms of historical and geographical scope. It is particularly well suited to testing the kinds of cross-national and long-run generalizations with which Harvard has provoked the contextualists.

The Harvard approach distinguishes four basic categories of strategy, summarized in Figure 5.1. The two relatively undiversified strategic categories are 'single business' and 'dominant business'. The two diversified categories are 'related' and 'unrelated' diversification. These categories reflect two underlying

---

[1] See Kono (1984) and Suzuki (1991) for Japan; Capon et al. (1987) for Australia; Hamilton and Shergill (1993) for New Zealand.

dimensions of diversity in the original Harvard view—the extent of diversification on the one hand, and the nature of diversification on the other (Rumelt, 1974: 11). In assessing the extent of diversification, the key measure is the proportion of turnover accounted for by the firm's largest individual business activity. Relatedness is defined operationally, in terms of market or technological relationships between businesses. Businesses are viewed quite broadly, which is why Rumelt (1974) preferred to talk in terms of business diversification rather than product diversification.

We can see better how these categories are operationalized by examining some examples. The simplest kind of business is the 'single' business, where at least 95 per cent of the firm's turnover is concentrated in a single type of business activity. A good example of a single business strategy is the British firm Dairy Crest, which, although it has a range of products (milk, butter, yoghurt, cheese), is defined here as essentially in the dairy business, on account of its common input factors and production processes.

The 'dominant' business strategy is slightly less concentrated. Firms included in this category have a core business that accounts for somewhere between 70 per cent and 95 per cent of total turnover. Often, though not necessarily, dominant business firms have expanded beyond their core business by entering activities related to their main business activities. Typical examples of this type of strategy can be found in the oil industry, where companies such as British Petroleum and Shell have expanded their activities outside their core business into related areas of activity such as chemicals.

In the two diversified categories, related and unrelated, no individual business activity accounts for 70 per cent or more of turnover. Firms assigned to the two categories differ in their market or technological relatedness, defined quite operationally. Market-based diversification underpins the strategy of Unilever, for example, whose foods and groceries businesses are not technologically closely related but which do all go through supermarkets to consumers. Technology-based relatedness can be illustrated by the diversification pattern of German optical company Zeiss, whose activities range from simple lenses to space telescopes, microscopes, and complex optical systems. An unrelated diversified firm has neither market nor technology relationships, as for example BAT operating in tobacco, insurance, and retailing. Unless otherwise qualified (i.e. by reference to corporate relatedness), it is these operationally based conceptions of relatedness and unrelatedness that we shall use consistently through this chapter.

Although the Harvard studies follow the same basic principles in all countries, each of the national researchers introduced slight variations that complicate both longitudinal and comparative analysis. We detail these differences in Appendix II, but we can note here the main effects of different schemes both across the Atlantic and within Europe. On account of a different treatment of vertical integration from the European, the scheme used by Rumelt (1974) and

Markides (1995) in the United States tends to inflate the 'dominant' category at the expense of the 'related diversified' category. Also, due to less weight being put on historical relationships, other things being equal, the Americans are more likely to classify diversified companies to the 'unrelated' category than are the European researchers. Other things are not quite equal, however, as the European researchers used different cut-off points regarding the proportion of unrelated business required to tip the classification into the conglomerate category. Here Channon's (1973) scheme for the United Kingdom is most conservative, Thanheiser's (1972) for Germany least so, and Dyas's (1972) for France is in between. On Channon's (1973) scheme, therefore, the extent of British conglomerate diversification will be understated by comparison with the levels obtainable on any other scheme. On the other hand, Thanheiser's (1972) scheme may exaggerate unrelated diversification in Germany even above the level obtainable by the Americans.

Given these variations in method, we categorize all companies two ways. For longitudinal analysis, we shall rely primarily on the various 'national' methods of the original Harvard researchers, simply extending their particular categorization scheme to the 1980s and 1990s. On the various 'national' methods, therefore, historical trend data for particular countries will always be consistent across the whole period 1950 to 1993. For comparative analysis, however, we reclassify all European companies according to the standard 'Rumeltian' scheme developed by Rumelt (1974) for his American sample. Although we shall not be able to apply this 'Rumeltian' scheme retrospectively to the 1950–70 period, for the 1980s and 1990s at least, it does give us a consistent basis for comparison both between European countries and between Europe and the United States. Again, whichever categorization scheme we are using, the terms relatedness and unrelatedness will refer to the Harvard definition in terms of operational relationships, unless specifically qualified.

We drew our information on the extent and relatedness of diversification primarily from documentary sources such as annual reports, analysts' reports, and press articles, supplemented by interviews in around a third of the companies (as described in Chapter 1). Classifications of companies to particular strategy categories were made independently by two judges on the basis of standardized information, with a third researcher involved to resolve any differences. Again, we are considering only the domestically based members of each country's Top 100 industrials. Further details about research and classification methods are available in Appendix II.

5.2. STRATEGY TRENDS AND TRANSITIONS

As we saw in the first chapter, Dyas and Thanheiser (1976) predicted continuing diversification across European industry. This prediction was founded on Scott's

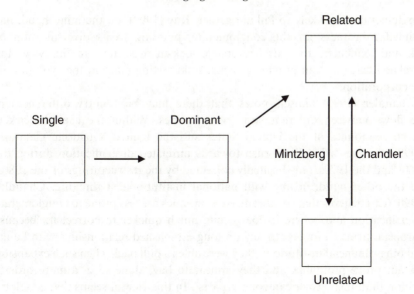

Figure 5.2. *Stages in Corporate Development*

(1973) three-stage model of corporate development, extended to four stages by
Mintzberg (1979) to allow for the rise of the conglomerate. According to
Harvard, therefore, the aggregate trend to diversification in particular countries should be underpinned by the transition of individual firms through
the various strategy categories towards increased diversification. Figure 5.2
describes the process of increasing diversification as a rightwards movement:
the final unrelated diversification stage does not necessarily represent more
diversification, only a different character of diversification. Thus firms should
develop steadily from the single business strategy, through the transitional
dominant business strategy, and then at least to related diversified strategy.
If Mintzberg's (1979) fourth stage is admitted, a final step will take these firms
to unrelated diversification. In the original formulations, a reverse flow in
the opposite direction towards less diversification was hard to visualize: 'once
adopted, the strategy of diversification tended to become institutionalized'
(Channon, 1973: 238).

Since the 1970s the flow has come to be seen as less unidirectional. The issue
is particularly unrelated diversification. The orthodox resource-based view is
hard on conglomerates, stigmatizing them as 'hopeful monsters' (Dosi et al.,
1992). Our own view is more appreciative of the short-run economic advantages available from corporate relationships, but sceptical about the longevity
of the top management resources capable of exploiting them. In both these
views, however, we should expect a reverse flow out of the conglomerate
category, towards either greater focus or greater relatedness. Otherwise,

conglomerates are likely to fail altogether. Kay (1997), on the other hand, has claimed robustness for the conglomerate, pointing to its diversification of risk and tendencies towards irreversible lock-in over time. In this view, the unrelated category can provide a secure final resting place in the evolution of the corporation.

Chandler (1990) himself notes that there may be country differences in the flows between different strategy categories. Within the capital market-driven economies of the United States and the United Kingdom, Chandler (1990) observes a headlong rush towards unrelated diversification during the 1960s and the 1970s, only belatedly corrected by the restructurings of the 1980s. On the other hand, in line with national institutionalist thinking, Chandler (1990: 626) believes that bank-centred economies are less prone to conglomerate diversification and, where it does occur, much quicker to correct it: 'because European firms continued to rely on long-established relationships with banks and other financial institutions, they were able to pull back when such expansion did not prove profitable, and they appear to have done so in a more orderly fashion than their American counterparts'. In this view, it seems that conglomerates are universally undesirable, but that countries are not equally able to undo them.

There is a case, then, for inserting a further Chandlerian arrow in Figure 5.2, reversing the flow back from the unrelated category to the time-honoured strategy of related diversification. However, the flows into and out of the conglomerate strategy would vary between countries. Continental Europe would see lighter flows in, earlier flows out. Capital-market Britain, on the other hand, would indulge most enthusiastically in conglomerate excess. And, once again, the British would be slowest to learn.

It is against this framework that we shall examine aggregate trends and company transitions in each of the three countries, taking them in turn before bringing the picture together as a whole. First we shall take France, from a national institutionalist point of view unlikely to be susceptible to diversification, at least of an unrelated kind. Then we shall consider Germany, again unfertile ground for diversification and, on Chandler's (1990) argument, particularly prompt to correct any uncharacteristic conglomeratization due to the strength of its banks. Finally, we examine the bogey-man of Europe, the United Kingdom, for whose financiers the conglomerate seems a fatal attraction.

France

France has the kind of relational financial system, extensive personal capitalism, and technical culture that national institutionalists at least would characterize as unamenable to enthusiastic diversification. Yet, as we see in Table 5.1, none of

Table 5.1. *Diversification Trends for Domestic Top 100 Industrial Firms in France, classification according to Dyas* (%)

	1950	1960	1970	1983	1993
Single	45	35	20	24.3	19.4
Dominant	18	22	27	10.8	15.2
Related diversified	31	36	43	52.7	51.5
Unrelated diversified	5	5	9	12.2	13.6

Sources: 1950–70, Dyas and Thanheiser (1976); this study, 1983—93

these factors appears to have kept French business from continuing down the path of increasing diversity already established in the immediate post-war years. Between 1970 and 1983 the percentage of domestically based Top 100 industrial firms pursuing diversification strategies increased from about 52 per cent to 65 per cent, continuing the established trend. Over the next decade, diversification appears to have stabilized, but there is no aggregate reversal. Although strategies of related diversification dominate, accounting for over half French large firms in the 1990s, the unrelated conglomerate strategy remains robust, at more than one in eight. Even between 1983 and 1993, a period when economic and managerial orthodoxy would lead us to expect otherwise, there has been no overall refocusing.

Between 1970 and 1983 the aggregate share of French firms pursuing the two least diversified strategies—single and dominant—fell markedly. Since then, however, there has been some plateauing, with the proportion of single and dominant companies fairly stable at just over a third, taken together. However, despite this aggregate stability, the least diversified single business strategy still lost ground in the 1980s and early 1990s to the more diversified dominant business strategy. Taking this shift towards dominant strategies into account, by 1993 French businesses were more inclined to diversification than ever before. Dyas (1972: 39) appears broadly to have been correct in expecting the future of French business to lie with the diversified enterprise.

These trends are aggregates for a shifting population. We need to explore the underlying processes in more detail. Figures 5.3 and 5.4 present a more detailed analysis of the pattern of strategic entry, exit, and stability among the domestically owned top industrial firms in France over the two periods 1970–83 and 1983–93. The figures within each strategy box indicate the numbers remaining within the same strategy category over the whole period. The arrows out of the strategy boxes show the numbers moving from one strategy category to another or, where ending in no strategy box, exiting entirely the population of top industrial firms (whether for reasons of takeover, bankruptcy, relative shrinkage in

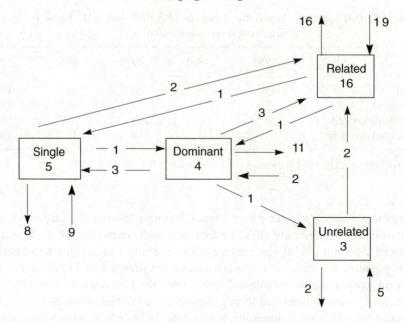

Figure 5.3. *Strategic Change in France, 1970–83*

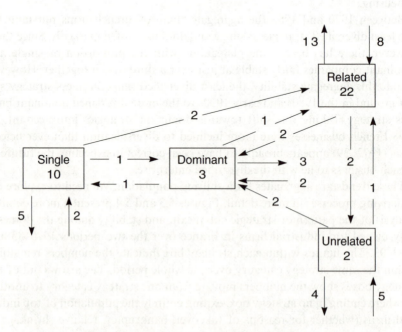

Figure 5.4. *Strategic Change in France, 1983–93*

Illustration 5.1. *Bongrain: Family-owned Specialist*

Bongrain's history is quite similar to many specialized French food companies, including Bel, Bridel, and Doux. Jean-Noël Bongrain founded his company in 1956, when he took over his father's small cheese-making company in the Haute-Marne region. The basis of Bongrain's success was the creation of the Caprice des Dieux cheese, one of the very first French mass-produced cheeses aimed at a national market in the early 1960s. Bongrain grew rapidly, acquiring a host of other cheeses all of which it re-oriented towards mass markets. The group was also quick to internationalize, establishing itself in Germany as early as 1962. In the United Kingdom, it acquired the Milway stilton company and in Switzerland it manufactured its own emmental, Fol Epi. In 1992 the company took a major step forward by acquiring the majority stake in the failing Union laitière normande, which, as well as improving integration into milk supply, offered the strong camembert brand, Coeur de Lion. Although Jean-Noël Bongrain did diversify into other food activities, such as chocolate, fish, and meat, these were controlled separately through the family holding company, Soparind.

Principal sources: Interview and *Figaro Economie*, 4 October 1993.

terms of turnover, or, occasionally, transition to service-dominated business).[2] The arrows with no source boxes represent new entrants into the populations of top industrial firms. Tracking firms over ten years or so, these transition analyses provide a first cut on the sustainability of different strategies. We shall consider the longer term record over the whole twenty-three years 1970–93 later when we discuss performance.

We will begin on the left-hand side of the figure with the fully focused single business strategy. As we have already suggested, one of the more surprising features about the French overall trends is the sustained importance of the single business strategy: one-fifth of French firms were still following this strategy in 1993 just as they had in 1970. However, comparison of the flows in and out of this single business strategy for the two periods reveals that different processes underpinned this aggregate stability. In the earlier period, many firms were both entering and exiting. Exits were often specialized businesses in declining industries such as textile firm Devanlay & Recoing and steel company Forges de Guegnon. Entrants into the single business strategy by 1983 were typically established firms enjoying rapid growth and coming from a range of sectors including food (Bongrain and Générale Biscuit), household appliances (Moulinex), and glassware (Verrerie Cristallerie d'Arques) (see Illustration 5.1).

---

[2] We have been inclusive rather than exclusive in interpreting continuity: as an instance at the margin, we count as surviving Moët-Hennessy, which, although it came under the control of Financière Agache and was merged with Louis Vuitton, by 1993 was still readily identifiable as the largest part of LVMH, an independent quoted company in our population. Where two companies are merged, it is only the larger or otherwise clearly dominant part that counts as surviving.

Over 1983–93, however, there was marked stability around the single business category: no less than ten companies stuck to their focused strategy, coming from a wide range of industries. Thus these stable single business companies included the food companies Bel and Bongrain, aerospace company Dassault, and cement producer Ciments Français. There have been, however, markedly fewer new entrants to the single business category in the more recent period, the only two companies being food-producer Doux and the established engineering company Technip.

From a Chandlerian perspective, what is most surprising about the French single business companies is how few 'progressed' on to more diversified strategies—just three in each time period. Even those that did diversify often did so conservatively. Thus the Pernod and Ricard drinks companies merged in 1974 and gradually added non-alcoholic beverages to their portfolio of spirits (e.g. pastis), wine, and champagne. Indeed, in the earlier period, more firms are entering the single business category from more diversified categories than are moving out towards Chandlerian diversification. It seems that at least some French firms have learned to love specialization.

Again, the pattern of movement around the dominant category shows the rarity of smooth transition from one category to the next. In the earlier period, just three firms out of twenty-two move on to related diversification (one goes straight to unrelated). Prominent among these firms following the approved track was L'Oréal, moving away from a mainly hair-care oriented profile towards a much broader based cosmetics company with a growing interest in pharmaceuticals. In the later period just one firm manages the transition from the dominant category to related diversification. This was the state-owned oil company Elf Aquitaine, moving heavily into chemicals and pharmaceuticals. Rather than serving as the classic transitional point to full diversification, therefore, the dominant category is more likely the path to decline. In the earlier period, half of the dominant firms drop out of the population of top industrials, mostly because of slow growth or takeover.

The position of the French related diversifiers, however, does conform more closely to the Chandlerian model. In both periods this is the largest group of firms and also relatively stable. Very few companies move backwards to more specialized strategies. The retreat of Bull from its broader base in industrial and building controls, aerospace and defence systems and test instruments, to its core computers business was the response of a notoriously weak player to successive crises. For L'Air liquide, the shift back to a dominant strategy simply reflected a regained importance for its core business, the production of industrial gases. These kind of strategic moves do not represent a radical refocusing of French industry.

The related business strategy is not, however, a guarantee of success. Many French firms exit the category, typically because of low relative growth or takeover. The pool of related businesses is replenished not so much by the switches of already large firms as by the number of growing firms entering this category directly. Among these entries we find many—such as Aussedat Rey and Arjormari-Prioux, Lesieur, SNPE, and Hachette—that drop out again in the later time period. However, there are also longer lasting direct entries such as engineering company Framatome and publisher Groupe de la Cité. It is this combination of longevity, inflow from other categories, and a rough balance of new entrants with exits that accounts for the overall stability of the related business strategy in France, at roughly half of all top industrials through 1983 to 1993.

The unrelated strategy also appears to hold a stable share of French business through our period. The aggregates mask a quite complex pattern. Surprisingly for the strict resource-based view, conglomerates are not condemned utterly to short life-spans. Three companies—Beghin Say, Boussac Saint Frères, and Schneider—manage to retain their unrelated conglomerate strategies through 1970 to 1983. The second period was less forgiving, with just two companies retaining their conglomerate strategies. Moreover, it does seem relatively easy to enter the population of large industrials through rapid growth based on unrelated diversification. Thus, over the 1970–83 period, Moët-Hennessy entered directly into the unrelated category as a producer not only of cognac and champagne but also of perfumes and other beauty products. Sellier Leblanc offered a very diverse range of businesses, from heating and fuels, road materials and packaging, to mineral water, the well-known Volvic. The problem, we shall see later, is sustaining the strategy over the very long term, more than the ten or so years in these transitions. Thus already in 1983 the textiles and retail conglomerate Boussac Saint Frères was involved in a spectacular and controversial financial crash, from which Bernard Arnault's Financière Agache was finally to profit. Paper and foods group Beghin Say would fall under the control of the Italians in the 1980s. Only Schneider would retain its unrelated pattern to 1993, and even in this case it was by then engaged in a series of divestments and rationalizations.

Overall, therefore, France conforms broadly to the Chandlerian expectation of steady diversification, especially related diversification. The transitions data have illuminated several anomalies, of course. In France, the single business strategy appears to be viable over the quite long term, with a good deal of stability especially over the last decade. Large firms do not typically progress through the stages towards increased diversification. Dominant strategies in particular relatively rarely play the stepping-stone role to diversificatory growth envisaged in the original Harvard model. In line with our reasoning in Chapter 3, conglomerates have shown themselves capable of advancing and some even of surviving reasonable lengths of time. This, however, is in line with our extension of the Chandlerian view, rather than a radical challenge. In the last decade of the century, related diversification remained the dominant strategy, one moreover that was sustained by many companies over good periods of time. In sum, the corporate model pioneered originally in the United States seems to be doing quite well in France, regardless of the swings and roundabouts of fashion or enduring differences in ownership and control.

Germany

For Chandler (1990), German industry, like that of the United States, was exemplary for its willingness to invest in scale and, more importantly here, scope. Thanheiser (1972) had indeed found German industry to have made substantial strides in diversification by the end-point of his original study. Thanheiser, of course, covered the more immediate post-war era, a time of reconstruction. The question for us is whether these trends continued from the 1970s onwards, into an era in which German post-war optimism gave way to a much more critical view of the country's competitiveness and economic prowess.

The overall trends depicted in Table 5.2 are clear: German industry did continue down the path of diversity. The aggregate proportion of firms in the two diversified categories increased continuously from 57 per cent in 1970 to 65 per cent in 1983 and almost 80 per cent in 1993. Both 'undiversified' categories find themselves in steady decline, each halving between 1970 and 1993. Of the two, the single business strategy remains the most important, at just under 13 per cent. Here we find automobile manufacturers such as Volkswagen and BMW, paper companies such as PWA and Haindl, and publishers such as the Bauer Verlag. The dominant business strategy has dwindled into insignificance with barely 8 per cent of firms following such a strategy. The remaining firms that do follow such a strategy include pharmaceutical firm Schering, sugar producer Südzucker, and beauty and hair-care specialist Wella.

However, the most surprising feature of the German picture is the success of the unrelated business strategy. This is awkward for national institutionalists, for the resource-based view, and, as we shall see, even for our own efforts at extension. Bank-centred, technically oriented German industry is not supposed to be inclined towards the conglomerate. If there had been any tendencies in that

Table 5.2. *Diversification Trends for Domestic Top 100 Industrial Firms in Germany, classification according to Thanheiser* (%)

	1950	1960	1970	1983	1993
Single	37	27	27	18.3	12.7
Dominant	22	24	15	16.7	7.9
Related diversified	31	38	38	40.0	47.6
Unrelated diversified	9	11	19	25.0	31.7

Sources: 1950–70, Dyas and Thanheiser (1976); this study, 1983–93

direction during the 1960s and early 1970s, Chandler (1990) had been particularly confident in the German capacity to correct them. A look at the transitions data will give a better understanding of the underlying processes of strategic change and stability. Our presentation will follow the same format as the earlier discussion of the French transitions.

The first impression we get from looking at Figures 5.5 and 5.6 is the predominant movement from left to right, from the less diverse to the more diverse categories. By comparison with France, in Germany the single and dominant categories are markedly unstable. The only notable exception to the rightward drift is in the 1970–1983 period, when a number of related-business companies reduced their overall diversity and moved towards the more focused dominant category. In fact the dominant category appears to be the focal point of activity, with a significant number of firms moving in and out of this category, particularly in the 1970–83 time period. It is worth pausing to consider these movements around the dominant category.

For two of the three companies moving from the single business to the dominant category between 1970 and 1983, Ruhrkohle and publisher Springer, this was the classic first step towards full diversification. Over the subsequent time period both firms moved towards a related-diversified strategy. For Springer, best known for publishing the *Bildzeitung* and *DIE WELT* newspapers, this meant a gradual expansion into areas such as book publishing and television.

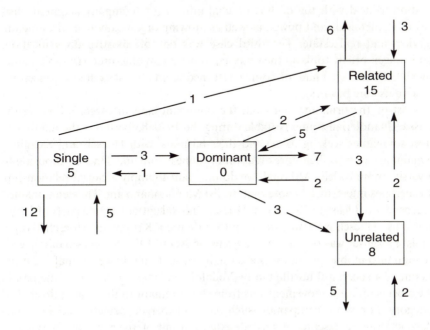

Figure 5.5. *Strategic Change in Germany, 1970–83*

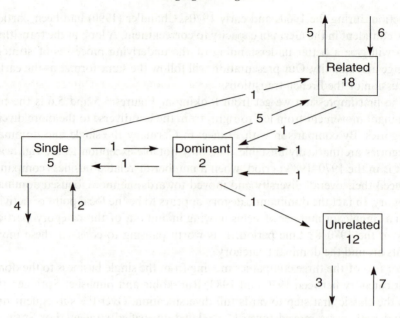

Figure 5.6. *Strategic Change in Germany, 1983–93*

The case at Ruhrkohle is somewhat more complex, involving government intervention to deal with the decline of coal mining: the company acquired businesses in chemicals and power, as well as growing organically in environmental services and real estate. The third case was one of abortive diversification: Volkswagen briefly took on the office equipment manufacturer Triumph–Adler. By 1993 Volkswagen had, of course, returned to an almost exclusive concentration on its core business.

Most of the firms moving from the dominant category were following the classic Chandlerian route. Notable during the 1970–83 period is the number of steel companies seeking to expand their business, with Hoesch and Salzgitter remaining closer to their core areas and Mannesmann and Thyssen choosing to diversify more widely. Although we do not want to imply a causal relationship, it is perhaps interesting to note that, whilst Mannesmann and Thyssen remained independent at least to 1993, both Hoesch and Salzgitter became parts of larger concerns. Hoesch was integrated into Friedrich Krupp, as Hoesch-Krupp, whilst Salzgitter was bought by the Preussag AG in 1989. Mannesman's diversification into mobile phones was eventually its undoing, however, making it the victim of a successful hostile bid by Vodafone in 2000. In the later time period the most significant movement was from the dominant to the related diversified category. For some companies, such as Heidelberger Zement and Deutsche Babcock, this represented a smooth extension out of their existing businesses. For others, such as Ruhrkohle, these moves represent very significant changes of their strategic orientation.

The approved related business strategy gradually gained ground, especially in the later period, both on account of a small surplus of inflow over exit and its ability to retain firms that had once moved in. We find a wide range of well-established companies among these 'stable' related diversifiers, including Siemens and most of Germany's chemical companies—the big three chemical companies BASF, Bayer, and Hoechst, as well as the smaller Merck AG, Wacker Chemie, and Beiersdorf. All these firms remained in the related diversified category over the entire time period, 1970–93. There is, however, one surprising exception to this overall stability, the five firms changing from the related-diversified to the dominant business category during 1970–83. Often these were firms for which their established core business gained in relative importance, such as ball bearings manufacturer FAG-Kugelfisher. For others, such as pharmaceutical company Boehringer Ingelheim, this marked a long-term commitment to their core business. The importance of Boehringer Ingelheim's pharmaceutical core business continued to increase over the following decade and by 1993 accounted for over 80 per cent of the company's turnover. Its remaining activities were typically closely related to this core and included veterinary medical products and food ingredients. The only company moving from a related to a dominant business strategy in the later time period is also a pharmaceutical firm, Schering. Over this time Schering increased its commitment to its pharmaceutical activities, divesting the techno-chemical divisions in 1992 and 1993 and initiating the restructuring of its agro-chemicals business. In a sense, then, these reversions to the dominant category often reflected success rather than retreat.

The most awkward feature of the German experience is the success of the conglomerate. Some allowance must be made for Thanheiser's (1972) more inclusive definition of conglomerates, but as we shall see it broadly holds even with standardization according to the Rumelt (1974) definitions. There are two main processes that explain the conglomerate's success: the rate of inflow and the degree of stability. Inflows were particularly marked in the earlier time period, as firms in seemingly mature businesses switched from the dominant and related business strategies to new unrelated business activities. By 1993 the engineering company Mannesmann ended up with a wide range of products, from pipes and mechanical engineering to automotive supplies and mobile communications. Over 1970–83, VIAG moved from its dominant business status by increasing its energy (electricity generation and gas) and chemicals activities compared to its traditional core business in aluminium. Over the following decade, to 1993, VIAG continued this strategy further, diversifying in areas such as PET packaging, glass and trade, distribution (including computers), and logistics. The only company to move towards an unrelated strategy in the later period, Degussa, had previously been a refocuser. However, in a major switch of strategy between 1983 and 1993, it diversified from its old core in precious metals to arrive at a portfolio including printed circuit boards, organic and inorganic chemicals, banking, and pharmaceuticals.

Illustration 5.2. *Friedrich Krupp AG—Hoesch-Krupp: Persistent Conglomerate*

The name Krupp is probably one of the most established in German industry. Dyas and Thanheiser (1976: 44) note that alongside firms such as Siemens and Thyssen Krupp had already established its leading position before 1914. Like most of Germany's steel and heavy engineering firms, the company developed as part of a family empire in the Ruhr region. Early diversification thereby followed a pattern of forward integration extending from its core in iron and steel manufacture leading to mechanical engineering, heavy machinery, and arms production (Dyas and Thanheiser, 1976: 95). Following post-war restructuring brought about by the allied powers the company diversified further afield. By the 1970s activities such as electronics, aerospace, and nuclear energy had been placed alongside iron and steel manufacture, shipbuilding, locomotive engines, and plant equipment. Whilst Krupp continued to strengthen its steel business (both steel production and steel-based manufacture) most notably through the merger with Hoesch, the company continued to engage in a wide portfolio of activities, which in the early 1990s included machinery (e.g. packaging machinery, plastics, wind-energy, and food technology), industrial plants (e.g. for the cement, coal, and chemical industries), automotives, and trade and services (apart from trade in steel this extended to recycling, heating systems, shipping, and travel agencies).

Principal sources: Interview; Dyas and Thanheiser, 1976.

The anomalous success of the unrelated strategy in Germany rests chiefly on its stability, in stark contrast to the turnover in the less diversified categories. Conglomerate refocusing is very rare. Among the exceptions were the chemicals company Henkel, which divested itself of its packaging machinery business, and publisher Bertelsman, which disposed of its agricultural interests. Taking the two time periods together, this conglomerate stability indeed was greater than that of the related business strategy, and even increased over time, despite the turn of business fashion against the conglomerate. Between 1983 and 1993, twelve of the fifteen unrelated diversifiers did not change their strategic orientation. These persistent conglomerates had their origins in a range of industries—from Krupp and Thyssen in heavy industry, to Oetcker and Tchibo in foods (see Illustration 5.2). In Germany the hopes of the conglomerate 'monster' (Dosi et al., 1992) were often not disappointed, at least over these periods of ten or so years.

As with the French case, therefore, the broad picture does confirm Chandlerian expectations regarding increased diversification, while yet offering some surprises in the detail. This time it is not the single business that is the anomaly but the unrelated conglomerate. National institutionalists predict a system-wide bias against this kind of strategy in the German context; Chandler (1990) had expected rapid banking correction. Somehow, though, the German conglomerate emerges as an enduring and important member of the local scene. We return to the longevity of the conglomerate both when we consider performance and in Chapter 7, when we examine ownership effects on strategy from the corporate political perspective: we shall find that powerful owners have a part to play. Otherwise, though, the pattern is largely as predicted. Germany emerges as substantially more diversified in 1993 than in 1970, even more so than France. Even with the surprising success of the conglomerate, it is still the approved strategy of related diversification that dominates. Despite stability in national institutions, Germany has achieved substantial strategic change over this period, and in the predicted direction.

United Kingdom

Expectations regarding the United Kingdom are very different to those for the two continental countries. First condemned by Chandler (1990) as a laggard in making the necessary investments in scale and scope—at least up until the early 1950s—the United Kingdom is now characterized, by Chandler and by national institutionalists, as particularly enthusiastic in its pursuit of the conglomerate extreme. At the original 1970 end point of the Harvard studies, the United Kingdom had already gone furthest down the road of diversification (Scott, 1973). At all points, therefore, the United Kingdom appears to be an outlier. We shall see how far capital markets and financial professionals have indeed driven British industry to conglomerate excess.

As we might expect, aggregate diversification has continued to advance in the United Kingdom. Between 1970 and 1983 the proportion of diversified firms increased from 63 to 77 per cent and then again to over 85 per cent by 1993. Table 5.3 again provides a more detailed breakdown. The single business strategy, already unimportant in 1970 has dwindled further, only Dairy Crest, Glaxo, and Wellcome remaining in this category by 1993. The dominant business strategy has declined even more dramatically, its share halving between 1970 and

Table 5.3. *Diversification Trends for Domestic Top 100 Industrial Firms in the United Kingdom, classification according to Channon (%)*

	1950	1960	1970	1983	1993
Single	24	18	6	6.7	4.5
Dominant	50	36	32	16.0	10.4
Related diversified	27	48	57	66.7	61.2
Unrelated diversified	—	—	6	10.7	23.9

Sources: 1950–70, Channon (1973); this study, 1983–93. Related figures include Unrelated for 1950–60

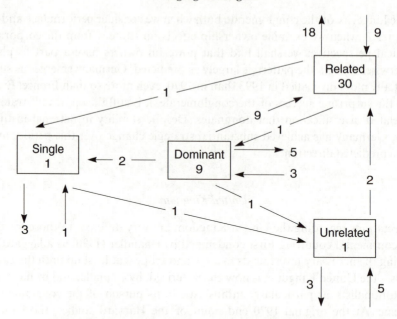

Figure 5.7. *Strategic Change in the United Kingdom, 1970–83*

1983, and falling further by 1993. On the face of it, these aggregate trends confirm expectations about the characteristic pattern of diversification in the United Kingdom. Unrelated business strategies have experienced a period of steady growth, while related business strategies slightly declined. There is no sign in this aggregate data of the corrective refocusing advocated during the 1980s and early 1990s.

However, the transition analyses of Figures 5.7 and 5.8 reveal a more complex picture. The single business category is much less populated in the United Kingdom than in the two Continental countries. It is also highly unstable. In each period only one firm survives as a single business enterprise. From 1970 until 1983 this is computer firm ICL, which, however, later became a subsidiary of Japanese electronics giant Fujitsu. In the later time period the only single business 'survivor' is the leading pharmaceutical firm Wellcome. Again, however, it is rare for established large firms to use this single business strategy as a successful base for diversification, at least while staying within the Top 100 firms. One exception was BAT, which between 1970 and 1983 embarked on an extensive programme of diversification into retail, insurance, paper, and cosmetics (see Illustration 5.3). Most firms in the single business category simply fail to stay within our large firm group either on grounds of insufficient growth or takeover.

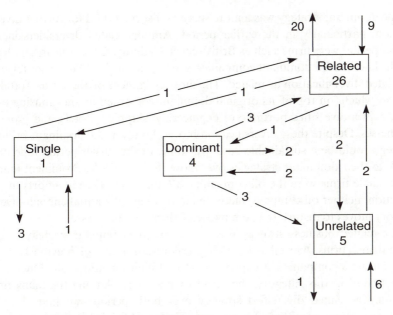

Figure 5.8. *Strategic Change in the United Kingdom, 1983–93*

Illustration 5.3. *BAT: Anglo-Saxon Conglomerate*

BAT started life as British American Tobacco in 1902, as a result of a market-sharing agreement between British tobacco manufacturers and the aggressive American Tobacco of James Buchanan Duke. As a result of tortuous cartel agreements and antitrust negotiations, BAT was initially obliged to concentrate on markets outside the United Kingdom. In 1952 BAT made its first substantial diversification move, acquiring Wiggins-Teape, the paper manufacturer. The 1960s and early 1970s saw the acquisition of several major perfume manufacturers, including Lenthéric and Yardley. During the late 1970s came a move into retail, including the Argos catalogue chain and the American Marshall Field's department stores. Paper activities were also developed with the acquisition of Appleton Papers. In 1984 a financial services leg was added to the diversified group with the acquisition of Eagle Star insurance, soon followed by Allied Dunbar and Farmers in the United States. An attempted hostile bid by Sir James Goldsmith's Hoylake Investments in 1989 prompted some refocusing, with the sale of Wiggins Teape Appleton, Argos, and many other retail activities. Financial services were retained, however, alongside a successful international tobacco business whose brands included Benson & Hedges, Kool, and Lucky Strike.

Principal sources: Interview and *International Directory of Company Histories*.

The dominant strategy was a more successful springboard for further diversification, particularly in the earlier period. Among related diversifiers in this earlier period were firms such as British Steel, Cadbury, GEC, Lucas, and RTZ. By the later period dominant companies were just as likely to adopt strategies of unrelated diversification as related. The most prominent of these was Trafalgar House, which, on top of its original dominant construction and housing business, built a diversified portfolio of engineering, shipping, hotels, and property businesses. Despite these diversification moves, however, the dominant business strategy could be a sustainable base over time. In the earlier period nine firms stuck to their dominant strategies over more than a decade. Prominent among these stable firms were the oil companies BP and Shell. Despite efforts in that direction, neither oil company succeeded in making substantial enough diversificatory moves to disturb the dominance of their core businesses.

The related business strategy was by far the most popular strategy among large British firms. As well as attracting a significant influx of previously dominant business companies, it enjoys a relatively high retention rate. Once firms have arrived in this category, they tend to stay there. Among the many firms retaining a related diversified strategy over both periods we find electrical companies such as GEC, Lucas, and Thorn EMI, food companies such as ABF and Cadbury Schweppes, and chemical company ICI. Taking both periods, only four firms abandoned related strategies in favour of more focused ones (while retaining their positions as leading industrials), two of these pharmaceuticals companies—Glaxo and Wellcome—for whom no doubt the profitability of their core businesses proved an irresistible attraction. In the later period, however, two firms moved from related to unrelated strategies, food company Unigate and engineering company TI.

With these firms we come to the most controversial characteristic attributed to British industry, adhesion to conglomerate strategies of unrelated diversification. As we have seen, this was a steadily growing strategy in the United Kingdom, by 1993 accounting for about a quarter of large firms. The transitional data indicate, however, that this growth is supported by two quite different processes in the two time periods. In the first period the unrelated business strategy is highly unstable, with only one company, Rank, remaining among the largest industrials while maintaining its highly diversified status. Although it divested itself of a number of far-flung activities in areas such as white goods manufacturing and retail, furniture, audio equipment, security systems, and industrial process control, Rank retained its interests in hotels and leisure and holiday facilities, film and television production and services (for example, in Pinewood studios), as well as a substantial participation in the document processing company Rank Xerox. Rank was exceptional. Reckitt & Coleman, and Standard Telephones and Cable reduced their unrelated activities. Sears Holdings, Slater Walker, and Thomas Tilling all dropped out of the largest industrials. With such changes the overall increase in the importance of the unrelated

strategy was basically a consequence of the new entries by such innovative conglomerates as BTR and Hanson, and also of growth by older established firms
such as Pearson, whose activities ranged from publishing and entertainment to
banking, specialist engineering, fine china, and oil.

In the second time period unrelated diversified firms were more successful at
retaining their places among the largest industrials: notable amongst these were
BTR, Hanson, and BAT. It seems that top management teams were learning to
exploit corporate relationships over quite long periods of time. Moreover, the
unrelated category also benefited from a new generation of conglomerates, such
as Charter, Siebe, Tomkins, and Williams Holdings. In this second period, too,
the trade between related and unrelated strategies was less to the disadvantage of
the conglomerates. Of those refocusing, Redland exhibited the clearest commitment to a focused strategy by fully concentrating on its construction and building materials ranging from roofing and bricks to building aggregates. It seems
that British industry, far from reverting to its core businesses in this period, was
learning to live with the monstrous conglomerate.

Overall, British industry had progressed in the direction of further diversification predicted by the Harvard group. By 1993 it was in aggregate the most diversified of the three countries, just as it had been at the start of the period. But, as
we shall see when we turn to the more systematic comparison, this difference
was marginal, and one of degree rather than tendency. Just as in every other
country, the most common strategy in British industry was overwhelmingly one
of related diversification, as approved by Chandler (1990). Britain may not have
rushed to refocus during the 1980s and early 1990s, but nor had any other
country. As we shall see more clearly in the next section, it is hard in this period
to maintain the caricature of British industry as either hopelessly laggard or
frenziedly conglomerate.

5.3. CROSS-NATIONAL COMPARISONS

The long-term patterns show broad progress in a Chandlerian direction, but
with national nuances. Here we shall examine the strategic trends more systematically, relying on the more strictly comparable Rumelt scheme for the years
1983 and 1993. This is the best basis for analysing whether enduring differences
in national institutions really mattered very much. The Rumeltian scheme also
allows us to make direct comparison with trends in the United States, where
Markides (1995) has suggested some limited disenchantment with the Chandlerian model in recent years. We might expect, with the international institutionalists, that the fashionable swing against American-style diversification will be
stronger away than at home.

Figure 5.9 combines the 'national' data for the earlier period with the
'Rumeltian' data for the later in order to provide a long-run comparative view.

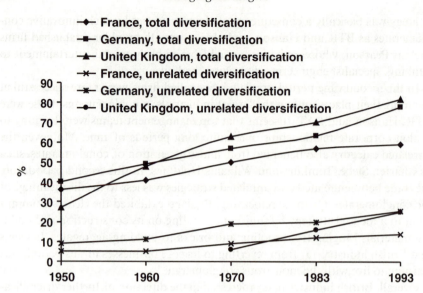

Figure 5.9. *Diversification in Post-War France, Germany, and the United Kingdom*

Note: 1950–70: figures based on 'national' classification schemes; 1983–93: figures based on 'Rumeltian' classification schemes

The main impression from post-war Europe is of parallel evolution towards greater diversification. Reckoning on the different schemes, all countries are markedly more diversified than in 1950 and substantially more diversified than in 1970. The United Kingdom and Germany in particular have become strikingly similar in terms of diversification strategy. It may be that the processes of diversification are different—with the United Kingdom prone to a more aggressive use of the takeover market (Prowse, 1995)—but the outcomes are effectively the same. By 1993 the proportion of British and German firms following strategies of unrelated diversification are identical; those for the related strategy are only slightly different. France lags a little bit, but even there three out of five large firms are diversified in one way or another by 1993. Despite some plateauing in trends, French business does not seem set on reversing the diversification achievement of the post-war period.

Surprisingly, Europe has accepted the American recipe of diversification as the United States has seemed to reject it. As we have seen, Markides's (1995) study found only about two in five of his large American corporations following either the related or the unrelated diversification strategy by 1987. Indeed, during the 1980s, the United States had seen some retreat away from strategies of unrelated diversification. We have noted already the issue of continuity between Rumelt's (1974) and Markides's (1995) groups of firms. On the face of it, however, Europe appears to have overtaken the United States in terms of diversification.

Taking the comparative picture overall, the original Harvard expectation that Europe would continue towards further diversification has been fulfilled. Neither the swings of business fashion nor enduring national institutions appear to have had much effect. Certainly, there are still some differences between the countries in detail, but in the 1990s Europe is more diversified than ever before. The approved related diversified strategy is the most widespread in all three countries and has shown itself to be stable over periods of ten years or so at least. Remarkably, the institutional opposites—Germany and the United Kingdom—are now particularly close. If British industry is to be castigated any more for its strategies, then so must German. Indeed, British firms have revealed themselves to be the more willing to correct conglomerate 'excesses'.

5.4. STRATEGY AND PERFORMANCE

The long-term trend towards increased diversification across Europe is certainly awkward for institutionalists, national and international. It does not seem that diversification was simply dictated by post-war American imperialism. The Europeans are now more enthusiastic diversifiers than the Americans. However, international institutionalists do raise sceptical questions about how far strategic change is driven by legitimacy rather than profit, while national institutionalists warn that the benefits of particular strategies may be skewed in different directions according to system-wide biases. These institutionalists would argue that the relationship between strategy and performance may either be quite insignificant or would vary according to national business systems.

Economic accounts of diversification are reluctant to allow institutional peculiarities to influence performance, at least in advanced economies with fairly efficient markets (cf. Khanna and Palepu, 1999). The orthodox resource-based view makes its predictions regardless: the related diversified firm is unequivocally superior because able to maximize utilization of resources; unrelated conglomerates are unequivocally inferior because lacking common operational resources and burdened with the extra costs and constraints of head offices. We share this interest in finding consistent performance relationships, at least within the kinds of economy represented by Western Europe, but have sought to extend the orthodox view to include conglomerates. Here Grant's (1988) introduction of corporate relationships has been useful, as outlined in Chapter 3. Given that conglomerates may be able to exploit corporate relationships and that they carry lower head-office costs than relatively interventionist and integrated related diversifiers, the financial performance differential relative to the related diversifier is likely to be less marked than in orthodoxy. This helps to explain why the diversification strategy and performance question remains one of the great unsolved mysteries of the strategic management discipline (Markides and Williamson, 1996). Moreover, these higher expectations for the financial performance of the conglomerate both predict better staying power than in the 'hopeful monsters' caricature and offer an explanation of why this otherwise ill-starred strategy continues to attract new entrants. We have added one caveat to the fortunes of the conglomerate, however. Although in the short term good financial performance will buoy the conglomerate up, in the longer term the strategy will be harder to sustain on account of the shallowness of its managerial resources. Short term, conglomerates will do better in terms of longevity and financial returns than the strict resource-based view allows; in competing for the long term, however, it is the related diversifier that will have the more puff.

Thus our analysis of strategy and performance will come at the question from two directions. We begin by examining relative sustainability, predicting similar longevity between related and unrelated diversifiers in the short term, superior longevity for the related diversifiers in the long term. This analysis of longevity is a useful additional measure of performance, given the inconclusive findings so far on financial performance. With coverage of twenty-three years, we also have substantially longer time periods than in the previous longevity studies of Hoskisson and Johnson (1992) and Kay (1997). These years, moreover, cover a period when the conglomerate strategy was no longer novel. We continue by considering financial performance. Here we are quite tentative, but we have one advantage. In the past studies have tended to use different methods, at different time points, and in different countries: not surprisingly, they have come up with different results. We shall be using common methods to see whether we can find strategy and performance relationships that are consistent across three countries in two distinct periods of time. Broadly, we expect benefits to diversification, but no great advantage of related diversification over unrelated. This comparison across six points is a tough test for claims to generalizability.

Our transitions data give us a first cut on sustainability, comparing the robustness of strategies over the thirteen years of 1970–83 and the ten years of 1983–93. Table 5.4 recapitulates the key survival figures in terms of relative percentages, both over the two shorter periods and over the twenty-three years as a whole. We count as survival the holding of the same strategy, while remaining within the Top 100 populations, at beginning and end-points in the shorter periods, and beginning, mid- and end-points over the whole twenty-three years. Survival is not assured. *Pace* Dosi et al. (1992), these have been testing selection environments, including the 1974 oil crisis, the 1987 financial crash, and the two severe recessions of the early 1980s and 1990s. Successful retention of the same strategy even over one of the shorter periods would be no small feat for any company, including monstrous conglomerates.

Over the shorter periods 1970–83 and 1983–93, the overall survival rates of related diversifiers and conglomerates are not markedly different (see Table 5.4). It is true that conglomerates did relatively badly in the early period in the United Kingdom and in the later period in France. On the other hand, German conglomerates did well in the earlier period and spectacularly in the later one;

Table 5.4. *Strategic Stability of Domestic Top 100 Survivors, 1970–93 (national classification schemes)*

	Single	Dominant	Related	Unrelated
France				
Numbers in 1970	16	22	34	7
Per cent same strategy: 1970–83	31.3	18.2	47.1	42.9
1983–93	55.6	37.5	56.4	22.2
1970–93	18.8	18.2	23.5	14.3
Germany				
Numbers in 1970	21	13	29	15
Per cent same strategy: 1970–83	23.8	0	51.7	53.3
1983–93	45.5	20.0	75.0	80.0
1970–93	9.5	0.0	37.9	33.0
United Kingdom				
Numbers in 1970	5	26	50	6
Per cent same strategy: 1970–83	20.0	34.6	60.0	16.7
1983–93	20.0	33.3	52.0	62.5
1970–93	0.0	15.4	30.0	0.0

Sources: 1970 Classifications based upon Channon (1973) and Dyas and Thanheiser (1976)

British conglomerates likewise proved themselves much better in the more recent period; French conglomerates ran a close second in the early period. These conglomerates also generally survived quite well by comparison with undiversified strategies, especially dominant strategies. Marked by recessions, oil crisis, or financial crash, neither of these two periods could be said to be relaxed selection environments. It seems the orthodox resource-based view is too damning with regard to the short-term prospects of the conglomerate. The improving short-term survival rates in Germany and the United Kingdom at least may even suggest that the increase in conglomerates over 1983–93 in these two countries is underpinned by rising skills in the management of corporate relationships.

We cannot, however, go as far as Kay (1997) in arguing for the long-term resilience of the conglomerate on grounds of risk dispersion and lock-in. No British conglomerates retained their strategies all twenty-three years, and only one French one. On the other hand, nearly a third of British related diversifiers successfully stuck to their strategies through the whole period, and nearly a quarter of French. Even in Germany, where one-third of conglomerates managed to sustain their strategies through all twenty-three years, the most stable strategy was still one of related diversification.[3] All in all, therefore, the

[3] Five German conglomerates survived all twenty-three years: Bosch, Krupp, Linde, Oetcker, and Preussag: Röchling retained the same conglomerate strategy, but dropped out temporarily of the Top 100 firms in 1983. We should recognize that the German conglomerates are being measured on the relatively inclusive Thanheiser (1972) definition: even so, only Bosch counts as switching to a related strategy under Rumelt's (1974) criteria.

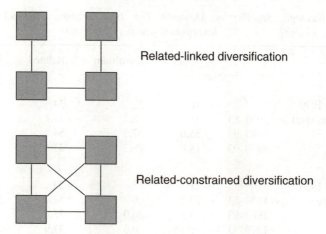

Figure 5.10. *Related-Constrained and Related-Linked Strategies*

conglomerate emerges in an intermediate position: more sustainable over the short term than allowed in severe interpretations of resource-based theory, but over the long term ultimately less resilient than the favoured related diversifier. This is consistent with our expectations based upon the value of corporate relationships but the relative shallowness of the top management resources necessary to exploit them.

This qualified rehabilitation of the conglomerate is confirmed by our analyses of financial performance. We should note at the outset that our financial expectations from Chapter 3 are less clear cut than expectations about longevity. Following Grant's (1988) emphasis on both corporate relationships and the relative costs of managing relationships, we maintained that conglomerates with corporate relationships could perform at least as well as (operationally) related diversifiers. However, as Harvard does not recognize corporate relationships, and they would be hard to discern in any case, we lack the measures to tell. Our overall position, then, is to expect that on average (operationally) related diversifiers would out-perform (operationally) unrelated diversifiers, but not necessarily very markedly.

Fortunately, the Harvard tradition has elaborated a further distinction that does allow a more refined examination, one moreover that acknowledges the costs of operational relatedness. For his performance analysis, Rumelt (1974) distinguished particularly between the diversification subcategories of 'related-constrained' and 'related-linked' (see Figure 5.10). In a related-constrained strategy the majority of a firm's businesses are related to 'virtually all other businesses taken one at a time' (Rumelt, 1974: 19). Diversification is constrained in that any move should be able to take advantage of relationships with more or less all other businesses. The related-linked strategy is looser. Here individual

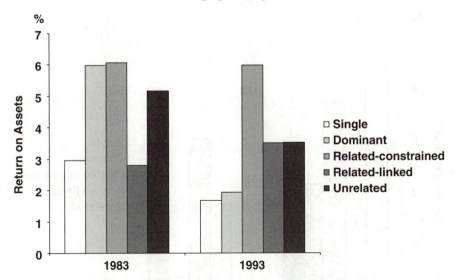

Figure 5.11. *Diversification and Performance in France*

businesses need only be related to each other one by one, the 'domino pattern' Dyas (1972: 121) identified as particularly common in France. Related-constrained and related-linked strategies may have very different implications for performance. Related-constrained strategies have an advantage because able to lever resource advantages across the whole range of their activities. Related-linked companies, on the other hand, have more limited relationships to exploit. They add, however, managerial costs of relatedness that simple conglomerates do not bear. Hoskisson and Johnson (1992: 626) have called the related-linked strategy a 'between' strategy, with the costs of relatedness but not all the benefits. It is possible that leaner conglomerates may even outperform them, either through leveraging corporate relationships or by exploiting market power.

Theory, then, establishes a hierarchy of expectations about the performance of the various Harvard categories. Whether for reasons of shared resources or market power, diversified firms are expected to out-perform undiversified firms; on account of their heightened resource advantages, related-constrained firms are expected to out-perform all others; and finally related-linked firms may suffer by comparison to conglomerates because carrying greater headquarters costs while lacking the full set of operational relationships (Rumelt, 1974; Grant, Jammine, and Thomas, 1988). This hierarchy is something that we can test, and a reasonable performance by conglomerates would also be in line with our expectations from Chapter 3.

The results of the performance analysis are summarized in Figures 5.11–5.13. The analysis is on a country-by-country basis, for two time periods each.[4] The

[4] A fuller regression analysis of performance, with a full set of control variables, is provided in Mayer (1999). The results do not substantially change.

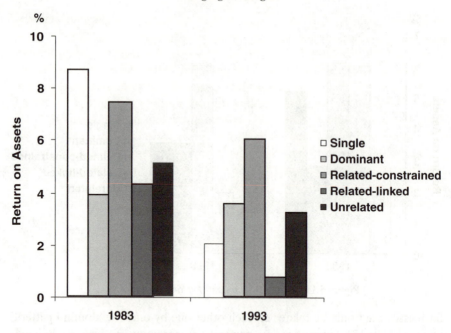

Figure 5.12. *Diversification and Performance in Germany*

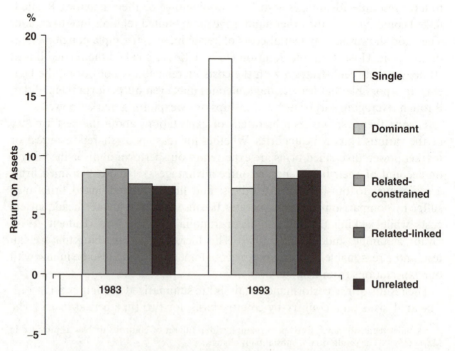

Figure 5.13. *Diversification and Performance in the United Kingdom*

profitability measure is return on assets, a good measure of efficiency and the most popular financial performance measure in the strategy field. In order to smooth any coincidental short-term fluctuations, three-year average returns were used with 1983 and 1993 as mid-points (Robins and Wiersema, 1995). The two time periods allow us to assess the extent to which performance relationships may be time sensitive. The comparison of countries separately avoids the perils of pooling financial data from different accounting regimes, as well as highlighting any possible business system effects on relative profitability. Our concern is whether the hierarchy of relative performance attributable to the various strategies holds broadly across the three countries and the two time periods.

Three things should be noted before we continue. First, on average, the British firms are substantially more profitable than either the German or the French. These favourable figures may be due to accounting differences, but are also consistent with Cassis's (1997) findings concerning the superior performance of British firms through most of this century. Second, it is important to note the unequal numbers in the various strategy categories, especially the often quite few firms in the undiversified categories.[5] Outliers may considerably exaggerate the average performances of these smaller undiversified categories in either direction, so that averages for these strategies are likely to be less consistent over time and across countries than for the larger diversified categories. We shall take care, therefore, to look at how individual companies may distort particular results and will also give more weight to the averages of the larger categories. Finally, we are comparing the populations of large firms, not samples, and so can fairly conclude in favour of one or other strategy on the comparisons of averages rather than statistical probability. However, our statistical tests do show that the differences in terms of average performance are generally very small. As Armour and Teece (1978) suggest, this is what we should expect as strategies 'mature' and firms find their new optima. With all this in mind, any conclusion in favour of a particular strategy should be made cautiously. None the less, the comparison across two time periods and three countries does give us six 'cases' of the strategy-performance relationship, a reasonably tough base for testing the robustness of performance relationships.

Theoretically, the related-constrained strategy is expected to do best, on account of its extensive set of relationships. This is indeed the case for France over both time periods, in Germany in 1993, and in the United Kingdom in 1983. The differences vary, however, with little to distinguish the performance of related-constrained from dominant firms in France and the United Kingdom in 1983. However, these dominant categories are quite small, easily distorted by a

---

[5] The distribution of firms by strategy for which there was adequate financial data for inclusion in the performance analysis was as follows (1983/1993): France: single, 13/10; dominant, 10/10; related-linked, 5/4; related-constrained, 18/22; unrelated, 8/8; Germany: single, 9/6; dominant, 9/6; related-linked, 6/10; related-constrained, 18/17; unrelated, 9/15; United Kingdom: single, 3/3; dominant, 13/9; related-linked, 16/12; related-constrained, 22/26; unrelated, 13/17.

few outliers. Thus the success of French dominant players in 1983 was partly due to the good financial results of the oil companies Elf-Aquitaine and Total. In the United Kingdom too an oil company, BP, contributed to the sound performance of dominant strategy firms, alongside firms such as Glaxo and Guinness.

Again in line with theoretical expectations, there is usually clear water between related-constrained and the undiversified single business firms. The exceptions to this rule are Germany 1983 and the United Kingdom 1993. In Germany the sound performance of the single business category is largely due to the success of the country's luxury car manufacturers, BMW, Daimler Benz, and Porsche. In the United Kingdom pharmaceutical companies Glaxo (refocused since 1983) and Wellcome performed particularly well. The spectacularly poor result for the British single business category in 1983 is down to the performances of British Leyland and Rolls Royce, both companies that had been nationalized after failure in the private sector. This instability around the single business strategy over time underlines the problem of small numbers.

The related-constrained companies perform consistently better than what is generally the second largest category, the unrelated diversifiers. This holds true across both time periods and all three countries. This is particularly remarkable because, as part of the related group more broadly, these firms are typically mature and stable in strategy. Unrelated diversifiers, however, are not poor performers. Usually they do not perform quite as well as those with related-constrained strategies, but better than single business firms. The exception here is again Germany in 1983. Apart from the results of the luxury car makers mentioned above, this was also affected by the more moderate results of unrelated diversifiers with substantial steel interests such as Krupp and Thyssen. We also need to mention the extremely poor performance of the Gutehoffnungshütte (GHH), the steel and engineering conglomerate. Undergoing a severe crisis, GHH soon entered into a fundamental restructuring ultimately resulting in the reformation of the concern in 1986 under the name of MAN, a former subsidiary.

It is when we compare the performance of unrelated diversifiers with the more loosely related-linked diversifiers that Rumelt's (1974) finer distinctions emerge as particularly useful. As expected, firms with unrelated diversified strategies generally have a slight edge on those following related-linked strategies. Only in the United Kingdom in 1983 is there some advantage for the related-linked strategy, influenced particularly by the solid performances of firms such as BICC, GEC, and Reckitt & Coleman. It is notable that the British were relatively highly committed to linked strategies in this period (see footnote 5). Without Rumelt's (1974) distinction, the performance of related-linked diversifiers would have pulled down the performance of related-constrained diversifiers, so obscuring differences with the simple conglomerate strategy. Overall, therefore, the conglomerate emerges in an intermediate position in terms of financial performance, generally better than the related-linked diversifier, poorer than the related-constrained.

In sum, although differences are small and not entirely consistent, certain patterns do emerge broadly in line with theory. The strategy most strongly favoured by the orthodox resource-based view, the tightly integrated strategy of related-constrained diversification, offers the most consistently superior financial returns. Where out-performed, it is only erratically and by categories with small numbers. This relative success for constrained diversification broadly holds across countries and across time. However, in line with our extension of the resource-based view to include corporate relationships, the conglomerate does quite respectably too: more often than not, it achieves better returns than the higher cost but less integrated related-linked diversifiers. The conglomerate is not so monstrous as orthodox resource-based theory would have it. Combining these findings on financial performance with those on longevity also produces an overall picture consistent with the model advanced in Chapter 3. Conglomerates survive longer and perform better than the orthodox resource-based view would predict, even if related diversification pays over the long term. By and large, these patterns predominate across the substantial majority of the six 'cases' provided by our three countries and two time periods. *Pace* the national institutionalists, economic models can account for patterns of diversification, survival, and performance even in quite different national contexts.

5.5. SUMMARY

As a strategy, diversification implies strong assumptions about the generalizability of managerial skills across different businesses. As scientific claim, Harvard's prediction for continued diversification across Europe expresses an equally strong confidence in the validity of general principles of management. By and large, the European experience seems to endorse both the notion of some generalizeable skill and the American project of constructing general principles of good management. In France, Germany, and the United Kingdom diversification has continued in the direction predicted by Harvard, by now dominating European industry. Moreover, the favoured strategy of related diversification appears to offer both the most sustainable recipe for continued growth and the best prospect of consistent, above-average financial returns. The success of the Chandlerian model has been dented neither by the fashionable reaction against diversification nor by the emergence of new financial techniques for the unbundling of corporations. Enduring differences in national institutions seem not to matter. The financially oriented managers of the United Kingdom end up with the same pattern of diversification as engineering-oriented, personal, and bank-centred Germany.

Nevertheless, our more detailed exploration of processes beneath the trends introduces some nuances to the original Harvard notion of diversification. The trends conceal, first of all, a great deal of complexity in the detailed patterns of transition. Diversification does not become as 'institutionalized' as Channon (1973) suggests. Although there is no evidence of aggregate refocusing in France, Germany, and the United Kingdom, the transition analyses make clear that firms are constantly refocusing individually. Refocusing and diversification are occurring simultaneously: it is just that there is more of the latter than the former. It is refocusing, however, that often claims the headlines. Break-ups and takeovers of established conglomerates get more attention than the surreptitious creep of new conglomerates into the lower end of our population of large firms. The impression of recent widespread downscoping may rely too much on one side of the equation. It takes careful analysis of entries as well as exits to get an overall grasp of diversification trends.

Diversification remains important, and it is clear that large firms owe their continuing positions as industrial leaders mainly to this rather than to development of core businesses. Yet, it is also clear, particularly from the French experience, that single business firms can more or less match the growth of their diversified counterparts and that the pressure for diversification is not ineluctable. Equally, the dominant strategy is not just one step upon a conveyor belt of increasing diversification. At the level of individual firms, the sort of evolutionary progression implied by Chandler's (1962) four chapters of enterprise, or Scott's (1973) three stages, is far from obligatory. As for Mintzberg's (1979) putative 'fourth stage' of unrelated diversification, there is no such thing. Once firms have reached related diversification (the third stage), they are unlikely either to go further towards conglomerate diversification or to retreat backwards towards more specialization. From what we can tell here, conglomerates are more likely to enter the unrelated strategy more or less directly rather than through measured progression through less diversified stages.

Mintzberg (1979) was right, though, to take the conglomerate seriously at least. The Chandlerian model of diversification should be extended to embrace the once unloved conglomerate. We find in the short run that conglomerates can achieve attractive levels of performance, accounting for the continuous direct infusion of such firms into the large firm population. Moreover, these conglomerates can survive quite long periods, more robust over the short term than severe versions of the resource-based view imply. The conglomerate cannot be dismissed as evolutionary freak, creation of over-active financial markets or creature of self-aggrandizing managerial interests. It is only over periods of two decades or more that conglomerates reveal themselves at a disadvantage to related diversifiers, as their thin top management resources finally begin to run out. In sum, although simple stage models of development are not followed strictly at the level of individual firms, in aggregate the strategic evolution of large European firms in Europe does seem to fit the extended Chandlerian model far better than theories of institutional dependence or managerial abuse. Generalization within certain temporal and territorial limits may be justified.

There is one surprising anomaly—the long-standing German conglomerates. Some of these prove able to survive two decades and more. We shall see in Chapter 7 that special ownership factors are partly at play here. However, we contradict Chandler (1990) by finding that the German banking system has been slower at unwinding conglomerates than British financial markets. With our more positive evaluation of conglomerates, we can be fairly relaxed about this apparent failure. After all, it looks as if a good deal of the German and British growth in overall diversification is driven both by the successful grasping of genuine new conglomerate opportunities and by improving capabilities in managing corporate relationships over time. The European trend towards diversification is not merely a matter of catch-up with some fixed strategic equilibrium. It involves European firms continually changing their strategies as they seek to take advantage of emergent opportunities and developing skills. This kind of process remorselessly undermines attempts at finality in the management sciences. Just as Chandler's (1962) elevation of related diversification had to be updated in line with the growing success of unrelated diversification, so even our model of Figure 3.3, with its rehabilitation of the conglomerate, must be given some provisionality. The balance between one strategy and another has a dynamic that is liable constantly to amend the demographics of diversification and the hierarchies of performance.

Chandler's (1962) famous prediction was that structure should follow strategy. The next chapter will examine the progress of the multidivisional form in Europe. Although Harvard would confidently predict steady divisionalization in line with diversification, institutionalists might feel more confident in their scepticism. After all, organizational issues touch more directly on politics, status, and culture than the simple economics of diversification.

6

Changing Structures

INTRODUCTION

Across all three major European economies, the large, diversified corporation is now the norm. The issue next is management. Chandler's (1962) prescriptions from scope, and Williamson's (1975) from scale, are unambiguous: the large diversified corporation requires the multidivisional structure. This structure, with its clear hierarchies, its division of responsibilities, and its systematic, objective procedures, is the contemporary translation of the Weberian ideal. For Chandler or Williamson, the multidivisional's artful combination of bureaucratic rationality with internal markets is the only way to manage the unprecedented scale and scope of late twentieth-century enterprise. Williamson (1975) even urged the export of American managers around the world to establish and administer this structural panacea. Indeed, as the original Harvard researchers regarded the opaque personalism of traditional European holding companies, it was clear to them that multidivisional transparency and professionalism were the future. Accountable and meritocratic, here was a governance system that could finally give modernity and dynamism to a hide-bound Europe.

As we have seen, so compelling seems this structural logic, that it becomes for Donaldson (1996) one of the touchstones of a positivist organization science. Quite simply, the universal corollary of diversification is divisionalization. But structures are touchy subjects. Making the economic case for combining technologies and markets through diversification is relatively easy. Structures, though, do not so directly translate to the bottom-line. Structures, too, are more obviously about the relationships between people. They are more than simple lines on organizational charts. They imply systems of control and accountability; they bring some people together, while excluding others; they prescribe what can be done and what cannot be done; they define essential managerial skills and likely routes to the top. The ramifications of structure are so pervasive that Rumelt (1974: 33) characterizes each structural type as a 'distinctive way of life'. Touching people so closely, the upwards path of the multidivisional may well be less smooth than for the economics of diversification.

There are good theoretical reasons for doubting whether the multidivisional really is either as universal or as perennial as once it seemed. As we have seen, theorists of national institutions and culture raise strong objections to the multidivisional's relevance across countries. After all, the multidivisional itself can be seen as a cultural artefact—its rationality, its impersonality, and its reductive modularity only too expressive of its American birthplace (Hampden-Turner and Trompenaars, 1993). If structure follows culture, then we may expect enduring resistance to the multidivisional principle in traditional Europe. The long-centralized French are not likely to take easily to the decentralized multidivisional. Solid institutional differences will reinforce cultural prejudices, too. The ideological hegemony of the multidivisional is circumscribed in countries where personal ownership and management still compete with managerial professionalism and meritocracy. The superiority of multidivisional surveillance is undercut where banks enjoy long-standing and intimate relationships with their networks of clients. As enduring institutional differences combine with cultural hangovers, there are good grounds to suspect continued lags and variation in the European adoption of the multidivisional.

Besides, fashion no longer favours the multidivisional. From an international institutionalist point of view, during the 1980s the tide turned decisively in favour of Japanese models, leaving American imports washed-up. Indeed, a strong economic case could be made against the multidivisional. The 'tyranny of the SBU' militates against the cultivation of core competences (Prahalad and Hamel, 1990). The rigid segmentation of division against division, corporation against corporation, is out of place in today's networked world. Technologies and markets move too rapidly for top management to stay safely aloof from operations. If we buy Ghoshal and Bartlett's (1998) vision of the 'individualized corporation', we are in the middle of another organizational revolution which is leaving the multidivisional behind as irretrievably as the functional structure was overtaken before. From this perspective, it is by no means clear that the multidivisional should have continued its advance into the 1980s and 1990s. Indeed, in this networked world, the wheel of fortune may even have turned to bring the fuzzy-boundaried, loosely controlled holding company back into favour (Mowery, 1992).

We think that many accounts of institutional context and organizational innovation are over-drawn. Just as the Chandlerian view of diversification can be extended to explain contemporary patterns of diversification across Europe, so can the multidivisional be developed to accommodate recent trends and experiments in organization. The multidivisional is not scarred indelibly by its modernist origins, but is an evolving and adaptive phenomenon. The network multidivisional concept that we introduced in Chapter 3 overcomes some of the stark divisiveness and remote detachment of earlier models, while preserving the essential principle of decentralization of operations, centralization of strategy. The multidivisional is changing, not dying.

This chapter will follow the progress of the multidivisional structure in contemporary Europe, as it struggles both against continuing institutional differences and against a shifting intellectual and economic climate. The next section recalls the main structural types used by Harvard and indicates how we operationalize them. We then go on to trace the structural trends in Europe over the period 1950–93. Our approach will be similar to the previous chapter's and we shall want to know whether the multidivisional has done as well as diversification. In addition to the trends and transitions, however, we shall also consider the transformation question, the extent to which the multidivisional has been changed, or even superseded, by new management approaches. Finally, as before, we shall consider performance, considering whether the multidivisional really deserves its place in contemporary Europe.

6.1. MEASURING STRUCTURE

Just as for diversification, Harvard uses four categories of organizational structure: functional, functional-holding, holding, and multidivisional. As we indicated in Chapter 3, the four categories are differentiated primarily according to patterns of centralization and control. Although the formal structures are quite straightforward, they require some skill to interpret in practice. The relevant information for classification ranges widely, beyond simple organization charts to include subsidiary ownership, management systems, organizational integration, and operating business overlap. In all these areas, our interviews were often particularly helpful in understanding companies' structures. Even where we did not interview, the interview experience helped considerably in interpreting the documentary data (press articles, annual reports, company directories, and the like) that were available. We again provide more detail on our procedures in Appendix II.

The functional organization is the simplest and most centralized, both strategically and operationally. Here the tasks immediately below chief executive level are organized along the lines of operating functions such as sales, marketing, and manufacturing (Rumelt 1974: 33; Dyas and Thanheiser 1976: 19). This is illustrated in Figure 6.1. Dairy Crest, with its centralized commercial, distribution, and dairy management functions, is one of the last examples of a functional organization remaining in our group of large industrials. The functional holding builds on the functional core simply by adding a periphery of subsidiaries or partly owned ventures, typically headed by general managers. This is illustrated in Figure 6.2. At Südzucker, for instance, the core sugar business was centralized, while its foods, milling, and agricultural businesses operated through decentralized subsidiaries. In the functional-holding, the subsidiaries remain small relative to the core, and report alongside the core's functional directors to the group chief executive. In the Harvard scheme, the functional-holding was often seen as a transitional structure to manage dominant-type diversification strategies, where the remaining preponderance of the core did not yet quite justify transition to a structure of equal, free-standing divisions.

The holding structure is another transitional one, at least in theory. The unsystematic *bête noire* of Harvard, it is seen in the United States as a purely temporary response to early twentieth-century antitrust regulation (Chandler,

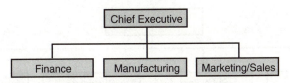

Figure 6.1. *Stylized Functional Structure*

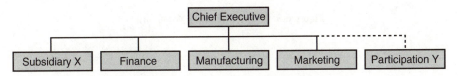

Figure 6.2. *Stylized Functional-Holding Structure*

1990: 72–3). As a consequence, the Harvard group tends to define it loosely and negatively. Thus for Dyas (1972: 154), the holding is 'defined more by its *not* being divisional than by any particular characteristic of its own' (emphasis added). The holding company appears in many guises, therefore, a common title that masks distinct national traditions of organization. In France the holding typically involves complex cascades of equity stakes, spinning out family or personal control in ever diminishing proportions (Couret and Martin, 1991; cf. Daems, 1978). In the United Kingdom, on the other hand, Channon (1973: 15) distinguished two more managerial types. In the first, corporate management was made up of the general managers of 'almost completely autonomous subsidiaries' and 'functional specialists generally drawn from the original parent concern' (Channon, 1973: 15). In the other, the only links between the corporate centre and the various subsidiaries were provided by members of the holding company board with seats on the boards of subsidiary companies (Channon, 1973: 15). These British holdings were often the historical product of a clubby propensity to manage competition through cartels and merger.

In both French and British cases, however, the holding company lacks a strong central management capable of independent strategic oversight of operations. This too is the defining characteristic of Rumelt's (1974: 38) American holdings, distinguished by the 'almost complete lack of management at the top'. In the general case of the holding, what relationships do exist between headquarters and operating units are typically 'limited and often unsystematic' (Williamson and Bhargava, 1972: 133). Subsidiaries, frequently only partially owned, may remain 'largely unconsolidated with the individual companies still retaining much of their original entities' (Channon, 1973: 139; discussion of Reyrolle Parsons). Overall this leads to a situation where the holding company's activities cannot be sufficiently monitored, where cash cannot circulate freely, and linkages are not exploited. Corporate management may have the ability to

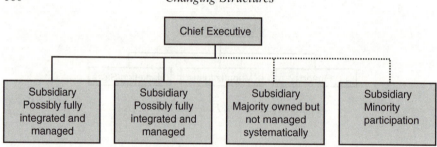

Figure 6.3. *Stylized Holding Company*

exit—as any investor—but it has little systematic control. In classifying holding companies, therefore, we looked particularly to the undermining of top management detachment by involvement in operations, the absence of common frameworks for accounting and planning, the extent to which businesses remain unconsolidated into coherent business units, and the degree to which central control over operating businesses was compromised by partial or minority ownership. Figure 6.3 provides a bare-bones organization chart of a typical holding. However, the details of Financière Agache, a successful holding of the early 1990s, give a richer picture of the real complexity of such organizations, particularly in France (see Illustration 6.1).

Illustration 6.1. *Financière Agache: Entrepreneurial Holding Company*

Financière Agache is the highest level managerial unit in a cascade of financial holdings and sub-holdings that include such famous names as Christian Dior, Bon Marché, and the various components of the LVMH group (including Louis Vuitton, Givenchy, Christian Lacroix, Moët et Chandon, and Hennessy). The group as a whole had a consolidated turnover in 1993 of FF27,000m, making it the thirty-third largest industrial company in France. One level higher than Financière Agache is the personal holding company of Bernard Arnault, the creator of the group by a series of daring acquisitions during the 1980s. However, at no level does Arnault hold complete ownership: indeed, the largest part of his business, LVMH, is only 46 per cent owned by a sub-holding far removed from Arnault's own ultimate holding (see figure). Arnault himself has depended on minority shareholders at various levels for the capital to support his newly constructed empire—most notably Guinness, Worms, and Crédit Lyonnais.

Although highly successful, managerial practice within the Financière Agache group departs somewhat from the multidivisional ideal. The company describes itself as 'a federation of small and medium-sized enterprises'. At the Financière

Agache level, there is a Direction des Ressources Humaines, which exercises oversight over personnel policy, especially regarding management development, for the group as a whole. LVMH, however, operates separate financial reporting and treasury functions from those of the rest of the group, in no sense depending on Financière Agache.

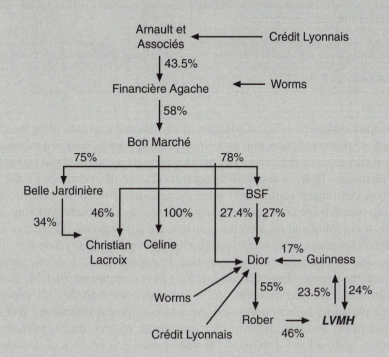

Within LVMH itself, clusters of subsidiaries are only gradually being co-ordinated—the seven main champagne brands not coming under a common directeur général until 1994—with members of the original owning families still prominent in management positions and retaining considerable shareholder rights. For example, in 1994, Arnault brought the perfume company Guerlain into the group, but left the owning family with a slight majority in the new subsidiary, with management control and with a 12 per cent share of the Christian Dior sub-holding. Subsidiaries owned at various levels are integrated only partially into coherent divisions: thus on the couture side, Celine and Christian Dior remained outside LVMH's couture operations, Christian Lacroix only being transferred in 1993.

Control and co-ordination are typically direct and informal, largely ensured by Bernard Arnault himself. Arnault is PDG not only of his ultimate personal financial holding company (Arnault et Associés), but of Christian Dior and LVMH. All subsidiary Présidents-Directeurs Généraux or Directeurs Généraux are brought together for bi-monthly meetings of the Comité d'Information et Renseignements

(*continued*)

Généraux, presided over by Arnault himself. Also, every two months, there are meetings by 'secteur' (not divisions) again presided over by Arnault personally. Arnault is not supported by a large head-office staff at group level (Financière Agache has thirty people; above this he operates a small personal 'cabinet'). In principle, synergies are negotiated voluntarily between subsidiaries, according to the opportunities that come to the attention of either Arnault or subsidiary presidents at any of their formal or informal interactions.

Principal sources: Interviews; Kerdellant, 1992; *Le Figaro*, 21 October 1991; *Challenges*, December 1991 and July–August 1994. Adapted with permission from Mayer and Whittington (1996), 'The Survival of the Holding Company', in R. Whitley and P. H. Kristensen (eds.). *The Changing European Firm*. Routledge, 98–9.

The multidivisional is less distinctive in its national characteristics than the holding, so that a common shift away from holdings can be seen as a movement towards convergence in Europe. The multidivisional has been defined rigorously by Williamson (1970) in terms of its decentralization of operations to discrete divisions, centralized control over strategy, and the existence of central staffs advising top management and monitoring divisions. Corporate planning, systematic accounting and information systems, and performance-related pay were all part of the package. However, the Harvard group was quite relaxed in interpreting divisionalization, recognizing that European practice often diverged from the theoretical ideal. Channon (1973: 217) commented that his British multidivisional companies 'tended to be less developed than the U.S. concerns in their planning, control and management development techniques, had not divorced policy and operations to the same degree, did not directly reward performance, and had not developed the widespread U.S. practice of a cadre of central staff general executives to monitor the activities of the division managers'. In order to preserve continuity with the original European studies, it is not the strict criteria of Williamson's (1970) ideal type, but the more relaxed operational definition of the Harvard researchers that we shall employ. In classifying divisionalized companies, we shall look particularly to the existence of distinct and coherent operating units (whether called divisions or not), a preference for substantial majority ownership of important and long-standing businesses, more or less standardized accounting and control systems, and the active integration of newly acquired operations. The earlier cases of DuPont in 1921 and 1999 (Figure 1.2) provide typical divisional organizational charts.

6.2. NATIONAL CONTEXT AND ORGANIZATIONAL STRUCTURE

For Chandler (1962) there was no doubt that the multidivisional organization was the end-point of the evolution of the modern industrial firm, and it was this

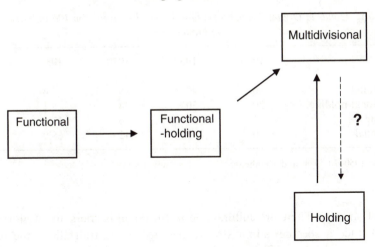

Figure 6.4. *Stages in Organizational Development*

view that informed the confident predictions of multidivisionalization in post-war Europe (Dyas, 1972; Thanheiser, 1972; Channon, 1973). As firms changed their strategies towards diversification, so they would change their structures to divisionalization. Again, a sequence of structural development was implied, though less elaborate than that of diversification. Although for the functional organization, the functional-holding structure might provide an intermediate stepping-stone, both for it and the holding company the multidivisional was the final chapter. There could be no reversion. Figure 6.4 summarizes the expected dominant patterns of transition, this time movement rightwards representing increased operational decentralization.

National institutionalists, of course, are sceptical of the irresistibility of this flow. International institutionalists—especially as the American model loses both political and ideological support—doubt its irreversibility. Radical talk of new organizational forms might even indicate movement from the modernist rigidities of the multidivisional to the flexible decentralization of the holding (Mowery, 1992). The dotted line in Figure 6.4 allows for such a new 'chapter' in the evolution of enterprise. This section will examine the overall trends and the patterns of transitions in each of the countries in turn, beginning with the two countries which differ most from the institutional home of the multidivisional, France and Germany.

France

France seems unpromising ground for the multidivisional. We have seen already that French industry has been most attached to the single business, undiversified

Table 6.1. *Trends in Organizational Structure Among Domestic Top 100 Industrial Firms in France* (%)

	1950	1960	1970	1983	1993
Functional	56	40	18	5.4	1.5
Functional-holding	20	30	24	8.1	9.1
Holding	24	24	16	17.6	13.6
Divisional	0	5	42	68.9	75.8

Sources: 1950–70, Dyas and Thanheiser (1976); this study, 1983–93

type of strategy. There are cultural and institutional barriers, too. Calori et al. (1997) trace a specific 'administrative heritage of centralization' due to the primary socialization effects of the rationalistic and hierarchical system of French schooling. These centralizing tendencies are reinforced both by the uniquely powerful French state, requiring centrally co-ordinated policy initiatives and responses (Zysman, 1994), and by the continued vitality of personal managerial control in family-owned enterprises. All these forces might be expected to reinforce loyalty to functional structures. Moreover, receptiveness to the multidivisional import is not likely to be assured in a country in which French 'exceptionalism' is a matter of pride and where Americanization has been an enduring 'dilemma' (Kuisel, 1993). The Americans may have been the liberators of Europe and models of modernity, yet from the presidency of de Gaulle to the controversy over Euro Disney, American economic and cultural imports have been regarded with deep ambivalence. If the French do decentralize, it is quite likely to be in the form of traditional holding companies, the loosely structured industrial groups and cascades of minority shareholdings that have long been a feature of French capitalism (Couret and Martin, 1991; Daems, 1978).

In practice, it seems that all these cultural and institutional barriers do not make a wit of difference. As Table 6.1 indicates, since 1970 the multidivisional organization has continued its steady trend towards dominance of the French industrial landscape. By 1993 over 75 per cent of the largest industrial firms in France had adopted this organizational form, up from the still relatively low level of 42 per cent in 1970. Even in centralizing France, the functional organization has almost completely collapsed, accounting for a negligible proportion of firms by 1993. The functional-holding company has undergone a similar decline, if maintaining a more significant niche. The holding company form of organization too has dropped in relative importance between 1970 and 1993, though again resisting extinction. Both the success of the multidivisional and the collapse of the functional form deserve more consideration, as do the continued resilience of holding and functional-holding forms.

The patterns of transition indicated in Figures 6.5 and 6.6 allow us to get a

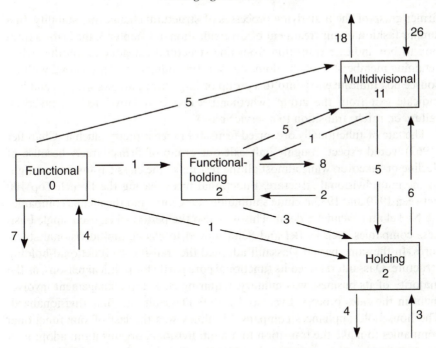

Figure 6.5. *Structural Change in France, 1970–83*

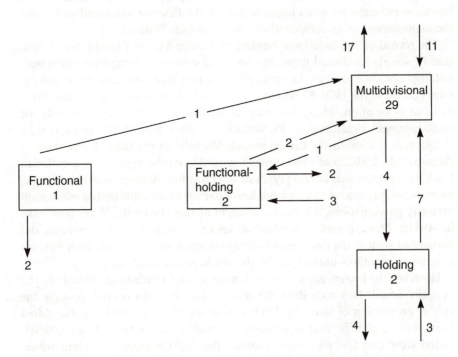

Figure 6.6. *Structural Change in France, 1983–93*

firmer grasp of the underlying processes of structural change and stability. In a similar fashion to our treatment of diversification in Chapter 5, the arrows from box to box indicate transition from one structural category to another while retaining membership of the domestic Top 100 industrial firms; arrows with no source box indicate entry into this group of large firms; arrows with no end box indicate exit from the group (whether because of relative decline, takeover, failure or, rarely, transition to a service base).

The fate of functionally organized firms in France is pretty much as Chandler (1962) would expect: roughly half exit our group of firms, largely because of decline or takeover, while almost all the rest make the classic transition straight to the multidivisional structure. Functional firms leaving the French Top 100 between 1970 and 1983 include shipbuilder La Ciotat and the metals companies Le Nickel and Wendel Sidelor. This was also the period when even single business companies such as Bel and Seita moved to classic multidivisional structures. In the same period Dassault adopted the transitional functional-holding structure. Dassault retained its functional core partly for political reasons, as the majority of its business was military, requiring close top management involvement in the sales process. Even so, by 1993 Dassault had fully divisionalized. The household appliances company Moulinex was the last of our functional companies to make the transition to a multidivisional organization, adopting a product-line based organization in 1986. By 1993 the only surviving functional organization was the Verrerie Cristallerie d'Arques, still single business, still based overwhelmingly in its home region of the Pas-de-Calais, and still under the management of its octogenerian gérant, Jacques Durand.

The record of the functional-holding in France has been hardly better than that of simple functional firms, the only real difference being that functional-holdings continue to enter the ranks of the largest industrial firms right into the later period. In the 1970–83 period, almost half of the functional-holding firms exit our population. Many, however, made the classic transition towards the multidivisional organization: for instance, Usinor Sacilor (Illustration 6.2), Peugeot, and Total in the earlier period, Michelin in the later. A few, such as Aérospatiale, EMC, and Fives Lille, departed from the approved Chandlerian track, moving towards holding types of organization. Aérospatiale, for example, owes its holding character to a weak headquarters and its substantial reliance on minority participations, the most prominent of these being the 38 per cent stake in Airbus. Nevertheless, a handful of relatively undiversified companies did manage to stick to the functional-holding structure for some time, with Renault remaining essentially unchanged for the whole period 1970–93.

However, the French are not exceptional enough to withstand the logic of the multidivisional. Not only does the multidivisional claim overwhelmingly the largest proportion of firms by 1993; this structure is also highly stable. Most firms that do change their organizational structure move towards a multidivisional structure; few who have adopted the multidivisional structure subse-

Illustration 6.2. *Usinor Sacilor: American-inspired French Multidivisional*

Usinor Sacilor was created in 1986 through the merger of France's two state-owned steel companies, Usinor and Sacilor. Usinor was the dominant component and had been an early divisionalizer, despite its focused business strategy. Claude Etchegaray, its Président-Directeur Général in the late 1970s and early 1980s, had worked for the American conglomerate ITT and was a strong believer in budgets, planning, and decentralization. He is quoted as saying of his regime: 'I applied the American method of management' (Godelier, 1995). François Mer, who took over the newly merged group in 1986, was a more classic product of the French system, being a polytechnicien and graduate of the Ecole des Mines. Nevertheless, he integrated the two companies into three main product divisions, flat products, long products, and stainless steel and special flat products. These divisions extended geographically, encompassing operations based in Germany, Spain, and Brazil. Horizontal committees were established to co-ordinate divisional supply to key customer sectors such as automobiles and construction. Rather contrary to the multidivisional spirit of detachment, Mer presided over the commercial committee of the flat products division, Usinor Sacilor's largest.

Principal sources: Interviews; Godelier (1995).

quently abandon it. Companies which stuck with the multidivisional structure throughout this period include BSN, l'Air Liquide, Pechiney, and Rhône-Poulenc. Most new entries into this set of large industrial firms are already divisionalized.

Few holding companies survive in France by 1993 and those that do tend eventually to reform. One example is the Schneider company. Classified in both 1970 and 1983 as a holding company, Schneider was a family group presiding over a loosely knit collection of partly owned steel and heavy engineering subsidiaries. In the early 1980s Schneider's largest subsidiary, the mechanical engineering company Creusot-Loire, was only 50 per cent owned and making huge losses. During the 1980s the group underwent substantial restructuring, with many divestments and closures (including the elimination of Creusot-Loire). By 1993 Schneider was reorganized into four core divisions, three owned 100 per cent and the fourth owned by substantial majority. Even persistent holding companies may undergo considerable transformation. Financière Agache was classified as a holding consistently in 1970, 1983, and 1993, but this surface continuity hides substantial changes in practice. Originally a textiles and stores group, Bernard Arnault transformed it during the 1980s into the personal vehicle for his luxury goods empire, of which LVMH was a critical but only partially owned component (see Illustration 6.1). Apart from some *haute couture* and a single department store, the original businesses were entirely disposed of.

There is a handful of cases where multidivisionals actually moved to holding company structures. Alcatel-Alsthom is a case of reversion from the

multidivisional that to some extent illustrates the structural challenges of contemporary international business. Originally a holding company as the Compagnie Générale d'Electricité, the company had rationalized considerably
during the early 1980s as nationalization allowed it to reduce its reliance on
minority participations and quoted subsidiaries. However, progress had been
only partial by the early 1990s, and growing involvement in international joint
ventures, notably GEC-Alsthom, had further inhibited efforts to integrate planning and accounting systems and consolidate activities. The group PDG, Pierre
Suard (who, incidentally, would later lose his job due to various business scan-
dals) also remained deeply involved in the operational management of the
largest Alcatel business, as had his predecessor, Ambroise Roux. Although we
can detect the pressures of international business in pushing Alcatel-Alsthom
back in a holding direction, we can also see the influence of a long heritage of
weak and unsystematic central control. There is little evidence in the transitions
of French companies for the adoption of holding-style structures as a response
to the new networked economy.

Overall, French business seems to have undergone exactly the transformation
predicted by the Harvard researchers. Despite its alleged cultural predisposi-
tions, its strong central state, and the extent of personal management control,
French industry has clearly abandoned the highly centralized functional structure. The French are now strongly committed to the American multidivisional
form.

Germany

Expectations regarding Germany pull both ways. Chandler (1990), of course,
had used the German experience as a stick to beat the British with, lauding such
early divisionalizers as Siemens. On the other hand, we have seen that extensive
personal control persisted in Germany right into the 1990s, and that the banks
continued to play an important part in the ownership of German industry. For
Cable and Dirrheimer (1983) bank-industry networks fulfil many of the

Table 6.2. *Trends in Organizational Structure Among Domestic Top 100 Industrial Firms in Germany* (%)

	1950	1960	1970	1983	1993
Functional	45	29	27	10.0	3.2
Functional-holding	40	53	21	23.3	14.3
Holding	14	14	14	10.0	12.7
Divisional	0	4	40	56.7	69.8

Sources: 1950–70, Dyas and Thanheiser (1976); this study, 1983–93

functions associated with the multidivisional firm by monitoring business performance and allocating capital between independent businesses. Where banking involvement can substitute, the attractions of divisionalization are reduced.

Again, however, the national peculiarities of Germany seem to have made no difference to the success of the multidivisional. Whilst in 1970, the end-point of the Harvard studies, multidivisional firms were still clearly in the minority, by 1983 they were already more important than all other forms of organization. Ten years later they clearly dominate the scene. By 1993 almost 70 per cent of German-owned Top 100 industrials had adopted a multidivisional structure. The functional organization, still accounting for a quarter of large German industrials in 1970, had practically disappeared by 1993. Perhaps the only surprise for Chandlerians is the survival of holding companies, and particularly functional-holding companies, into the 1990s: together they still accounted for more than a quarter of German firms. The success of the multidivisional and the persistence of holding types of organization both deserve some unpicking.

The structural transitions represented in Figures 6.7 and 6.8 underline the decline of the functional organization. Many functional firms simply drop out, due either to relative decline or to takeover. More successful firms seem to move equally to either functional-holding or divisional structures, just as the Harvard

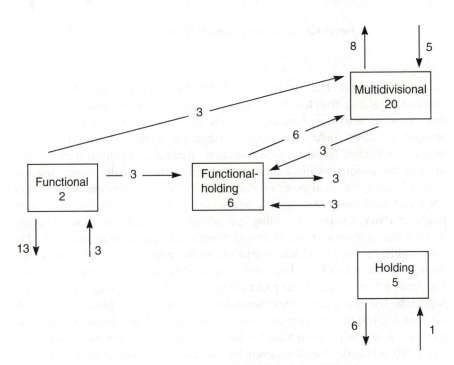

Figure 6.7. *Structural Change in Germany, 1970–83*

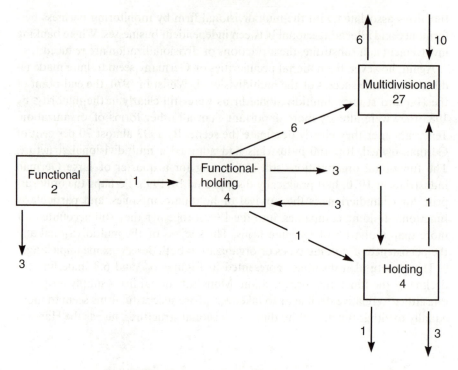

Figure 6.8. *Structural Change in Germany, 1983–93*

model would expect. The coal producer Ruhrkohle exemplifies the adoption of a functional-holding structure as a result of gradual diversification. Ruhrkohle's new non-coal activities were kept outside the functional core and formally brought together under the RAG-Beteiligungs GmbH. Under this RAG umbrella, so-called 'Führungsgesellschaften' (leading companies) were formed to head the various business areas. For instance, the partially owned Rütger-swerke became the focal point of Ruhrkohle's chemical activities. Other functional companies moved straight to multidivisionalization, as for example paper producer PWA. Despite remaining specialized as a single business company, in 1979 the company replaced its old functional organization with a highly decentralized structure, which, apart from minor adjustments, remained intact through to the mid-1990s. Ten, later nine, lead companies were grouped into four business areas (graphical papers, hygiene paper, packaging, and speciality papers) to balance synergy and responsiveness. PWA put in place a very 'lean' corporate centre that concentrated on financial control and developed strategic plans in close co-operation with the lead companies. The functional structure was rarely adequate, therefore, even for successful specialized firms. The only company to retain its functional structure through the whole period 1970–93 was the undiversified BMW, and even this would change after its unfortunate acquisition of the British car producer Rover in 1994.

The functional-holding structure, however, was more stable in Germany. Five companies managed to retain this structure in both periods (none retained this structure over the whole period 1970–93). There were also new entries such as the family-owned and controlled paper producer Haindl. Haindl's policy was to retain central control of its paper-making activities in Germany under the legal umbrella of the Haindl Papier GmbH. East German paper mills acquired in the early 1990s, for instance, were integrated into this main core of the company. However, paper-related activities outside of Germany and non-paper activities in Germany, notably a small airline (Interot), retained their independent status. Here the holding element assisted both internationalization and partial diversification, while allowing continued central control of the core.

However, internationalization of even fairly specialized businesses could also be managed by divisionalization. An example here is Volkswagen, originally a functional-holding company. Volkswagen made a number of international acquisitions, notably of Seat and Skoda, which were allowed to retain their legally independent status and put alongside the Audi and core 'Volkswagen' divisions. Nevertheless, the centralized heritage remained powerful, with central functions originating in the core business continuing to exert a strong influence more widely. It was product diversification that pushed another functional-holding company, Daimler Benz, towards divisionalization. The acquisition of electrical company AEG and aerospace manufacturer MBB were followed by the adoption of a multidivisional structure. The cultural and business dominance of the original automobile business has meant, however, that this structure has taken a long time to bed down (Hahn, 1994).

Just as theory would have it, the multidivisional organization does act as a sort of final resting point. Despite the substantial number of multidivisional firms only four multidivisional firms move away from this structure in almost a quarter century. Among the stable multidivisional firms we find all of the large German chemical companies—Bayer, BASF, and Hoechst—alongside diverse firms such as Deutsche Babcock and automotive supplier ZF-Friedrichshafen. The almost classic case of a multidivisional organization in Germany is the electrical company Siemens, whose historical commitment to this organizational form is recorded by Germany's leading business historian Kocka (1999) as an illustration of one of the earliest non-American multidivisional structures (see Illustration 6.3). These divisional structures could be used quite flexibly. ZF-Friedrichshafen, for instance, moved from a simple divisional structure towards a relatively complex structure with six divisions and three fully controlled German subsidiaries. Five of the divisions were product-oriented (commercial vehicles, car transmissions, off road transmissions, steering systems, suspension technology) and one had a regional orientation (North and South America).

Illustration 6.3. *Siemens: Established German Multidivisional*

Founded by Werner von Siemens in 1874 as Siemens & Halske, Siemens has played a central role in Germany's electrical industry and remains one of the most prestigious and established names in German industry. Throughout its early history the company has been closely associated with Germany's industrial development and for Chandler (1990) represents one of the first cases of multidivisional style management in Germany.

In the post-war era the company underwent two major structural changes, both of which were aimed at increasing the extent of decentralization and operational flexibility whilst maintaining the ability to exploit and develop organizational synergies. The first took place over the 1966–9 period. Here six, later seven, divisions were created. The company formed five central units for planning/organization, finance, personnel, R&D, and distribution. This structure was in place until 1989. Coming under pressure by both a significant increase in size as well as the rapid changes in the electrical and electronic markets, Siemens adopted a revised structure in 1989 which introduced smaller, more focused 'divisions'. It is notable that in contrast to trends in many other organizations (for example, at Daimler Benz) most of these were not given legally independent status. The initial exceptions to this rule were the OSRAM GmbH (founded in 1920 under participation of the AEG), the newly formed Siemens Nixdorf Informationssysteme AG, and, of course, the joint venture Bosch-Siemens.

Principal sources: Interview, *Manager Magazin*, September 1992; *Wirtschaftswoche*, 25 September 1992.

This structural development at ZF-Friedrichshafen was strongly influenced by pressures towards 'systems' selling in the automotive industry.

The success of the multidivisional in Germany is not quite complete, however. The story of the holding company in Germany has parallels with the surprising robustness of the conglomerate. Only two companies moved to holding company status in the whole period, 1970–93, and both of these, Tchibo and Henkel, were family-owned. There were a number of prominent holding company departures from the Top 100 ranks, most notably the two personalized Quandt and Flick groups. However, there was also a good degree of structural stability, the only holding company switching to a multidivisional structure, while retaining membership of the Top 100, being the conglomerate Gutehoffnungshütte. In this case, Gutehoffnungshütte only changed after severe financial crisis, leading to the former subsidiary MAN becoming the new corporate centre with more complete control of the firm's streamlined activities (see Illustration 6.4). It is notable, however, that many of the stable holdings had ownership peculiarities, such as VIAG and Zeiss, both with state connections, and the family owned Oetcker conglomerate. The 'purest' stable holding company is perhaps the AGIV. This company retained numerous partial participations in areas such as mechanical engineering, electronics, construction, and transport. With a small central staff, the AGIV only rarely intervened in the activities of its

Illustration 6.4. *GHH/MAN: From Failed Holding Company to
Successful Multidivisional*

The origins of MAN (Maschinenfabrik Augsburg Nürnberg), one of Europe's
leading capital goods producers, go back to 1840 when it was founded as a mechanical manufacturing company with early interests in printing machinery. The most
notable development during these early years, however, was the co-operation with
Rudolf Diesel in the development of the diesel engine. In 1921 MAN was integrated
into the GHH (Gutehoffnungshütte) which had grown out of one of the first
iron/steel firms in the German Ruhr area (founded in 1758). The GHH developed
into a widely diversified industrial concern with activities ranging from plant equipment and machinery to trucks, locomotives, cables, and shipbuilding. The GHH's
influence over its subsidiaries, however, remained by and large confined to its position on the various supervisory boards. Though there were attempts to implement
'planning' processes these were far from systematic and typically were restricted to
meetings at the location of the subsidiaries. The lack of a unified strategy combined
with the inability adequately to allocate and re-allocate financial resources contributed to a serious financial crisis. This led to a reformation of the firm under the
name MAN, which, although still highly decentralized, developed clear, multidivisional style management processes and systems. Corporation-wide accounting and
control systems were put into place as were corporate treasury functions and management development systems. The corporate centre provides certain services, such
as market research though R&D remains decentralized. In addition to its chairman,
the executive board comprises two members with corporate responsibilities (for
example, finance) and four chief executives of leading subsidiaries.

Principal sources: Interview, Liedtke, 1993.

subsidiaries. We shall return to the AGIV in the next chapter, exploring its
unique relationship to the BHF-Bank.

It is clear that these holdings are both a small minority and somewhat anomalous in terms of ownership. The corporate politics of ownership are the subject
of the next chapter. Here, however, we can conclude that the German experience
does indeed confirm Chandlerian expectations. By 1993 less than a third of the
studied firms fail to conform to the multidivisional template, leaving the role of
non-multidivisional firms only slightly more pronounced than in France. We will
reflect on the implications of this finding later, but now we turn to a country for
which the predictions of the institutionalists and those of the Harvard studies
point in the same direction, the United Kingdom.

United Kingdom

In the pre-war period Chandler (1990) clearly labels the United Kingdom as a
laggard in its investment in modern organizational capabilities. Later, however,

the United Kingdom emerged as a leader in the adoption of the multidivisional structure, significantly ahead of France and Germany by 1970 (Dyas and Thanheiser, 1976: 29). Institutional factors support this leadership in more recent times. As we have seen, by the 1980s and 1990s, British firms were much more likely to be under dispersed ownership and professional management than their Continental counterparts. Finance professionals, managing by numbers, were a powerful force in the boardroom. Diversification, moreover, had continued, ahead of France and equal to Germany. Yet observers of the British scene do sometimes like to have it both ways. Channon (1973) had admitted that the early divisional experiments were not as complete as the American, and since then critics have been happy to harp on about British structural weaknesses. For Guillén (1994: 265), the adoption of the multidivisional structure was often 'defensive' in style, state-led, and merely mimetic. Kogut and Parkinson (1993: 197) and Gospel (1992: 110–11) likewise suspect British multidivisionals, both because building on old holding companies and because distorted by the financial imperatives of conglomerate strategies. In these accounts, the British have been enthusiastic adopters of half-baked divisionalization.

Table 6.3 is compelling. Already in 1970 over 70 per cent of large, industrial British firms had opted for a multidivisional structure. By 1983 almost 90 per cent of firms were multidivisionals. Over the following time period the proportion of multidivisionals stabilized at this high level. Both functional and functional-holding companies have disappeared from the corporate landscape. In contrast to the two Continental countries, the intermediate step of a functional-holding structure seems very rarely to have been considered a viable option. Only in 1983 do we find any trace of such an organizational form. The fate of the holding company has been somewhat more varied. Between 1970 and 1983 it did undergo rapid decline, falling from more than a fifth to almost complete extinction. Over the following decade, however, there was some revival. Given the interest in holding-like networked forms, this is something worth exploring further through the transitional data. Overall, though, the statistics imply that,

Table 6.3. *Trends in Organizational Structure Among Domestic Top 100 Industrial Firms in the United Kingdom* (%)

	1950	1960	1970	1983	1993
Functional	—	—	8	4.0	1.5
Functional-holding	—	—	1	1.3	0
Holding	—	—	18	5.3	9.0
Divisional	6	22	74	89.3	89.5

Sources: 1950–70, Channon (1973); this study, 1983–93. Only divisional totals available before 1970

after its slow pre-war start, British industry has adopted the multidivisional with the enthusiasm of the convert.

The transitions data in Figures 6.9 and 6.10 confirm the overall picture. Between 1970 and 1983 only one firm maintains its functional structure, state-owned computer company ICL. The two multidivisional firms moving back to functional structures are also crisis-ridden state corporations, British Steel and Rolls Royce. By 1993, back in private ownership, both these companies have returned to multidivisional structures (see Illustration 6.5). ICL meanwhile had come under the control of Japanese company Fujitsu. None of the 1970 functional-holding companies survives as such within our group to 1983. The only functional-holding company of 1983, Guinness, had reverted to full holding company status by 1993, as it had been in 1970 (Channon, 1973). The company had by then largely recovered from the legacy of its 1980s chief execu-tive, the scandal-ridden Ernest Saunders, but with a third of its assets invested in French partner LVMH, it was still limited in the extent of central control over key activities. This is, perhaps, more a case of international networking than tra-ditional holding.

Some of the other holding companies also had substantial overseas activities

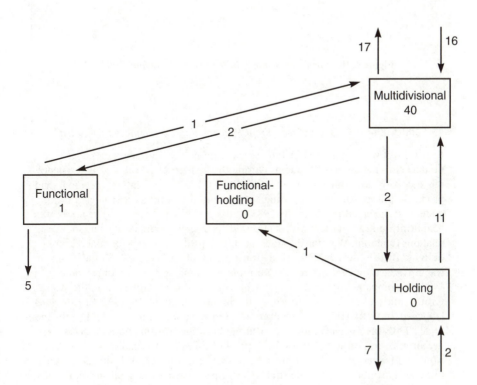

Figure 6.9. *Structural Change in the United Kingdom, 1970–83*

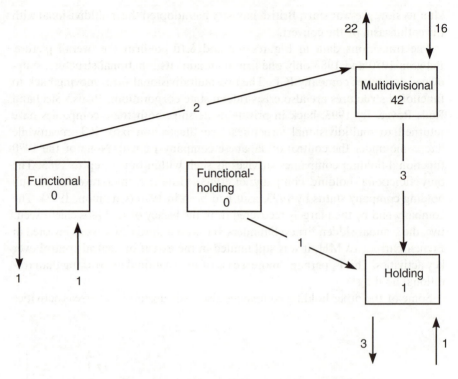

Figure 6.10. *Structural Change in the United Kingdom, 1983–93*

Illustration 6.5. *British Steel: From Functional to Divisionalized Specialist*

British Steel was established in 1967 to incorporate the fourteen nationalized steel producers in the United Kingdom. During the first ten or so years of its existence, the company experimented with various forms of organization—regional and product—but exerting an increasingly tight central control as it struggled to integrate its fragmented portfolio. By 1983 British Steel had 'divisions', but power was held firmly at headquarters with centralized commercial, purchasing, and industrial relations functions. With the divisions lacking control over policy for either inputs or outputs, British Steel was effectively functionally organized. In 1988 the company was privatized and moved to a more profit-accountable form of organization. In 1990 the company bought the major United Kingdom steel distributor, the Walker Group, and subsequently formed a distribution division. In 1992 British Steel launched its ORCHIDS reorganization—'Organization, Changes in Depth and Style'. This was designed radically to curtail headquarters functions and costs, and decentralize responsibility to twelve separate businesses. Crucially, business heads would no longer sit on the executive board but report to relatively detached executive board members. Corporate strategy and operations would finally be separated.

Principal sources: Interview; *International Directory of Company Histories*.

over which they had only partial control. Central control at RTZ, always noted for its lean management, was further handicapped by its minority position in the Australian company CRA, as well as other joint ventures. Caradon in 1993 still had a large proportion of its assets invested in the international Carnaud Metal Box joint venture, though was on track to dispose of them. Another holding company on the way to reform was Charter Consolidated, whose soon-to-be-sold stake in Johnson Matthey, a publicly quoted company, was equivalent to half its turnover. These were clearly reluctant 'networked' corporations, keen to become more strictly multidivisional. One traditional holding company was ABF, whose owner chairman operated a small head office and insisted on all subsidiary directors reporting directly to him rather than to any central executive committee. But ABF was the exception. Overall, there were few British holding companies, and, by 1993, many of these were marginal cases and clearly signalling imminent transformation to conventional multidivisional structures.

The multidivisional structure is overwhelmingly the dominant organizational form in late twentieth-century British industry. The period 1970–83 sees a rush of divisionalization among old established holding companies. Included here among companies making this transition are Babcock, John Brown, Hawker Siddely, Coats Viyella, Distillers, United Biscuits, Glaxo, Bowater, and Wellcome. The multidivisional form itself is highly stable in both time periods. Companies such as Allied Lyons, BICC, BAT, Burmah, Cadbury, ICI, RMC, Shell, and Unilever retain this structure over the entire period. A notably lower proportion of multidivisional firms drops out of the largest industrials, though the numbers are significant in absolute terms. To this point, the multidivisional effectively is the final 'chapter' of British enterprise.

As we compare the British experience with the French and German (Figure 6.11), we can see that all three countries have continued strongly to divisionalize through the 1980s and 1990s. This has been regardless of enduring national cultural and institutional differences, on the one hand, and the 'collapse of the American mystique' (Locke, 1996), on the other. In all three countries, nationally distinctive holding companies have declined, leaving the multidivisional accounting for the overwhelming majority of large firms. Both in France and the United Kingdom, the multidivisional had reached at least the same level of penetration as in the United States at the end of the 1960s (Rumelt, 1974); Germany lagged only slightly behind. The success of the multidivisional has been such that even single business firms have taken it up: by 1993, 77 per cent of remaining French single business firms, exactly half of German single business firms, and two-thirds of British single business firms had adopted the multidivisional structure. Given the nature of our firms as leading industrials, it seems that Williamson's (1970) scale effects are working for the multidivisional as well as Chandler's (1962) scope.

It is worth remarking on how British firms have consistently been the most advanced in adopting the multidivisional, right from 1950. This might surprise Chandler (1990) and elicit scepticism from those who suspect British managers

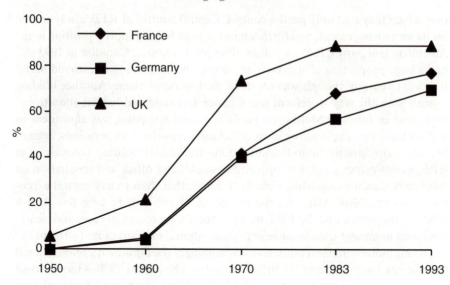

Figure 6.11. *Divisionalization in Europe, by Domestic Top 100 Firms*

of half-hearted acceptance of the multidivisional (Kogut and Parkinson, 1993; Gospel, 1992; Guillén, 1994). Yet the sheer numbers of multidivisionals, the long-standing nature of the structural arrangements, the scrutiny of capital markets, and the professionalism of management all seem to undercut the suggestion that British divisionalization is somehow less committed than French or German. Our interview experience tends to favour the British case as well. Granted, our interviews were not detailed audits, so we cannot tell for sure. Yet quite often, French and German managers would refer to quirks in their multi-divisional structures that were unusual in British firms. And even the British holding companies were typically less complex and opaque than their Continental counterparts. Our judgement is that the relative incompetence of British divi-sionalization is simply a canard.

6.3. THE NETWORK MULTIDIVISIONAL

Our interviews did, however, allow us to explore the question of multidivisional transformation. If we are to credit recent modish talk about new 'postmodern' (Volberda, 1998), 'federal' (Handy, 1992), 'network' (Miles and Snow, 1992), 'internal market' (Halal, 1993), or 'management holding' (Bühner, 1992) types of organization, then the multidivisional form itself is now as anachronistic as the functional or traditional holding forms. Allegedly, we are moving 'beyond the multidivisional' (Bartlett and Ghoshal, 1993; Ghoshal and Bartlett, 1998), even towards a new N-form (Hedlund, 1994). Times have certainly moved on since the birth of the original M-form in pre-war corporate America. All the same, we find little evidence for a fundamental break in organizing principles among our large industrials.

In Chapter 3 we suggested instead that some companies were developing flatter, more flexible, and horizontal organizations in the form of the 'network multidivisional'. We did find several examples of these kinds of initiatives and we detail the cases of Rhône-Poulenc (Aventis) and Unilever in particular (see Illustrations 6.6 and 6.7). However, in all of these cases the essential principle of decentralized operations and centralized corporate strategy, first emphasized by Alfred Chandler, seemed to be at least maintained intact, and in some respects extended.

Both Rhône-Poulenc and Unilever (see Illustrations 6.6. and 6.7) have been making equivalent organizational innovations to those at ABB, so often the model for new forms of organizing. Both invested heavily in more horizontal, cross-boundary network activities: at Rhône-Poulenc through the professional networks and the *comité d'orientation*; at Unilever through the innovation centres, the international business teams, and the functional networks. At both companies, too, these networks have strong informal and self-directive elements: 'synergies must appear of their own accord'. Vertical relationships have changed, as central services have been placed on a customer–contractor

---

Illustration 6.6. *Rhône-Poulenc: Decentralizing and Disentangling*

At the beginning of the 1990s, Rhône-Poulenc was France's largest chemicals company, with a turnover of over FF86,000m. State-owned, it had expanded rapidly overseas by acquisition, especially in the United States. Since 1969 the company had been based on a classic multidivisional structure, introduced by McKinsey itself and with eight main divisions. However, as it began to digest its acquisitions, the company recognized the need for further adaptation of its basic structure.

Jean-René Fourtou, PDG since 1986 and an ex-consultant himself (from Bossard, France's leading firm), reorganized Rhône-Poulenc around five sectors, split into a total of fifty Strategic Business Units. These SBUs were themselves broken down into typically three or more 'entreprises', each focused on a particular activity and market. It is these entreprises—about 300 in all—that became the effective profit centres. The SBUs themselves exist less as managerial sub-units than as groupings to bring together related entreprises for common strategic co-ordination and reflection. 'Country delegates' provide lateral co-ordination, representing Rhône-Poulenc locally as well.

This decentralization to entreprises has been reinforced by substantial changes at the centre. The headquarters staff was cut from 900 to 250. Central planning fell

(continued)

from 30 to 3 professional staff: the company stopped producing consolidated plans for Rhône-Poulenc as a whole. Formerly central functions were either decentralized towards sectors, as was R&D, or constituted as internal contracting central services, as was engineering. Remaining central functional staffs were now confined to the definition and auditing of central policies—of which there remained very few—and the cultivation of professional networks between decentralized operating units (for instance, the finance and R&D staffs networks).

The top *comité exécutif* was reduced (seven against nine members) and now included only three of the five sectoral chiefs. Meeting two days a month, it had a simplified agenda: overall group performance, with basic sectoral (rather than SBU or entreprise) figures; strategic items, for instance adjustments to the portfolio; and human resources. Human resources became a regular agenda item because the effectiveness of decentralization depends on the quality of its managers. The *comité exécutif* only reviewed sector investment decisions exceptionally. It considered its role as primarily allocating broad capital totals to sectors at the beginning of the year, the sectors themselves deciding how to spend them. Some oversight was maintained by the five *conseils de secteur*, typically including two or three members of the *comité exécutif* as well as representatives of central functions and meeting three times a year. It was up to the conseils and the sectoral presidents to decide whether to refer anything up to the *comité exécutif*—there were few compulsory rules. Treasury functions were centralized, however, and all sectors had to conform to common reporting systems.

Although the *comité exécutif* diffused clear statements of corporate vision, values, and management principles, it did not directly enforce internal co-operation from the top. In the words of a senior manager: 'The synergies must appear of their own accord; if they don't appear, they're not true synergies.' Within sectors, synergy was facilitated by the loosely structured SBUs and through interventions by sectoral management. Between sectors, synergy and other corporate strategic issues were addressed through the professional networks, internally contracted central services and the *comité d'orientation*, a group of sixty top managers from around the world who would meet three times a year for two-day seminars on key corporate themes. Common managerial training policies and extensive transfers between sectors, entreprises and countries reinforced personal networks. 'The problem of decentralisation is not a problem of organigrams. It is a problem of behaviour. . . . Decentralisation is not a design. It lies in the principles of management and the sort of people who go with it.'

In 1999 Rhône-Poulenc merged with the German chemicals company Hoecht to form a new European corporation, Aventis. The new corporation is to be decentralized into two main groups, Pharma and Agriculture, and its headquarters, with just 180 people, is being built at Strasbourg, the centre of Europe. The corporate language is now English.

Principal sources: Interview; internal documents; *L'Usine nouvelle*, 1 April 1993; *L'Expansion*, 21 October 1999.
Adapted with permission from Whittington, R. and Mayer, M. (1997). 'Beyond or Behind the M-Form', in H. Thomas, D. O'Neal, and M. Ghertman (eds.), *Strategy, Structure and Style*. Chichester: John Wiley. Copyright John Wiley & Sons Limited. Reproduced with permission.

Illustration 6.7. *Unilever: Fulfilling the Chandlerian Ideal*

The Anglo-Dutch Unilever is an international food and home and personal care group that radically reorganized during the 1990s. Traditionally Unilever had been highly decentralized in character, with a great deal of autonomy within the national subsidiary companies. During the late 1980s and early 1990s the company began to introduce new innovation and strategy processes, at the same time as clarifying its core businesses. However, the Shaping for Outstanding Performance programme launched in 1996 achieved a substantial change in structure as well.

Until 1996 power had been vested in a Special Committee—composed of the Dutch and UK company chairmen, plus the chairman designate—and a fifteen-person executive board, comprising functional, product, and regional directors. The structure as a whole was a matrix, with the product 'co-ordinators' (directors) having prime profit responsibility in Western Europe and the United States and regional directors having profit responsibility in remaining regions. Responsibilities often got blurred. According to an internal document: 'We need clarity of purpose and role: the board finds itself too involved in operations at the expense of strategic leadership.'

Shaping for Outstanding Performance abolished both the Special Committee and the regional director level. In its place was put an eight (later seven)-person executive committee made up of the chairmen plus functional and category (i.e. food and home and personal care) directors. Reporting to them, with clear profit responsibility, were thirteen (later twelve) Business Group presidents, typically with complete profit responsibility for their category within a particular region. Global strategic leadership was clearly placed at the level of the executive committee; operating performance was the direct responsibility of the business groups.

Beneath this formal structure, international co-ordination was facilitated by the existence of many formal and semi-formal networks. Research and development was assured by international networks of innovation centres, leadership typically going to centres of expertise rather than automatically to the Netherlands or the United Kingdom. Product and brand networks—International Business Teams—worked globally to co-ordinate branding and marketing. At the same time, functional networks worked on a succession of projects in order to achieve global co-ordination on critical issues, such as recruitment and organizational effectiveness. All these networks relied heavily on informal leadership and social processes, as well as increasing investment in electronic mail and intranet technology. Participation was largely determined and funded by the Business Groups rather than corporate headquarters.

Principal sources: Interviews and internal documents as part of the INNFORM programme on innovative forms of organizing, led by Professor Andrew Pettigrew (Pettigrew and Fenton, 2000).

principle at Rhône-Poulenc and the former category co-ordination functions at the centre of Unilever have moved into a facilitative role with the international business teams. Both companies have downsized or delayered: at Rhône-Poulenc by radically pruning headquarters staff; at Unilever by the elimination of the regional director level.

These kinds of initiatives are alien to the hierarchical and segmented multidivisionals of Chandler's and Williamson's original archetypes. Yet there are fundamental continuities. The simplified agenda of Rhône-Poulenc's *comité exécutif* is focused precisely on the broad strategic and monitoring issues of the classic multidivisional. Human resources have entered onto the agenda, but this is purely in line with the rise of knowledge and people as critical resources for strategic allocation and control. The formal strategic planning that was characteristic of an earlier generation of multidivisional has, on the other hand, been radically demoted at Rhône-Poulenc. At Unilever one of the driving motives for the Shaping for Outstanding Performance initiative was precisely the need to achieve the separation of strategy and operations. The new executive committee was explicitly removed from direct profit responsibility, with the Business Groups reporting to them from outside. Making some allowances for an earlier faith in planning, the rationale almost precisely echoes Chandler's (1962: 309) earlier diagnosis of the multidivisional's success: 'it clearly removed the executives responsible for the destiny of the entire enterprise from the more routine operational activities, and so gave them the time, information, and even psychological commitment for long-term planning and appraisal'.

Rhône-Poulenc and Unilever are both making significant organizational innovations. Their emphasis on horizontal networks is particularly novel and important. However, we do not conceive of these as representing a radical break, rather as utterly consistent with the notion of the 'network multidivisional'. Informal exchanges have always existed within organizations. The difference with the network multidivisional is both that it is so much more reliant on these unmanaged exchanges and that it is much more deliberate in creating the framework in which they can take place. Our conclusion, then, is that these innovative structures do not go 'beyond' the multidivisional; they simply extend and develop certain principles that were always more or less latent within either the ideal or the practice of previous multidivisionals. Moreover, the new features of this networked multidivisional do not make redundant those of previous generations: old considerations for capital allocation or scale and scope are not displaced, simply complemented by a more explicit concern for knowledge. In the same vein, the network model is no more likely to become a universally triumphant model than its predecessors. Just as the managerial model never extinguished the investor model, and the multidivisional as a whole has not entirely driven out the holding, so can we expect the network version finally to exist alongside other forms of organization, not to supersede them entirely. The appropriate model will depend, as ever, on contingency factors such as scale, scope, knowledge intensity, and both competitive and institutional environments (Whittington et al., 1999). We should abandon the language of 'beyond', with its teleological undertones, and talk more of 'beside'.

6.4. STRUCTURE AND PERFORMANCE

The multidivisional organization now dominates European industry. The trend began in the early post-war period and continued at least until the end-point of this study. Both for Chandlerians and organizational economists such as Williamson, this development is not surprising. In both traditions organizational change is ultimately seen to be driven by the relative efficiencies of alternative organizational arrangements. Both claim the multidivisional as the superior organizational form for the large, usually diversified, enterprises we are studying.

But these claims are now contested. National institutionalists insist that the multidivisional is not equally suited to all terrains. Where somehow foisted inappropriately, it is likely to suffer poor performance. International institutionalists deride the multidivisional as washed-up residue of American power. Even managerial critics of the multidivisional condemn it as a redundant anachronism, a mere 'fossil' (Bettis, 1991). Where still clung on to, again poor performance is likely to be the result. The superiority of the multidivisional is certainly now moot.

One simple cut on the multidivisional's performance is again to consider survival, as we did for diversification. We have already remarked on the relative stability of the multidivisional in our transitions analysis. Table 6.4 summarizes the survival rates from one period to another while remaining within the populations of Top 100 firms. The superior stability of the multidivisional is so striking, and the theoretical need to distinguish the long term is not so important, that we shall confine ourselves just to summarizing the shorter period survival patterns. The contrast between 1970 and 1983 and 1983 and 1993 is particularly

Table 6.4. *Structural Stability of Domestic Top 100 Survivors*

	Functional	Functional-holding	Divisional	Holding
France				
Per cent same structure: 1970–83	0	11.1	31.4	16.7
1983–93	25.0	33.3	56.9	15.4
Germany				
Per cent same structure: 1970–83	9.5	40.0	64.5	45.5
1983–93	33.3	28.6	79.4	66.7
United Kingdom				
Per cent same structure: 1970–83	14.3	0	65.6	0
1983–93	33.3	0	62.7	25.0

Sources: 1970 classifications based upon Channon (1973), and Dyas and Thanheiser (1976)

relevant: the first period being when the American hegemonic decline had just begun; the second being when it was emphatically confirmed. Following the international institutionalists, one might expect inferior stability for the multidivisional in the second period.

The summary of the shorter period transitions data in Table 6.4 is strong in its support for the multidivisional. Even in Germany the multidivisional is markedly the most stable structure, while in France and the United Kingdom its superiority is overwhelming. Quite contrary to expectations that one might draw from international institutionalist theory, the robustness of the multidivisional broadly increases over time, even as the influence of the United States declines. The only other structure to display even remotely comparable levels of sustainability is the German holding company, but this seems to be highly specific. Indeed, three German holdings—Oetker, Viag, and Zeiss—managed to sustain their structures through all twenty-three years 1970–93. No French or British holding survived as long. Both functional-holdings and pure functional structures appear largely unsustainable.

Our financial performance data broadly support the multidivisional's economic effectiveness across countries. The performance analysis is summarized in Figures 6.12–6.14. The analysis follows the same pattern as that of the strategic categories. The evaluation was conducted on a country-by-country basis, for two time periods each.[1] Although profitability may not be directly compared on a cross-national basis, the hierarchy of relative performances within nations categories can. We offer evaluations at two time periods to assess the extent to which performance relations may be time-sensitive or alter with learning effects. As in the previous chapter the analysis is based on the most popular financial performance measure of the field, return on assets. In order to eliminate any coincidental short-term fluctuations, three-year averages were used with 1983 and 1993 as mid-points (Robins and Wiersema, 1995). We should be alert to the danger that the average performance attributed to small structural categories— effectively all categories bar multidivisional—may easily be distorted by the exceptional performance of just one or two firms.[2]

At first glance, there is no overwhelming evidence from Figures 6.12–6.14 that multidivisional firms out-perform non-multidivisionals. In France multidivisional and functional-holding firms perform well in both time periods. In 1983 there is even a slight advantage for the functional-holding form with companies such as Arjomari-Prioux, Essilor, and Perrier achieving good

---

[1] A fuller regression analysis of performance, controlling, for instance, for strategy and industry membership, is provided in Mayer (1999). This analysis does not substantially alter our main conclusions here.

[2] The distribution of firms by structure for which there was adequate financial data for inclusion in the performance analysis was as follows (1983/1993): France: functional, 2/0; functional-holding, 5/5; holding, 9/8; multidivisional, 38/41; Germany: functional, 4/2; functional-holding, 13/6; holding, 5/6; multidivisional, 29/40; United Kingdom: functional, 2/1; functional-holding, 1/0; holding, 3/6; multidivisional, 61/60.

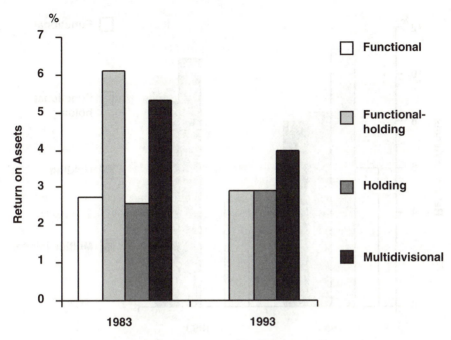

Figure 6.12. *Structure and Performance in France*

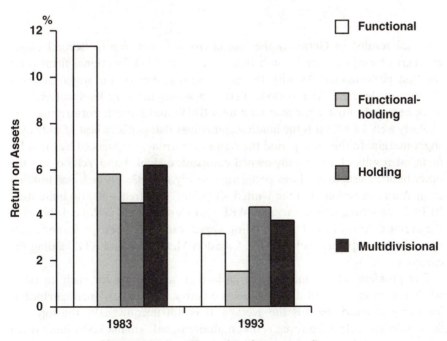

Figure 6.13. *Structure and Performance in Germany*

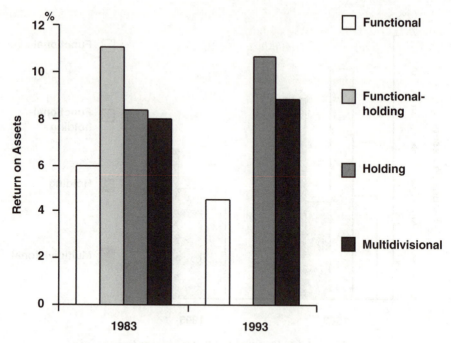

Figure 6.14. *Structure and Performance in the United Kingdom*

financial results. In Germany the multidivisional firms are in 'second place' in terms of performance in both time periods. In 1983 functional firms offer the best performance. As with the good performance of the single business strategy in the same time period, there is a strong industry level influence at work here, with luxury car manufacturers BMW and Porsche performing particularly well. In 1993 it is the holding companies that perform best, if only by a slight margin. In this time period the results are strongly influenced by the solid financial results of two family-owned companies, Henkel and Tchibo. On the other hand, German holdings performed poorly in 1983. Though few holding companies can be found in the United Kingdom, they frequently do quite well. In 1983 the strong performance of ABF and Consolidated Goldfields boosted the average. Again in 1993 the holding appears to be the best performing category, with companies such as ABF, Caradon/Metal Box, and RTZ leading the category.

The problem for the multidivisional is that, accounting for such an overwhelming proportion of firms in each country, its financial performance is inevitably dragged towards the average. It is not unequivocally the top performer. What is clear, however, is that multidivisionals are markedly more often near the top of the ranking than the bottom. Their average performance is either best or second best in five out of six possible comparison points.[3] None of the other structures does so well, with their average performances fluctuating wildly. We have seen already that the multidivisional is typically a stable structure over time. Here it seems that, financially as well, the multidivisional is a solid and consistent performer. There is no evident national bias—the country where the multidivisional does marginally worst turns out to be the United Kingdom. Again, the multidivisional meets Chandlerian expectations for performance, in terms of robustness at least.

6.5. SUMMARY

Corporate organization in Europe has changed dramatically. In the early 1950s almost no multidivisional firms were to be found. Forty years later the massive majority of large industrial firms had adopted this American invention. In the United Kingdom, which has been at the forefront of multidivisionalization since the early post-war period, the transformation has been almost complete. Notwithstanding Chandler's (1990) scolding for the pre-war period, the British have proved themselves now to be no slouches at divisionalization. In France and Germany there are still small groups of functional-holding and holding companies clinging on—we shall explore these further in the next chapter. Even so, the overwhelming majority of companies in both countries have divisional-ized and the trend is steadily in the upwards direction. National institutions seem to offer little obstacle. Fashionable swings against the modernistic multidi-visional have altered the fundamental logics of organization not at all.

In the network economy, the multidivisional is changing, but it is not going. Its essential principle of operational decentralization is only being accentuated by the extreme fragmentation into many small operating units practised by com-panies such as ABB, Rhône-Poulenc, and Unilever. This fragmentation is far from the old anarchy of the holding company. In the 'network multidivisional', advanced information systems continue to ensure tight headquarters control. In a sense, the multidivisional is further perfecting itself in its combination of extreme operational decentralization with heightened surveillance from the centre. Indeed, the multidivisional principle of operational decentralization is now finding itself increasingly relevant even to undiversified companies. Most of our single business companies had adopted the multidivisional structure by 1993. Once adopted, moreover, the multidivisional structure is rarely aban-doned. By and large, the multidivisional offers the best chance of steady and respectable financial returns.

[3] A similar comparison of the performance of diversified multidivisionals with non-diversified multidivisionals showed superior performance for the former in both time periods in France and Germany, and in 1982–4 in the United Kingdom. There is some support here for divisionalization fitting better to scope, following Chandler (1962), than to scale, following Williamson (1975).

This is good news for the new management sciences. In broad terms, the general principles of corporate organization developed by Alfred Chandler in the early 1960s have proved correct. These principles have stood the tests of time and place remarkably well. Although the speed of change may differ, all three major European economies are going steadily in the same direction. The trend is driven by pursuit of a basic but constantly developing source of organizational advantage. Managerial knowledge does appear to be transferable across national boundaries and renewable over time. The multidivisional was not simply foisted on Europe at a time of relative weakness. Although it may not do so always, for the moment at least it seems that the changing multidivisional still offers the most efficient, transparent, and accountable means for organizing the large corporations of contemporary business life.

7

Strategy, Structure, and Politics

INTRODUCTION

As the last two chapters have shown, big business in post-war Western Europe has been moving steadily towards the model of the diversified, divisionalized firm pioneered in the United States in the 1920s. Details of the original model may have changed, but the core has proved remarkably robust. By and large, related diversification and multidivisional structures appear to offer stable end-points in corporate development. Equally, they seem to yield good performance pretty consistently across time and countries. All this is against a background of distinct and enduring national institutions of ownership, control, and manager-ial careers. There seems little sign here that national systems affect either the dif-fusion or the performance of the American model. Economic generalizations predict better than sociological contextualism.

Yet we do know from Chapter 4 that France and Germany especially are still rife with the kinds of institutional idiosyncrasies that appear very 'unAmeri-can'. Personal ownership is still common; many firms are still run by founders or their successors; the state meddles, especially in France; and firms frequently risk compromising their strategic interests by taking or accepting shareholdings in other firms. It seems that the prevalence of these institutional idiosyncrasies does not introduce system-wide distortions. However, it is quite possible that such idiosyncratic conditions might make a difference to particular firms, in a manner easily obscured by aggregate trends. After all, the previous two chapters have left us with anomalies still to be explained, particularly the survival of single business firms in France and the stubborn conglomerates and holding companies of Germany. These anomalies may not be large enough to ascribe to system effects, but they are persistent enough to deserve more exploration.

This chapter, then, picks up the American corporate political work of Fligstein (1987) and Palmer et al. (1987; 1993), to examine the strongest likely particular effect, that of different kinds of ownership upon strategy and struc-ture at the level of the individual firm. The chapter begins by spelling out the kinds of ownership effects frequently predicted, whether of families and entre-preneurs, of banks and financial institutions, of the state or of other firms. It then goes on to examine the actual impacts of these different kinds of owner-ship in the three countries. We shall find that many kinds of shareholder have been unjustly accused. Families, banks, and the state are all more or less equally competent and enthusiastic in following the economic logics of diversification and divisionalization.

7.1. THE POLITICS OF STRATEGY AND STRUCTURE

The corporate political approach we shall take up here makes use of many of the institutional characteristics emphasized by the national institutionalists, but points them in the opposite direction. Again, ownership, control, and dominant managerial expertise are argued to influence corporate strategy and structure in certain ways (Fligstein, 1987; Fligstein and Brantley, 1992; Palmer et al., 1993). However, unlike the national institutionalists, the political approach is interested more in how these factors may motivate deviations from system norms rather than conformity to them. The approach is 'political' because these deviations are explained in terms of the self-interest, defined in various ways, of powerful actors.

We shall focus on the influence of potentially the strongest political resource, ownership. Ever since Berle and Means (1932), social scientists have worried about the implications of different forms of ownership for business behaviour. Fears go in two directions. We have seen that the Harvard group itself was concerned about the effects of continuing family ownership and control, especially in the United Kingdom of the pre-war period (Chandler, 1990). Incompetently managed and overly obsessed with income and security, family firms were held to have unduly resisted both the demands of diversification and the disciplines of the multidivisional form. Principal-agent theorists, however, reverse the argument. Their fear is that, in the absence of strong shareholders, firms will fall into the hands of sectional managerial interests. Careless of shareholder rights, managers will pursue prestige and income through excessive growth and diversification rather than return surplus funds to their rightful owners (Marris, 1964; Roll, 1986). Here managers are a barrier to good practice.

Fligstein and Brantley (1992) and Palmer et al. (1993) have extended these kinds of argument to test formally the effects of different forms of ownership on corporate strategy and structure in large American firms. The focus is not on system-wide patterns of ownership, but on how particular types of ownership in particular cases might distort strategy and structure from the dominant pattern. In this account, families and entrepreneurs are preoccupied with control. Personal ownership is held to obstruct adoption of the multidivisional form because of its implications for decentralization and accountability. Diversification is restricted because of the risk of increasing dependence upon external sources of finance or on professional managers. Firms with significant bank ownership are similarly supposed to be more resistant to the diversified, divisionalized ideal. Banks are reluctant to support diversification because able to spread their risks perfectly adequately through stakes in separate firms. They are suspicious of the multidivisional for fear of its challenge to the banks' role in capital allocation. Firms without powerful shareholders, on the other hand, are supposed to have fallen under managerial control. Either through sheer professional profit maximization, or through self-interested aggrandizement, such firms are deemed likely to be enthusiasts for growth by diversification and, possibly, divisionalization.

In the United States, the evidence for such politically motivated influences on strategic and structural choice is quite patchy (Fligstein and Brantley, 1992; Palmer et al., 1993). However, Europe may represent more fertile ground for the play of political influences. On the one hand, as we have seen, European business is characterized by the prevalence of very significant private ownership interests, much more than in the United States. On the other hand, European decision-makers may enjoy a greater margin of discretion as less oppressed by the disciplines of an active market for corporate control or large, open product markets. Moreover—unlike in the United States where antitrust plays such a strong role and the state acts chiefly from the wings—in Europe there are two further important types of interest that frequently hold power in large corporations. First, as we have seen, the state is still a substantial shareholder in many European firms, especially in France. Second, many large European firms, particularly in France and Germany, are constrained by the presence of substantial shareholding stakes from other large industrial firms. It is very likely that the state as shareholder will not pursue the theoretically profit-maximizing strategy of related diversification, either ignoring new business opportunities or tacking them on to existing businesses for reasons of political convenience more than real economic synergy (Dyas and Thanheiser, 1976: 166–71). For political reasons, too, states may prefer the opaque flexibility of the holding over the strict disciplines of the multidivisional. Again, firms under the ownership of other firms may find themselves constrained from diversification for reasons of conflicting interests, so that they will restrain themselves to narrower portfolios than they would freely adopt (Dyas and Thanheiser, 1976: 80–8).

As we trace the effect on strategy and structure of particular ownership configurations, we shall be following directly in the tracks of American scholars such as Fligstein and Palmer. However, we shall be exploring a relatively novel path in considering systematically the implications of state ownership and firm ownership, issues neglected in the United States. We shall also recognize the complexity of the European financial system by separating out the effects of bank ownership from ownership by other kinds of financial institution. Here there is little guidance from previous studies, but given the strikingly different positions of banks and financial institutions in the United Kingdom and the two Continental European economies, the distinction is due. As we may recall from Chapter 4, in the United Kingdom, banks are negligible while other financial institutions are pervasive, if rather weak. In France and Germany, on the other hand, banks are frequently major shareholders, alongside a range of other powerful financial institutions. It is not theoretically clear whether these other financial institutions, typically insurance companies, will have the same resistance to diversification and divisionalization as attributed to banking interests. These financial institutions are at least as capable of diversifying on their own account as banks, but they may be less disturbed by the multidivisional's role in capital allocation. A further implication of the complex European pattern of ownership is that we should explore effects by country rather than by simple pooling: the size of typical stakes held by banks and financial institution varies widely between the United Kingdom and the Continental countries, so their impacts on strategy and structure are not likely to be the same. We shall also explore these effects separately according to the two time periods, 1983 and 1993, to test for their consistency over time.

Our measures and categories for ownership are the same as in Chapter 4. Firms with no shareholders with 5 per cent or more of the voting stock are classified as under dispersed ownership and implicitly under managerial control, as in the agency and corporate governance literatures (Schleifer and Vishny, 1996; Palmer et al., 1987, 1993). Key owners of firms under more concentrated ownership are identified broadly according to the schema developed in the American studies of Palmer et al. (1987, 1993), distinguishing between personal ownership, bank ownership, and ownership by other financial institutions. We shall add two ownership categories particularly relevant to the European context, that is the state and other non-financial firms. To save clumsiness, we shall generally describe firms as 'personally owned', 'state owned', and so on where there exists a 5 per cent or larger stake, whether or not the stake is majority. In that sense, a particular firm may be 'owned' by two or more sorts of institution. As before, we are concerned with just the home-based members of the Top 100 industrials in each country. Our strategy categories are Rumeltian.

7.2. OWNERSHIP AND STRATEGY

France

We start with a country where the stakes of banks and financial institutions are both increasingly prevalent and typically quite large (see Chapter 4). France is also a country with a surprisingly robust pattern of family and entrepreneurial ownership and a persistent state sector. Many large industrial firms are also under the partial ownership of other industrial firms. There are reasonable theoretical grounds to expect all these factors to inhibit diversification.

As we cast our eyes over the patterns of strategy adoption in Figures 7.1. and 7.2, what is generally most striking is the absence of any consistent effect over time. It is true that in 1983 firms under dispersed ownership and hence without any dominant shareholder constraints are more enthusiastic for diversification

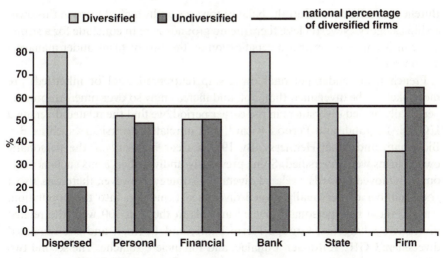

Figure 7.1. *Ownership and Diversification in France, 1983*

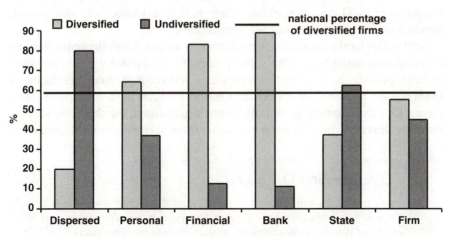

Figure 7.2. *Ownership and Diversification in France, 1993*

than almost any other category, just as both Chandlerian and agency theory might predict: 80 per cent of firms under dispersed ownership (in other words, with no shareholder holding more than 5 per cent of the equity) are diversified. However, in the next period, this effect is precisely reversed: now only 20 per cent of firms under dispersed ownership are diversified. This reversal should, of course, be understood in relation to the relatively small number of firms under dispersed ownership. With some diversified firms such as Sellier Leblanc and SAT dropping out, new entries by the dominant business firms Arcadie and

Burelle are sufficient to shift the balance towards undiversified firms in this ownership category. Nevertheless, there are no grounds here to conclude for a strong and consistent bent towards diversification on the part of firms under managerial control.

French firms under personal ownership (entrepreneurial or inherited) are more likely to be diversified than not, and increasingly so over time. Among the personally owned diversifiers in the earlier period, we find the related diversified L'Oréal, Legrand, and Pernod Ricard, and unrelated diversifiers such as Bic, Biderman, and Moët-Hennessy. By 1993 a clear majority of the personally owned firms were diversified. Some previously undiversified firms such as Guyomarc'h moved towards a related diversified strategy. However, there was also a good number of personally owned diversified firms new into the population. Among these new personally owned arrivals in the Top 100 were the related diversifiers Chargeurs, Groupe Pierre Fabre, and Labinal, and the unrelated diversifiers CGIP, Taittinger, Fimalac, and Financière Agache. The second two of these were fast-growing entrepreneurial creations, but the first two were old-established family groups. As the example of CGIP indicates (Illustration 7.1), such old family groups could re-invent themselves to invest in dynamic new sectors such as IT and consulting. There is little evidence here that French personal capitalism was strategically conservative.

Neither did banks constrain diversification—indeed, quite the opposite. The overwhelming majority of firms with significant banking stakes were diversified in both periods. Rare exceptions pursuing undiversified strategies included Olida et Caby in the earlier period and Ciments Français in the later period. The picture for other financial institutions is not so consistent, but the tendency is in the same direction. In 1983 firms with other financial institutions as significant

Illustration 7.1. *The CGIP: Ancient French Holding*

The Compagnie générale d'industrie et participations (CGIP) is the holding company of the de Wendel family, able to trace its history back to Lorraine steel interests established in 1704. Effective nationalization of its core business, Sacilor, in 1978 stimulated a significant reorientation and revival around a more dynamic set of interests. By 1993 these interests included a 25 per cent stake in CarnaudMetalbox (independently quoted), a dominant stake in the information technology and consulting group Cap Gemini Sogeti (also independently quoted), and a 55 per cent stake in CEDEST, a cement company (again independently quoted). The group was managed actively by the Baron Ernest-Antoine Seillière de Laborde. Seillière de Laborde was not just the nephew of Henri de Wendel, the eighth in a line of de Wendel industrialists stretching back nearly three hundred years, he was also an énarque, graduate of Harvard and former protégé of the influential Michel David-Weil, director of the powerful Lazard Frères investment bank.

Principal sources: *Tertiel*, 38, July 1988; *L'Expansion*, 3–16 June 1988.

shareholders were equally balanced between diversification and non-diversification. Given the overall preference for diversification by then in France, some inhibiting affect might be attributed. However, by 1993 all firms with stakes from other financial institutions were diversified. Despite their power in France, it is hard to maintain that French banks and financial institutions resisted corporate diversification out of their own self-interest.

However, it should be noted that banks and other financial institutions in France were very frequently co-owners alongside other substantial interests. For instance, in 1983 Hachette and Perrier, both related diversified firms, were under the joint ownership of a financial institution and a personal owner, while the conglomerate Beghin-Say was jointly owned by Suez and the Italian Ferruzi group. The same is true of banks, so that Crédit Lyonnais was a minority partner in power-station producer Framatome, alongside the state nuclear energy company CEA, and in Aérospatiale, alongside the French state.

This observation leads us to the state-owned firms, a group of considerable significance in the French economy. Here we again find a switch in the relative frequency of undiversified and diversified firms between 1983 and 1993, but this time against diversification. In 1983 a small majority of state-owned firms were diversified. Most of these were related diversifiers, for instance Aérospatiale, CEA, CGE, EMC, IMETAL, and Pechiney. However, there was also the formerly private conglomerate Boussac Saint-Frères, undergoing a state-led rescue, and Charbonnages de France, the state-owned coal company attempting to diversify out of decline. By 1993 less than 40 per cent of state-owned firms were diversified. This was partly as a result of privatization of diversified companies such as CGE, Boussac, and Pechiney, and partly because of the refocusing of some formerly diversified companies such as Charbonnages de France and EMC. The other undiversified state-owned firms were predominantly sectoral national champions, for instance Renault in automobiles, Usinor Sacilor in steel, and Bull in computers. It could be said, therefore, that by the end of our period state ownership was associated with non-diversification. However, examination of particular cases does not reveal this influence to be necessarily reactionary. Many of the state-owned undiversified firms were in sectors such as automobiles, steel, and computers, where substantial specialization is in fact the global norm; others were firms that had undergone much needed rationalization. If the state did constrain diversification, it did not do so for obviously special reasons.

The other distinctive feature of Continental Europe is the role of other (non-financial) firms in the ownership of industrial corporations. Stakeholdings by such other firms are expected to inhibit diversification. It is true that in 1983 a clear majority of externally held firms still followed undiversified strategies. Here are included single business firms Ciments Français (in that year still without bank involvement), Roquette, and Sacilor, as well as dominant business companies such as Carnaud, Chausson, Peugeot, and Poclain. In many of these

Again we begin our considerations with the firms under dispersed ownership, where managerial interests are expected to drive firms towards excessive diversification. As in France we need to recall that this category is relatively insignificant: in Germany, most firms are under concentrated ownership. As the data show, those firms that are under dispersed ownership have typically opted for a diversified strategy. With only 20 per cent of firms remaining undiversified in 1983 this was even more pronounced in this earlier time period than in 1993, where the figure held at not quite 29 per cent. Taking the two years together, we can certainly accept that dispersed ownership favoured diversification, but by 1993 at least there is no case for managerial excess.

Personal ownership, on the other hand, is expected to inhibit diversification. The French findings already cast some doubt on this assumption, but Germany is different as lacking a vigorous entrepreneurial class (see Chapter 4). Nevertheless, despite the growing proportion of inherited personal ownership in Germany, the tendency is broadly the same as in France. True, in 1983 a higher proportion of firms under personal ownership is undiversified than for those under dispersed ownership, but by 1993 the reverse obtains. Moreover, in both time periods companies in some of the other categories, such as those under ownership of other firms, are more likely to be undiversified. And, most obviously, in both time periods most firms under personal ownership are diversified.

The single business firms under personal ownership include the luxury car manufacturer Porsche, owned by the related families Porsche and Piëch; and BMW, in which the Quandt family holds significant shares. It is quite notable that both firms have not attempted to follow (bank-backed) Daimler Benz in diversifying further afield, opting instead to remain close to their core business. For BMW this is defined slightly more broadly and includes its well-known motorcycle production. BMW, however, at least tried to expand within its own specialization, attempting to rehabilitate the ailing British Rover company. The Quandt family also is engaged with a further single business company included in both 1983 and 1993, the battery producer Varta (see Illustration 7.2). A number of undiversified firms under personal ownership in 1983 later passed out of the control of the respective families or entrepreneurs. Some fell under the control of larger concerns, such as the computer company Nixdorf and sportswear company Adidas, whilst the ball-bearing manufacturer FAG-Kugelfischer passed into dispersed ownership. The diversified firms under personal ownership were largely more successful at retaining their independent status in the Top 100 to 1993. Here we include related diversified companies such as engineering company Benteler, the white goods manufacturer Miele, and the media companies Springer and Bertelsmann. Successful unrelated family-owned companies include Oetcker, with a wide range of participations in banks, brewers, hotels, and private clinics, and Tchibo, involved in both coffee and, through its stake in Beiersdorf, cosmetics.

The largest participation in Beiersdorf, however, is that of German insurance

Illustration 7.2. *Quandt: Shaping Germany's Industrial Landscape*

As one of Germany's leading industrialist families, the Quandt family has historical associations with four of the largest German industrial enterprises in 1993: the chemical and foods company Altana, the automobile manufacturers BMW and Daimler Benz, and the battery producer VARTA. The roots of the Quandt family's industrial heritage lie in the textile manufacturing activities of Emil Quandt, begun in the later years of the nineteenth century. Under the leadership of Emil's son, Günther Quandt, the family's interests soon expanded significantly in both scale and scope with the Accumulatorenfabrik AG (the later VARTA AG) becoming the core of its industrial holdings. The rise of the Quandt family as a major force in Germany's industrial landscape, however, is associated with the name of Herbert Quandt, who assembled a diversified set of industrial holdings in areas such as chemicals, mechanical engineering, and automobiles. The most noteworthy move came in 1959, when Herbert Quandt gained effective control of BMW in the wake of a severe financial crisis that had threatened the survival of the automobile manufacturer. Although remaining a minority partner, Quandt also played a significant role at Daimler Benz. With the strategic development of Daimler Benz over the late 1960s and early 1970s effectively being negotiated between Quandt, the Deutsche Bank, and Flick, Dyas and Thanheiser (1976) ascribe the limited involvement of Daimler Benz in the restructuring of the automobile industry during that era, as well as its long reluctance to diversify, to disagreements between the three owners. In 1977 the Quandt holding company was divided, with Altana and VARTA, among others, gaining independent status. Herbert Quandt himself continued as chief executive of the Altana AG until 1980. Throughout the 1980s and 1990s various branches of the Quandt family retained controlling interests in Altana, BMW, and VARTA, with Johanna Quandt emerging as the family's most prominent representative.

Principal sources: www.h.-quandt-stiftung.de (1999); Dyas and Thanheiser (1976).

giant Allianz. We should turn then to the role of financial institutions, starting with non-banking institutions such as the Allianz insurance giant. In 1983 the level of diversification among firms with significant financial institutional shareholders is close to the average at 60 per cent. Notable among the Allianz's participations at this time was Daimler Benz, which was soon to embark on a radical strategy of diversification, and the conglomerate GHH. By 1993 all firms with non-banking financial institutions as significant shareholders had become diversified. There is no evidence here that these financial institutions are reluctant to delegate the diversification of risk to their corporate partners.

As in the case of Daimler Benz, where Deutsche Bank was the dominant shareholder, these non-banking financial institutions are often shareholders alongside powerful banks. Banks occupy a controversial role in the German economy, but from the data here there is little evidence that they exert an undue influence. There is little difference between the diversification pattern of bank owned firms and those with other types of shareholders, apart from non-financial companies. Most of the companies we can mention here are familiar already, such as BMW, Daimler Benz, and GHH. Others are the unrelated diversified Preussag, whose activities range from metals, to petroleum and chemicals, to construction, coal, and transport. The clearest connection between bank ownership and firm strategy is, however, to be found in the relationship between the Berliner Handels und Frankfurter Bank (BHF) and the AGIV. The AGIV was effectively formed to manage the BHF's existing participations in industrial and transport companies, thus contributing to the diverse profile of the AGIV in 1983 and 1993 where its activities ranged from construction, a wide range of mechanical engineering activities, as well as energy and transport services. We shall return to consider this company again in our discussions of the relationships between ownership and structure. For the moment, we can see that far from wanting to inhibit diversification, for BHF the AGIV's strategy was the means to manage its diversification.

State ownership in Germany is clearly much less significant than in France. Nevertheless, where state authorities are engaged, there is no indication that this has restrained diversification—if anything state-owned firms are more likely to have diversified than their counterparts in other ownership categories. In 1983 many of the state participations were in the expected sectors of energy and heavy industry, as for instance in the cases of company Saarbergwerke and steel firm Salzgitter. The unrelated diversified status of the VIAG in 1983 is due to its role in managing many of the German federal state's industrial participations. Although the federal state began to sell off its holding over the decade, the Bavarian state developed its influence via the relationship between the Bayernwerk, Bavaria's state-owned energy concern, and the VIAG. It is clear, anyway, that the German federal state can be absolved of any resistance to diversification.

As we have mentioned, inter-firm ownership is particularly common in Germany and this might readily introduce constraints on diversification. There is certainly evidence for this in 1983 when firm-owned is the only category for which we can identify more undiversified than diversified firms. By 1993 the balance had shifted, but still firms with other firms as shareholders were the least likely to be diversified. Often there are good business reasons for the specialization of these quasi-subsidiary firms. For example, the Oberrheinische Mineralölwerke (OMW) conducts refining activities and is owned by a number of oil and energy companies, including VEBA. The Norddeutsche Affinerie, part owned by the chemicals and metals firm Degussa, has similarly remained focused on its metals business. In these cases, it is not clear whether the emphasis should be put on the restrictions to diversification imposed on quasi-subsidiaries or on the limited vertical integration of the dominant shareholding firm. Where firm-owned companies have diversified, however, they have often opted for the tighter knit related strategy. This is evident at the paper producer

PWA, part owned by the Bayernwerk, and the Klöckner-Werke (see Figure 4.2). There are, therefore, some signs of restraint on diversification exerted by firm shareholdings, but, as in the case of partial integration, these are not always obviously for reasons of political self-interest.

Last of all we should consider the enduring anomaly of the German conglomerate. As we saw in Chapter 5, Germany is remarkable for the importance and staying power of its conglomerates. Six conglomerates survived from 1970 to 1993 with their basic strategic orientation unchanged: Bosch, Krupp, Linde, Oetcker, Preussag, and Röchling. In all of these cases, it may be that the presence of large, understanding shareholders provided an effective guarantee for the security of this otherwise typically unstable strategy. Bosch was firmly in the hands of the Robert Bosch Stiftung and the original Bosch family. Krupp, too, had a powerful family foundation involved, with the Alfred Krupp von Bohlen und Halbach-Stiftung the majority shareholder. Oetker was wholly family-owned. At Linde and Preussag close relationships with financial institutions may have helped. In the case of Linde the Allianz was the largest shareholder, with 14 per cent in 1993, with other major stakes held by Commerzbank and Deutsche Bank. The Westdeutsche Landesbank owned 30 per cent of Preussag (as well as a substantial stake in Krupp). Röchling was family-controlled. While it is clear that families and financial institutions will readily support the more approved strategy of related diversification, it is noticeable that all the most enduring conglomerates do have these large stakes. Powerful families and financial institutions by no means insist on conglomerate strategies, but their support is highly valuable for firms wishing to resist rationalization.

Ownership interests, therefore, do play some role in Germany, but not quite as expected. As in France, though to a lesser degree, banks and other financial institutions are supporters of diversification. Despite the growing decrepitude of personal capitalism in Germany, firms under personal ownership do not by and large resist diversification. Indeed, there are some instances of striking family loyalty to conglomerate diversification. The rather incestuous linkages between German industrial firms do restrain diversification levels in aggregate, but examination of particular cases often reveals the problem to be more of limited vertical integration. Throughout it is clear that the corporate politics of ownership are neither simple nor deterministic.

The United Kingdom

The relationship between ownership and diversification in the United Kingdom is likely to be very different from that in France and Germany. Whereas concentrated ownership is the norm in the two Continental countries, the majority of firms in the United Kingdom lacks any single shareholder above 5 per cent. One result is that a number of ownership categories are either marginal or nonexistent. We shall therefore not consider bank ownership in any of the time

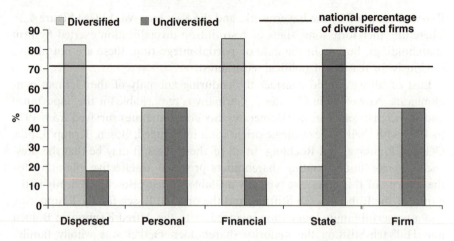

Figure 7.5. *Ownership and Diversification in the United Kingdom, 1983*

periods, whilst state ownership is only relevant in 1983. Another issue is that where there is some concentration, the level of shareholding is typically still quite small, as in the case of insurance companies where stakes are always less than 10 per cent. Strong political effects are not, therefore, to be expected.

Clearly, British firms with some concentrated ownership are already exceptional by this very fact. However, this makes little consistent difference to their strategies. It is true that in 1983 firms with dispersed ownership were markedly more diversified than the generality of firms with concentrated ownership, but in 1993 this no longer holds true at all (Figures 7.5 and 7.6).[1] For both periods firms with financial institutions as substantial shareholders seem as enthusiastic diversifiers as the rest. By the early 1990s all firms under personal ownership are diversified.

In the British case, therefore, there is not much of an ownership problem to be explained at all. However, since the United Kingdom's pre-war personal capitalists have been particularly the butt of Alfred Chandler (1990), it is worth pausing momentarily to consider their more recent energy. Neither Lord Hanson, coming from a well-established business family but creator of Hanson Trust, or third-generation Gary Weston of ABF, showed much sign of family decadence. Hanson created the prototypical Anglo-American conglomerate of the 1980s (Brummer and Cowe, 1994), while Weston acquired British Sugar at the age of 65. The family-controlled Pearson Group was busy in newspapers, publishing, television, family attractions, and even banking. Entrepreneurs such as Green at Carlton and Solomon and Thompson at Hillsdown were vigorously

---

[1] Figure 7.6 excludes the state and bank-owned categories on grounds of small numbers: only one-third of these are diversified. The same applies to Figure 7.12.

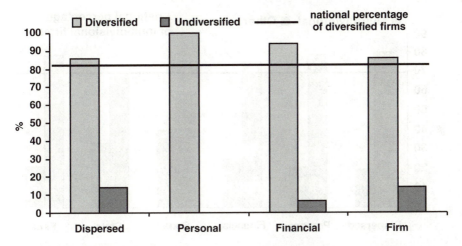

Figure 7.6. *Ownership and Diversification in the United Kingdom, 1993*

creating new diversified groups. Personal capitalism in post-war British industry might have been limited, but it was certainly not lacklustre.

Overall, then, for the dispersed British as much as for the concentrated French and Germans, the special interests of owners appear not to make much difference to strategy. Banks and financial institutions do not resist diversification and families and entrepreneurs are willing diversifiers. Firms under dispersed ownership, whose managers are presumed to be less constrained, are broadly no more likely to diversify than any others. Let us see now whether political interests are more influential in matters of organization. Expectations here might be higher. After all, with structure we are dealing directly with issues of power and control.

7.3. OWNERSHIP AND STRUCTURE

France

As we know, France is characterized by at least three groups of powerful shareholders alleged to be reluctant adopters of the multidivisional form. Families and entrepreneurs dislike the decentralization and accountability involved. Banks resent the multidivisional's role in capital allocation. The state prefers the flexible obscurity of complex holdings. These, anyway, are the starting premises.

Two observations immediately catch the eye when looking at the broad pattern of French structure adoption presented in Figures 7.7 and 7.8. The first is that, by and large, ownership seems to make very little difference to the propensity to divisionalize. Only one type of owner seems to offer any special

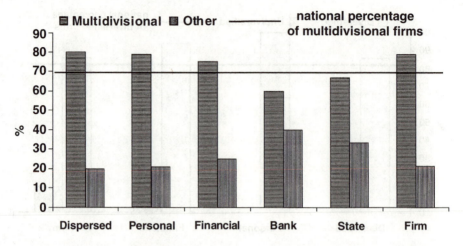

Figure 7.7. *Ownership and Structure in France, 1983*

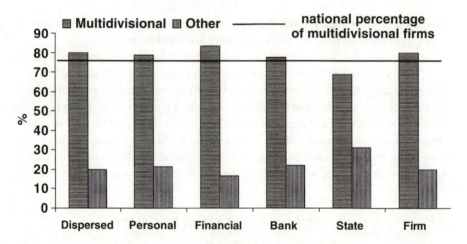

Figure 7.8. *Ownership and Structure in France, 1993*

resistance to divisionalization, the state. The second observation is the stability of the distributions, with changes by and large taking place only at the margins. For these reasons, our discussion will focus on personal ownership, the old *bête noire* of Harvard, and state ownership, clearly something of a barrier.

Despite all the suspicions in the literature, it is striking that personally owned firms have almost exactly the same level of multidivisionalization as the firms under dispersed ownership: 79 per cent in both time periods. Even some of the non-divisionalized exceptions have their excuses. Chandler (1962) at least would have to forgive the most outstandingly persistent functional firm, the Verrerie

Illustration 7.3. *Elf Aquitaine: State-owned-Holding*

In the early 1990s Elf was the largest company in France, and until 1994 was major-ity-owned by the French state. At the point of privatization, it had three main busi-nesses—hydrocarbons, chemicals, and health—each organized as *branches*. On the face of it, Elf was a conventional multidivisional firm.

However, the operating businesses had high autonomy, especially the African operations, chemicals and health. To take health as an example, this *branche* was actually an independently quoted company, of which Elf owned a proportion fluc-tuating around 50–60 per cent. Its chief executive had founded the business in 1973, and had seen three group heads come and go over the life-time of his power. He had his own personal team surrounding him and there were very few managerial trans-fers with the parent company. But even within the health *branche*, subsidiaries had great autonomy. Within the beauty division, there was a string of partial ownerships and independent managements. At Yves Rocher voting control still rested with the family and Didier Rocher, son of the founder, was chief executive. At Nina Ricci, where Elf held 55 per cent of the shares, the company was still run by the son-in-law of Robert Ricci. At YSL the previous owner and Yves Saint-Laurent himself were guaranteed continued managerial control of the 'couture' side of the business.

Principal sources: Interview; *Le Figaro*, 21 February 1994; *L'Expansion*, 7–20, October 1994.

Cristallerie d'Arques, as it follows a consistent single business strategy through-out this period. Bongrain and DMC were both family-owned holding compa-nies that switched to multidivisional structures. Fimalac and Financière Agache are more hastily constructed entrepreneurial conglomerates, whose holding structures may simply reflect constraints of capital. Although these firms had acquired an extensive set of subsidiaries, these are often partially owned because of the limited financial resources of their founders, Ladreit de Lacharrière and Bernard Arnault. These two individuals may well have chosen deliberately to share ownership in some of their subsidiaries rather than to subject themselves to capital-rich external shareholders at the apex of their holdings. For the moment, they could rely on the force of their personalities rather than strong majority ownership to exert control over their various activities. These holdings, then, had a sort of logic, even if not strictly managerial.

State-owned firms are, however, just slightly more resistant to the multidivi-sional structure than the rest. There is no clear pattern among these non-divisionalized state-owned firms, except for a marginal preference for holding-type structures. In 1983 we find the functional-holding, Dassault, and the holding companies Aérospatiale and EMC. Aérospatiale retains its holding company status in 1993, where it is joined by CEA, Elf, and Thomson (see Illus-tration 7.3). It seems that the state is indeed less anxious to impose the rational transparency of the multidivisional on its interests, but that this reluctance is not particularly marked.

Overall, then, ownership interests seem to have little impact on corporate structure in France. All types of owners are more likely to divisionalize than not, including even the most reluctant divisionalizer, the state. Personal owners do not seem unable to find the courage and skills to divisionalize. Banks do not resent the multidivisional's role in capital allocation. Even if the French state may have a sneaking propensity for holding structures, it seems to keep this tendency well under control.

Germany

Like France, Germany has strong personal shareholders and powerful financial institutions. It also has a particularly introverted set of inter-corporate linkages and a continuing role for the state. It is true that the overwhelming majority of German firms have adopted multidivisional structures, but there is a particularly stubborn group of holding companies to explain. Perhaps the case against ownership interests will be stronger in Germany than France.

Indeed, Figures 7.9 and 7.10 do indicate that non-divisionalization in Germany is associated with concentrated ownership, in particular that by other firms and the state. In 1983 most of the companies with banks, the state, or other firms as owners had not adopted multidivisional structures. By 1993 the aggregate tendency towards diversification had produced some corrections, but still firms under concentrated ownership were less likely to be divisionalized. It is striking that in both time periods firms under dispersed ownership, where managers are presumed to have more control, are 100 per cent divisionalized. There is a case to answer here.

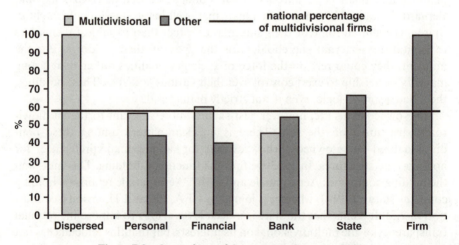

Figure 7.9. *Ownership and Structure in Germany, 1983*

Personal owners in Germany are not altogether reluctant divisionalizers. For them, multidivisional firms are a clear majority in both periods. Indeed some personally owned firms can be found among the earliest multidivisionalizers. Freudenberg was a wholly family-owned company which was already classified as a multidivisional by Thanheiser (1972). At Bertelsmann the great grandson of the company's founder, Reinhard Mohn, brought together his social ideas with the multidivisional's principles of decentralization and accountability to create a strong emphasis on entrepreneurial behaviour and open communication. However, not all personally owned companies embraced such clearly defined and systematically integrated structures.

In some cases firms under personal ownership serve to channel the owning families' participations in other companies which are held alongside the usually more tightly integrated and managed core activities. Within Tchibo, for instance, there resides a 25 per cent stake in the cosmetics firm Beiersdorf, whilst by 1993 the Henkel family moved its participations in Degussa under the Henkel company's umbrella. At Röchling matters are more complex. Here two legally separate companies are placed at the centre of the organization. The Gebr. Röchling KG (a limited partnership) is under the exclusive ownership of about 150 Röchling family members. Next to this there exists a limited liability company, the Röchling Industry Verwaltungs GmbH, in which outside share-holders hold about a half of the capital but have no voting rights. Although the top management of these is identical, this legal form places certain barriers on full integration of the company's activities. In addition to this Röchling holds a number of partial participations, the most notable being a 66 per cent stake in Rheinmetall, itself more than half the size of Röchling. Together with a very hands-off approach to managing the various participations, the company is

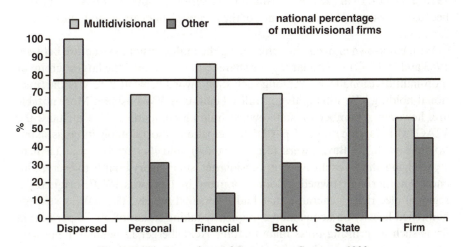

Figure 7.10. *Ownership and Structure in Germany, 1993*

closer to a traditional German holding company than a multidivisional (see Mayer and Whittington, 1996, for further discussion of this case).

As discussed earlier, commentaries on German industry have frequently argued that banks fulfil an important co-ordinative role which may replace some of the functions associated with the multidivisional organization (for example, Cable and Dirrheimer, 1983). It is true that a slight majority of bank-owned firms are not divisionalized in 1983 and that there are indeed cases where bank-owned firms have long resisted multidivisionalization. Here the case of the AGIV is perhaps the most obvious example. As noted in our discussion of ownership and strategy, the origin of the AGIV lies in an attempt of the Berliner Handels und Frankfurter Bank (BHF) to find a new way in which to manage its industrial participations. This led to the formation of the AGIV, one of two transport companies founded by the Berliner Handelsgesellschaft, the precurser of the BHF, in 1881. Through the 1980s and early 1990s the AGIV remained closely linked to the BHF. Many of the AGIV's participations remained below 75 per cent, with control typically being exerted via the supervisory boards of the subsidiaries. Here the AGIV's managers were frequently joined by representatives of the BHF itself, thus further inhibiting the development of full multidivisional style management structures and processes (a more fundamental reorganization was initiated only in 1995, supported by the Boston Consulting Group).

However, although we can find banks associated with resistance to multidivisionalization, we can also find them very active in the opposite direction. The most dramatic case is at the Gutehoffnungshütte, where the Commerzbank supported fundamental structural change during the 1980s to create the MAN. Beiersdorf, Daimler Benz, PWA, and Thyssen were all prominent firms with large banking stakes that underwent divisionalization in our period. By the early 1990s it is hard to argue that German banks seriously opposed divisionalization because of some putative threat to their capital allocation and monitoring functions.

With bank-owned firms thus embracing the multidivisional structure between 1983 and 1993, firms with large state shareholders remained the largest group of 'non-multidivisionalizers'. Among such state-owned firms in 1983 was the functional-holding VW, still highly centralized in its core VW business. More notable are, however, a number of state-owned holding companies. This includes the VIAG, with its wide range of partial participations, most notably its cross shareholdings with the Bayernwerk (see Chapter 4), and its detached management style relying almost exclusively on subsidiaries' supervisory boards to exert influence. Another state-owned holding company in 1993 was RWE, originally a regional electricity generator that had diversified widely. The RWE's strategy had relied heavily on acquisitions, frequently taking stakes of 50–70 per cent in firms such as printing-press manufacturer Heidelberger Druckmaschinen and construction company Hochtief, the chief executive of which in turn sat on the

RWE board. Further complications enter via the involvement of the municipalities which together hold the majority of RWE's voting stock. Press reports suggest that interventions frequently led to politically motivated appointments at RWE (*Wirtschaftswoche*, 25 September 1994).

The presence of minority stakes from other (non-financial) firms accounted for a notable number of non-divisionalized firms as well. Typical examples are the oil refiner Oberrheinische Mineralölwerke, which was functionally organized in both 1983 and 1993, and metals company Norddeutsche Affinerie, which was organized in a classic functional-holding manner, with an operationally centralized core business and subsidiaries outside of this core. Bosch-Siemens underwent a reorganization between 1983 and 1993 moving it from a functional-holding status towards a full multidivisional status in 1993.

Finally, we should consider the anomalous case of the stubborn German holding companies. Oetker, VIAG, and Zeiss were the only European firms to have survived across all of 1970–93 as unreconstructed holdings. Again, ownership has something to answer for in all three cases. However, as with the German conglomerates, it is not that particular types of owner were positively associated with these anachronistic structures, but that in some cases powerful owners were able to sustain them for long periods of time. Oetker, also one of Germany's stable conglomerates, is firmly under family ownership (see Illustration 7.4). VIAG is state-owned, its original function being precisely to hold a diverse range of industrial participations. Zeiss is held by the Carl Zeiss Stiftung, effectively under the control of the Baden-Württemberg state government.

In Germany, then, there is a stronger case for the role of ownership interests in obstructing divisionalization than in France. Even so, the characterization of this role should be nuanced. By 1993 it is only state-owned firms that are more likely to have resisted the multidivisional than otherwise. Families and banks seem perfectly capable of adopting the multidivisional form, and do so overwhelmingly. There are ownership effects, but these are confined to state-owned firms and a few persistent holding companies, neither of which are representative of wider German industry.

The United Kingdom

In considering the relationship between ownership and structure in the United Kingdom we again face a quite different set of contextual factors from those in France and Germany. First, the general level of multidivisionalization is even higher in the United Kingdom than in the two Continental countries. This, of course, leaves less deviation from the multidivisional ideal to be explained. Second, we again must note the fundamental difference in ownership patterns between the United Kingdom and France and Germany. In the United Kingdom most firms are under dispersed ownership. In fact one can characterize the typical firm as a multidivisional under dispersed ownership.

Illustration 7.4. *Oetker: Family-owned Holding*

Since the pharmacist Dr August Oetker founded the company in 1891 generations of family members—and the relationships between them—have shaped the development of this family-owned firm. In the post-war period Rudolf August Oetker, grandson of the company's founder, initiated a period of extensive diversification, following his motto 'not to put all eggs in one basket'. Oetker became a widely diversified organization, with activities ranging from its core food business to shipping, banking, insurance, publishing, advertising, chemicals, retailing, and luxury hotels. The management style was loose, with strategic direction set by Rudolf August Oetker at his famous 'Saturday morning meetings'.

The Oetker dynasty had a talent for familial capitalism. After differences between Rudolf August Oetker and his sister had led to a partition of the company in the late 1960s, Arndt Oetker, one of Rudolf August Oetker's nephews, moved to transform his part of the inheritance, notably the sewing machine manufacturer Kochs Adler and later the jam/conserve company Schwartau (a well-known brand name in Germany). Arendt turned both into successful businesses before settling to manage a diverse portfolio of personal business interests in areas such as food, trade, shipping, and sports-marketing. By the early 1990s relationships between the two parts of the family had improved when another nephew of Rudolf August Oetker, Roland, took up a supervisory function in Oetker's Lampe Bank, after stints at Deutsche Bank and the successful building of his own network of participations. Meanwhile succession had become an issue at the heart of the Oetker empire. Attempts in the early 1990s by younger generation and American-educated August Oetker to implant modern management techniques met strong resistance from the 'old guard' around Rudolf August Oetker. Rudolf August retained control and continued to define the broad strategic direction of the firm at his traditional 'Saturday morning' meetings.

Principal sources: Liedtke, 1993; *Wirtschaftswoche*, 11 October 1991.

This becomes immediately obvious when considering the relationship between dispersed ownership and structure adoption depicted in Figures 7.11 and 7.12. In 1983 almost 96 per cent of dispersed ownership firms, which account for 60 per cent of all firms in that year, are multidivisionals. In 1993 the level of divisionalization is at 94 per cent, accounting for 57 per cent of all firms in that year. These putatively managerially controlled firms are clearly enthusiastic adopters of the Harvard organizational model. However, there are only two types of owner that seemed to show any consistent reluctance towards the multidivisional—firms with significant state or personal shareholders—and we shall concentrate the remainder of our discussion on them.

The majority of state-owned firms in 1983 were already divisionalized. Here we can include British Leyland, British Petroleum, and British Shipbuilders. However, there were also some that resisted, including the functionally organized British Steel, ICL, and Rolls Royce. As these were all undiversified, there is

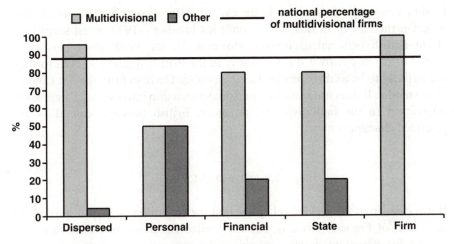

Figure 7.11. *Ownership and Structure in United Kingdom, 1983*

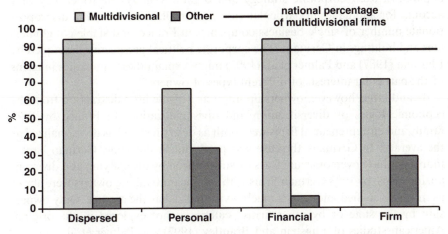

Figure 7.12. *Ownership and Structure in United Kingdom, 1993*

good theoretical excuse. By 1993 there was only one state-owned firm left, Dairy Crest, and this too was functionally organized. Again, however, it was undiversified. It seems then that the state's apparent reluctance to divisionalize reflects only its portfolio of specialized businesses.

The case against personal ownership is stronger, especially initially. We should recognize the very small numbers involved, but nevertheless in 1983 50 per cent of personally owned firms are not divisionalized, and in 1993 the figure is still 33 per cent. Firms with large personal stakes seem to have a slight propensity for holding company structures, as in the case of ABF, Western United, and Guinness. On the face of it, this would confirm Chandler's (1990) worst suspicions about British personal capitalism. However, by the 1990s these personally owned firms are clearly a small minority in the British system and even so they are as likely to be as divisionalized as the average German firm, the old Chandlerian model. It does not seem that personal ownership interests offer significant opposition to the multidivisional anymore. British personal capitalists are reformed characters now.

7.4. SUMMARY

It was clear from the previous chapters that the very different institutional characteristics of France, Germany, and the United Kingdom were of little consequence for dominant patterns of corporate strategy and organization. This chapter has, in a sense, given institutional differences a second chance, focusing particularly on the direct effects of ownership. If ownership differences do not, apparently, skew corporate strategy and organization system-wide, they may account for anomalies in particular cases. After all, there are still a disproportionate number of single business companies in France, and stable conglomerates and holdings in Germany. The corporate political perspective developed by Fligstein (1987) and Palmer et al. (1993) might explain these anomalies in terms of the particular interests of different types of owners.

By and large, however, ownership interests provide little distraction from the economic logics of diversification and divisionalization. In France by 1993 family and entrepreneurial firms were both as diversified and as divisionalized as the average. In Germany the case was pretty much the same. German banks, moreover, have overcome any fears of substitution by diversifying and divisionalizing firms: by 1993 German firms with significant banking owners were about as much diversified and just as much divisionalized as the average. Only ownership by the state or by other firms—categories not explored in the original American studies of Fligstein and Brantley (1992) and Palmer et al. (1993)—seem to make much difference, and by 1993 in both France and Germany the majority of state-owned and firm-owned firms are at least divisionalized anyway. The main role of ownership seems to have been in protecting over the long run a handful of anomalous German conglomerates and holding companies from the rationalizations that were the normal fate of their peers. None of these was under dispersed ownership.

Disappointing as it might be for certain social scientists, this absence of substantial corporate political influence on strategy and structure is welcome. The special interests of ownership are not subverting the economics of big business in contemporary Europe. Families and entrepreneurs have learnt to love the diversified, divisionalized firm, putting aside any fears about control and overcoming former inadequacies in managerial professionalism. This detachment of ownership from policy is both good for economic dynamism and good for the survival of distinctive national traditions of capitalism. In a sense, the condition of continued differences in ownership in Europe is that these should make no difference to the big issues of economic performance. For strategy and structure, ownership does not matter.

8

Concluding for the Corporation

INTRODUCTION

Harvard's original programme on corporate strategy and structure was a foundational one for our understanding of large, diversified corporations. It was a pioneer in the systematic long-range comparison of evolving business practice in an international context. To a large extent, it developed the basic concepts and methods of the emerging discipline of strategic management. It provided a rationale for the ways in which big business was developing in the 1960s and 1970s, at the same time as posing critical questions regarding international convergence and national performance. For Scott (1973) and Dyas and Thanheiser (1976), there was little doubt that business around the world was set firmly on the same track towards the American model of the diversified, multidivisional corporation.

All this, however, was way back in the middle decades of the twentieth century. The Harvard programme bears the heavy stamp of its time and place. After modernism and with the end of the American mystique, we might reasonably be sceptical about the continued progress of the diversified, divisionalized corporation. At the very least, then, tracking the development of Europe's largest industrial companies has allowed us to catch up with the story, to check up on how things have really turned out since 1970. But we can do more than simply satisfy historical curiosity. Returning to the inverted triangle of Figure 1.1, the development of European big business gives us insight into at least three further kinds of questions—about performance, about convergence, and about the scope of the social sciences.

This closing chapter reviews what the unfolding story of European big business can tell us on these three questions. We start with the issue of effective strategies and structures. Here, despite the rise and alleged fall of the conglomerate and notwithstanding claims for a new networked, N-form economy, we find that the Chandlerian model holds more or less true. Heedful of Toulmin (1990) and Mouzelis (1995), we must amend and renew the original model, yet its essential principles endure. On convergence, we find a mixed picture. There has been less of a managerial revolution in Continental Europe than the original Harvard scholars might have expected, yet corporations of all sorts—entrepreneurial, inherited, state, or managerial—have steadily been adopting the common business school model. This very combination of institutional stability with corporate change speaks strongly to the economic advantages of the Chandlerian corporation. Finally, we shall consider implications for the social sciences. Over a period of several decades and across stubbornly different national patterns of ownership and control, we have found the Harvard group's original predictions and prescriptions to hold remarkably well. At one level, and within particular temporal and territorial boundaries, we have discovered a sphere for cautious generalization. Context must be acknowledged and probed, but there is no need to sink into a disabling relativism. A boundedly generalizing social science is possible. We can accept the Chandlerian model as a provisional and adaptive conception of the firm, while leaving behind the modernistic, universalism of Chandlerism.

8.1. THE CHANDLERIAN MODEL RENEWED

There are two fundamental principles at the core of the Chandlerian model of the large corporation. The first is that there are attractive economic benefits to be had from the more efficient use of critical resources through diversification. The second is that decentralization of operations and the independence of strategy are important for the effective extraction of these benefits. The principles of diversification and divisionalization were first elaborated on the other side of the Atlantic in the early part of the twentieth century. Many decades later, European corporations are not only adopting these principles but renewing them to match the challenges and opportunities of more recent times.

Strategy

We should begin by recalling the historically novel nature of the diversified corporation. In 1949 just 30 per cent of large American industrial firms were diversified (Rumelt, 1974). In France at the beginning of the 1950s the proportion was 36 per cent; in Germany, 40 per cent; in the United Kingdom, 27 per cent (Tables 5.1, 5.2, 5.3). The post-war ascent of big business in these economies is strongly associated with the rise of diversification. By 1969 already two-thirds of American businesses were diversified (Rumelt, 1974). By the early-to-mid-1990s, substantially more than two-thirds of large British and German corporations were diversified, with the French hovering not far below. Diversification can claim to be a defining characteristic of big business in these contemporary advanced economies.

Dyas and Thanheiser (1976) were essentially right, therefore, to predict the continuing advance of diversification in Europe. The trouble is, not all of this diversification has been by the book—conglomerates represent a vigorous and substantial proportion of European diversification. We have poor theoretical resources to account for this conglomerate success. It will not do to blame conglomerates on the distortions of finance or the abuses of managerial power. They perform too well and too evenly over distinct and changing national environments for such easy dismissal. Prevailing economic accounts are not much better. Chandler's (1962) original four chapters predate the rise of the conglomerate; the orthodox resource-based view prejudges it. Nevertheless, the fundamental reasoning involved in these economic accounts does provide an essential core on which to build a more comprehensive model of diversification.

The orthodox view favours diversification in order to make efficient use of resources. It falls short only in focusing too exclusively on the transfer and sharing of resources between operationally related activities. It is Robert Grant's (1988) extension of relatedness to include corporate relationships that allows the framework to cover the patterns of diversification, performance, and longevity that we observe in Europe. This extension involves no fundamental break with either the original Chandlerian model or the resource-based view, and indeed recalls Penrose's (1959) original emphasis on managerial resources. Once corporate similarities are admitted, then top management teams can be recognized as a resource with quite general application, regardless of operational linkages in terms of markets or technologies. So long as the corporate relationships exist, these top management teams can add value without all the expense of the complexly integrated related diversifier. For a time at least the conglomerate's prospects can be much better than allowed in severe interpretations of the resource-based view.

We wish to rehabilitate conglomerates, therefore. As we saw in Chapter 5, conglomerates perform financially quite well, often better than related-linked diversifiers. They seem, too, to be able to ride out quite severe economic storms, no less able to survive either of the given ten-year or so periods than the approved related diversifiers. The conglomerate strategy only comes apart over the very long term, as the break-up of original management teams renders corporate relationships finally intractable. It takes periods of two decades or more for the managerial investments of the related diversifiers to pay off, through the creation of successive generations of corporate leadership capable of sustaining them for the long run. Conglomerates are not the 'hopeful monsters' of the orthodox resource-based view (Dosi et al., 1992), even if they do not have quite the staying power of the related diversifier so approved in the original four chapters of enterprise.

Intriguing practical implications emerge from the success of our conglomerates. Prescriptions for the future must be conditioned by the bounded nature of our empirical base, but with this warning we venture some remarks. The transitions examined in Chapter 5 suggest that conglomerates more typically enter into the ranks of the Top 100 by direct entry, rather than by gradual evolution through other strategies. The strategy does, moreover, pay quite well. Conglomerate-building is thus a potentially rapid way to riches. There are good prospects of milking profits for an ample ten years or so. After that, however, conglomerates tend to hit a brick wall, entering a period of either decline, takeover, or break-up. The Achilles' heel of the conglomerate appears to be its top management resource. Except in Germany, where special ownership factors kick in, it does not yet seem possible to exploit corporate relationships effectively over the long term. The challenge for conglomerates is either to find the means for developing the second generation of top managers capable of exploiting these corporate relationships or to act promptly to manage decline on their own terms. It was this kind of graceful retirement that Hanson, the archetypal conglomerate of the 1980s, achieved with its voluntary de-merger in 1996. Its old rival BTR struggled miserably on, only to sink finally into the arms of Siebe (now Invensys) in 1999. Conglomerates need to know when to be practitioners of corporate euthanasia.

The most successful long-term strategy, however, remains related diversification, especially constrained diversification. Great related diversifiers, such as Cadbury Schweppes and Unilever, BASF and Siemens, BSN (Danone) and Pechiney, seem to have discovered secrets of longevity that elude the conglomerate. Even in their maturity related-constrained diversifiers are more profitable than conglomerate upstarts. The success of related diversifiers over such long periods of time and in such different environments encourages us to believe that their strategies are likely to be robust quite widely. Operational relationships endure, and the managerial skills required to exploit them can be passed from one generation to another. We can incorporate the conglomerate within our framework, but as we do so we must reaffirm the early preferences of the basic Chandlerian model: related strategies, and especially the most tightly integrated strategy of constrained diversification, still seem to offer the best prospects of long-term prosperity.

Structure

The multidivisional structure is the corporate success story of post-war Europe. Hardly known in Europe in 1950, by the 1990s the rate of divisionalization in France, Germany, and the United Kingdom lay between 70 per cent and 90 per cent (Tables 6.1, 6.2, 6.3). Nationally distinctive holding companies and centralized functional structures are giving way to the rigorous decentralization of the multidivisional. The model's attractions are so great that even most undiversified single businesses are now divisionalized. Multidivisional companies are much more likely to stick to their structures than companies organized any other way. Financial comparisons are difficult because of the unbalanced numbers, but there is evidence at least to suggest that multidivisional organization delivers steady and satisfactory performance.

In the face of this success, we find the sociological theorists of institutions too sceptical. Europe's adoption of the multidivisional is more than the product of American political, economic, and managerial hegemony (Djelic, 1998; Guillén,

1994; McKenna, 1997). It continued long after the decline of American power and mystique. The rise of Japan did not disturb one jot the upwards trajectory of the multidivisional. What we owe to American hegemony in the 1950s and 1960s is not the imposition of an alien form, but rapid diffusion of an effective model of management. National cultures and institutions (Hofstede, 1980; Whitley, 1994) appear to make little difference. The centralizing French turn out to be more attached to the multidivisional than the federal Germans. Families, entrepreneurs, and banks do not blanch at adopting multidivisional structures that might be against their corporate political interests (Palmer et al., 1993). In imagining objections to the multidivisional structure, it seems that the sociologists are more the practitioners of dismal science than the economists.

The decentralization of operations, the fluent movement of resources, and the internal transparency of the multidivisional can clearly yield economic benefits. Managers are better able to concentrate on their responsibilities and are more accountable for their success. The multidivisional frees and motivates. These are enduring principles around which the multidivisional seems capable of reinventing itself. The network society (Castells, 1996), far from rendering it redundant, has pushed the contemporary multidivisional to new degrees of decentralization and transparency. What we have called the 'network multidivisional' (Table 3.1) extends the fundamental principle of operational decentralization, strategic centralization, at the same time as adding a new horizontal dimension. Formal, semi-formal, and informal networks within and across divisions overcome the 'tyranny of the SBU' feared by proponents of core competences (Prahalad and Hamel, 1990). Just as capital was distributed within the early multidivisional, so can knowledge be exchanged within the network multidivisional.

The multidivisional can, therefore, be 'an enduring source of value', in the phrase of Hoskisson et al. (1993). But we should recognize it for more than this. We should recall the sense of shock and anxiety experienced by Americans and American-trained scholars as they contemplated the Europe of the 1950s and early 1960s. Europe was a dark continent, historically the home of undemocratic fascism, then still threatened by undemocratic communism. While Soviet Europe seemed to be mustering huge economies of scale, industry in Western Europe was fragmented by history and borders. Western European business élites were untrained, stagnant, and incestuous; they had already shown themselves compliant in the face of military occupation and dictatorship (Cassis, 1997: 219–22). The baroque family holding companies of European tradition might hold some charm for us now, but in the eyes of contemporary Americans they were the dangerous centres of conservative and unaccountable economic power. On the Continent, they had collaborated with fascism; in Britain, they were tightly bound to a failing empire. The multidivisional, as it challenged the hierarchies of centralized functional organizations, and as it opened up the opaque complexities of holding companies, was part of a democratic as well as economic project. The transparency, meritocracy, and accountability of the multidivisional might have been limited—they were—but on the whole the new structure was much better than what went before. It was Europe's good fortune that democratic and economic interests coincided even to this extent.

As we review the history of Europe's commitment to diversification and divisionalization, we can surely conclude that the Chandlerian model has survived its modernist origins. Certainly, it has amended its rigid segmentalism and extended its valuable relationships, but that does not detract from its success. Rather, the model has shown itself to have the flexibility to adapt to changing times, proving itself to be of far more than passing and local interest. Indeed, its tenacity in the diverse and evolving contexts of Western Europe has substantial implications for how we characterize national approaches to business and evaluate prospects for reform.

8.2. STRATEGY, STRUCTURE, AND NATIONS

The Chandlerian model, therefore, has continuing relevance to business long after its first formulation and on both sides of the Atlantic. This success challenges national and international institutionalist accounts head on. At the same time, it has intriguing implications for the possibility of economic reform in other economies currently suffering an equivalent 'corporate deficit' to that of Western Europe in the early post-war period.

The challenge for the institutionalists can be understood by recalling the general predictions developed in Table 2.1. As it turns out, by the 1990s there is scarcely any discernible diversity in the corporate profiles of big business in Western Europe; there has been no significant flux over time to disturb the onward progress of the Chandlerian model. Although—as we shall underline in the next section—we shall insist on certain limits, the evolution of strategy and structure in post-war France, Germany, and the United Kingdom conforms very closely to the predictions of the economic universalists. European business has converged on the American corporate model. If we go on to compare experience with the more specific predictions of Whitley's (1994) 'business systems' theory (Figure 3.6), we find in fact that business in all three countries is now piling into the same north-western quadrant—diversified in strategy, decentralized in structure. This is regardless of enduring institutional differences in terms of ownership, control, and top management careers. The engineering-orientated and bank-connected Germans are just as diversified as the financially driven British. The statist, hierarchical French are even more divisionalized than the federal Germans.

This kind of disarticulation between national macro-institutional characteristics and meso-level corporations requires a radical revision of business systems theory. National institutional effects do not work in Europe according to the tightly integrated, all-embracing pattern suggested by Whitley (1994) or by Hollingsworth and Boyer (1997). The paths of European development can be understood in two ways: either the meso-level can change far faster than the macro-level, or the macro-level does not need to change as fast as the meso-level. In the first view, meso-corporations are cast strongly as potential leaders in economic and social reform. Europe's top managers have brought steadily more and more businesses under their control and provided them with a structure in which transparency, accountability, and the optimal allocation of resources are the norm. In the second view, it looks like a condition for the survival of macro-traditions and idiosyncrasies that they do not block reform at the lower level. Family firms persist in Europe not because they draw in some introverted way upon local traditions of strategy and organization, but precisely because they are ready to embrace the new and the foreign. In either case, the self-reinforcing circular conservatism of national systems no longer applies. In the advanced economies of Western Europe at least, change is endemic and may have different velocities at different levels.

A revised appreciation of national institutions has implications for economic reform more generally. As one considers the institutional structures of any particular country, the concern shifts from characterizing them as 'systems' towards establishing their degrees of 'systemness' (Mayer and Whittington, 1999). Prospects and programmes for economic change will vary radically between tightly integrated nations, with high degrees of systemness, and more loosely articulated nations, with low degrees of systemness. In loosely articulated systems, reforms may be more continuous and selective, with changes at one level or of one kind not necessarily requiring wider changes elsewhere. In this kind of loose system, moreover, change is likely to gather its own internal momentum, as particular agents within the system are able to advance limited kinds of reform without taking on the institutional structure as a whole. A diagnosis of tight systems, on the other hand, sets expectations of long periods of inertia punctuated by episodes of revolutionary crisis. Change when it comes will be radical and system-wide. It will be of such catastrophic proportions, and so alien to domestic traditions, as likely to require the intervention of outside agents. Presumptions of tight integration, as in the notions of Whitley (1994) and Hollingsworth and Boyer (1997), actually raise the obstacles to change by casting it in such unpalatable and unmanageable terms. An appreciation of national systems as variable in their degrees of openness and flexibility lowers the stakes and so widens the possibilities of gradual and self-regenerating economic reform.

In this way, we confirm our affinity with Harvard's own original mission for the reform of European industry. In struggling economies, the corporation is a ripe target for change and, occupying such a strategic economic position, may then become an effective vehicle for wider transformation. We have to say, though, that the original Chandlerians exaggerated the direct significance of corporate strategy and structure and probably cast the wrong country in the role of villain. In particular, Chandler's (1990) own extension of his model of corporate development from the level of the firm to that of the nation entails several mistranslations in detail.

As we have seen, for Chandler (1990) investment in scale, scope, and structure was not just a matter for performance at the level of the firm, but had implications for national economic performance as well. Chandler had been most directly concerned for the failures of British 'personal capitalism' before the war: even here, it seems, his thesis is much disputed, both as to the degree of under-investment in British firms and to the extent and causality of British under-performance (Hannah, 1991; Broadberry, 1997; Cassis, 1997). However, Chandler comments also on the implications of corporate-level change for relative economic performance more recently, again contrasting the United Kingdom unfavourably with Germany. This time, British managers have failed their country by being *too* American, over-enthusiastic adopters of the alleged conglomerate excesses of the 1960s and 1970s (Chandler, 1990: 627–8). Here the link from corporate development to national economic performance is probably a step too far.

To start with, British firms can no longer be accused of retrograde personalism. As Chapter 4 established, by the 1980s at least, it was German firms that were substantially the more likely to be personally owned and controlled. It is true that the processes of German diversification rely less on the techniques of hostile takeovers than the British acquisitive diversifiers such as BTR and Hanson, but nevertheless, the two countries have ended up with equivalent levels of conglomeratization. Moreover, the German conglomerates appeared to be slower to unwind, despite being financially out-performed by theoretically approved related-constrained diversifiers. As for organizational structure, British firms were substantially ahead of German firms in terms of divisionalization throughout the whole post-war period. Chandler's (1990) favoured Germans seem in practice to have been more than a little recalcitrant in following his prescriptions.

The recalcitrance of the Germans and the near-model behaviour of the British seem to have had no obvious affect on national economic performance. If one compares relative levels of growth in industrial production—a finer measure than Chandler's (1990) original one of Gross Domestic Product—with trends in industrial firms' corporate development, no obvious pattern emerges. It is true that from the 1950s to the 1970s, British industry consistently underperformed French and German in terms of growth (see Figure 8.1). This period of under-performance was one during which the British were clearly ahead in terms of divisionalization at least, although it is harder to make direct comparisons in terms of diversification or management. This is awkward for Chandler's thesis, but should not be taken too seriously. During the 1980s and the first half

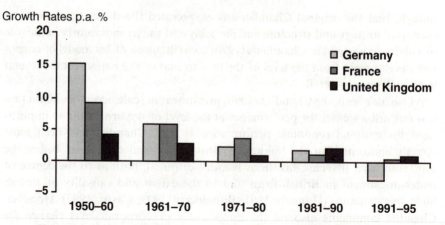

Figure 8.1. *Industrial Production in Europe: Average Annual Growth Rates*

Sources: Mitchell, B. R. (1976), *European Historical Statistics*, London: Macmillan; *Handbook of International Economic Statistics,* Washington: Central Intelligence Agency. Reproduced with permission from Whittington, R., Mayer, M. and Curto, F. (2000), 'Strategy, Structure and Performance in European History: Corporate and National Perspectives'. In *National Capitalisms, Global Competition and Economic Performance*. Edited by Sigrid Quack, Glenn Morgan, and Richard Whitley. John Benjamins Publishing Co., 2000, Amsterdam/Philadelphia. Graph on page 114.

of the 1990s, the performance advantage returned, slightly, to the British. Relative recovery was not accompanied by any obvious change in corporate-level trends in France, Germany, or the United Kingdom. As Jones (1997) comments, the correlation between British Americanization in the 1950s and 1960s and relatively poor economic performance looks to be just a coincidence. Indeed, the overall pattern at the level of national performance is not one of establishing clear winners and losers, but of convergence on similarly low levels of industrial growth. In a sense, the evolution of relative national economic performance is just another instance of wider processes of international convergence over this period.

As Dosi and Kogut (1993) suggest, repeated episodes of more or less gradual convergence are exactly what we would expect in a world where competitive pressures for efficiency prevail, but there remain sufficient institutional differences both to impose some frictions and to generate new and distinctive ideas about managing and organizing. Thus Europe has slowly but quite surely adopted the American corporate model, and more recently shared with the United States the effort of absorbing the managerial innovations emerging from Japan. There is enough institutional diversity in the world to ensure continued innovation, but not enough institutional perversity to prevent constant imitation. In this view, the so-called 'decline of the American mystique' (Locke, 1996) was an exaggerated reaction to the catch-up of European and Japanese business in the 1980s. The success of European and Japanese corporations was more a compliment than a challenge to the American corporate model. As it was adopted by other advanced economies, naturally the American model could no longer be a source of advantage. New but imitable sources of advantage were springing up. In a world of innovation and imitation, both national specificities and national advantages are likely to be short-term phenomena (Dosi and Kogut, 1993: 258). Japan's stagnation during the 1990s can in part be seen as the result of American and European success in adopting the quality revolution of the 1980s. At the turn of the century, with its internet boom, the United States again looks to be the source of innovation. Its great old corporations—General Electric, Ford, and IBM—are once more showing themselves to be skilful and flexible riders of another wave of change. We can expect that European and Japanese corporations will eventually catch up with them this time as well.

8.3. THE SCIENCE OF THE CORPORATION

The Harvard group, and the business schools and consultancies they inspired, were themselves important contributors to European catch-up. Their basic model of the corporation, with its emphasis on diversification and decentralization, has proven to be of enduring and transferable value. Their rigorous attempts to test the model in the United States, and their readiness to prove it in different territories, represents a substantial achievement for the social sciences. The model has certainly had to adapt to changing times, but its core ideas remain robust.

After modernism, and now even 'past postmodernism' (Callas and Smircich, 1999), we can recognize the essence of the Chandlerian programme for the conditional and bounded success it is. In the advanced economies of America and Europe there is sound sense to diversification and divisionalization. There is no necessary determinism in the Chandlerian prescriptions: as the examples of the German holdings demonstrate, in particular circumstances companies may choose to ignore them, even if at risk of a certain cost. The prescriptions are not rigid either: evolving capabilities in managing corporate relationships and new means of fostering horizontal networks have already changed the manner in which diversification and divisionalization are actually done. We can accept the basic good sense of the Chandlerian formula without adopting the modernist universalism of Chandler's original formulation. We acknowledge the limits of time, territory, and practice, only draw them less tightly and less definitely than do the contextualists. The success has been specific to post-war Western Europe, but it has been achieved over such rugged territory and over such turbulent times that there are good grounds for suspecting the model's essential robustness—if not everywhere and for ever, at least further afield and longer into the future. It is true that the sheer facts of their diffusion and longevity tell us little about how diversification and divisionalization are actually initiated, sustained, and developed (Whittington, 2000), but nevertheless the articulation of these principles remains of continued practical relevance. Harvard Business School and McKinsey & Co. have been offering sound advice.

Leaving Chandlerism behind, therefore, we have in the basic Chandlerian model modestly generalizeable principles worthy of inclusion in a bounded management science of the corporation. This Chandlerian model is both an expression of scientific rationality and an achievement of social scientific endeavour. To engage in diversification, and to adopt the multidivisional structure, is to trust in the value of abstract, generalizeable knowledge. The success of the diversified multidivisional represents a continuing endorsement of the possibility of such rational abstraction. As to the model itself, social science first projected it, and social scientists have since validated it, doing so over a widening temporal and territorial sphere. In this, the Harvard researchers were pioneers, the very first to pursue the systematic study of organizations from a longitudinal and comparative perspective. There are other kinds of knowledge with value to the scientific understanding of management, but the Chandlerians have shown that theirs is at least one kind of social science that can provide enduring and widely relevant foundations to the management sciences. Even if we might now be more inclusive in our definition of scientific knowledge, the original ambitions of the Ford and Carnegie reports on management education (Gordon and Howell, 1959; Pierson et al., 1959) were worthy and far-reaching ones. There is some science to management—thank goodness.

However, this science is necessarily provisional and adaptive. European corporations have not simply been chasing some corporate equilibrium set finally in America three decades or so ago. Rather they are taking advantage of the constantly-shifting matrix of opportunities and capabilites afforded by changing environments and growing experience. As in the cases of diversification and divisionalization, improving skills—in the long-term management of corporate relationships, for instance—or new managerial technologies (the network multidivisional) critically alter the balance of advantage. Of course, this balance can alter in another direction. In any case, our long-run perspective on strategic and structural evolution helps in pointing to a more general conclusion. The management sciences should avoid hard-and-fast prescriptions—one strategy, or one structure, over another. They will become more practical not as they promise fixed hierarchies of performance, but as they give to their models both dynamism and provisionality.

As in Mouzelis's (1995) conceptual and empirical pragmatism, the point now is to keep exploring the sphere over which this scientific knowledge is actually applicable. There is no need to take fixed positions in the debate over universal relevance and contextual relativism, for there is a fluid space between. Just as corporations constantly amend their boundaries through diversification and divestment, so we should expect the scope of the management sciences to be continually shifting, as research probes and amends the outer limits of their relevance to a changing world. In this sense, then, the arguments between modernism and postmodernism, structural contingency theory and institutional contextualism, are not likely ever to be finally resolved by argument alone. In large part, the question of generalization in the management sciences is an empirical one. The 'paradigm warriors' (Aldrich, 1988) can lay down their arms and get on with the ordinary business of research.

For the moment, we believe that the development paths in Europe demonstrate a potentially wide scope for scientific generalization, at least at the corporate level. Returning to the 'adjustable vice' of Chapter 1, it seems that the pressures for convergence have dominated the idiosyncrasies of national cultures and institutions. British, French, and German firms have amended their corporate profiles in a common and 'American' direction. The enduring performance advantages of Chandlerian patterns of strategy and structure suggest that it is not international institutional effects but market pressures for efficiency that drive this conformity. Diversification and divisionalization have easily survived the decline of the American mystique. Rather than decaying, these strategies and structures have extended and renewed themselves. True, as we see in continued variations in ownership and management, the vice is not yet so tight as to squeeze out all national differences. There is no inevitability either that the vice will not be adjusted and processes reversed. Yet our companies are marching sufficiently in step for us to speak with increasing confidence, not of *The Emerging European Enterprise*—Dyas and Thanheiser's (1976) book title—but of the European corporation.

Appendix I: Strategic and Structural Classification of French, German, and United Kingdom Firms

For diversification strategy, firms are classified both according to their 'national' scheme (Channon, Dyas, or Thanheiser) and by Rumelt's scheme, for comparison across countries and with the United States. See Appendix II for explanation of strategy and structural classification schemes. Firms are categorized by main broad industry sector.

Key:

S	Single business
D	Dominant business
R	Related diversified
RL	Related-linked diversified
RC	Related-constrained diversified
U	Unrelated diversified.
F	Functional structure
FH	Functional-holding structure
H	Holding structure
M	Multidivisional structure

Main sector, strategy, and structure of large industrial firms, France, 1983

Company	Largest sector of activity	Strategy		Structure
		'Dyas'	'Rumelt'	
Aérospatiale	transportation equipment	R	RC	H
Arjomari-Prioux	printing, paper, publishing	R	D	FH
Aussedat Rey	printing, paper, publishing	R	D	M
Beghin Say	food, drink, and tobacco	U	U	M
Besnier	food, drink, and tobacco	S	S	M
Bic	rubber and plastics	U	U	M
Biderman	textiles and clothing	D	D	M
Bongrain	food, drink, and tobacco	S	S	H
Boussac Saint Frères	textiles and clothing	U	U	M
Bridel	food, drink, and tobacco	R	RC	F
BSN	food, drink, and tobacco	R	RC	M
Carnaud	mechanical engineering and metals	R	D	M
CEA	electrical and instrument engineering	R	RC	M

Company	Largest sector of activity	Strategy		Structure
		'Dyas'	'Rumelt'	
CGE	electrical and instrument engineering	R	RL	M
Charbonnages de France	mining and extraction	U	U	H
Chausson	transportation equipment	D	D	H
Cii Honeywell Bull	electrical and instrument engineering	S	S	H
Ciments Français	brick, pottery, glass, and cement	S	S	H
Dassault	transportation equipment	S	S	FH
Dollfus Mieg et cie	textiles and clothing	R	RC	M
EBF	mechanical engineering and metals	R	RC	M
Electronique Serge Dassault	electrical and instrument engineering	R	RC	M
Elf Aquitaine	petroleum	D	D	M
EMC	chemicals and pharmaceuticals	R	RC	H
Essilor	brick, pottery, glass, and cement	D	D	FH
Fives Lille	mechanical engineering and metals	R	U	H
Fromageries Bel	food, drink, and tobacco	S	S	M
Générale Biscuit	food, drink, and tobacco	S	S	M
Guyomarc'h	food, drink, and tobacco	R	D	M
Hachette	printing, paper, publishing	R	RC	M
IMETAL	mechanical engineering and metals	R	RL	M
L'Air liquide	chemicals and pharmaceuticals	R	RC	M
L'Oréal	chemicals and pharmaceuticals	R	RC	M
Lafarge Coppée	brick, pottery, glass, and cement	R	RC	M
Legrand	electrical and instrument engineering	R	RC	M
Leroy Sommer	mechanical engineering and metals	R	U	M
Lesieur	food, drink, and tobacco	R	RC	M

Company	Largest sector of activity	Strategy		Structure
		'Dyas'	'Rumelt'	
Lilles Bonnières Colombes	mechanical engineering and metals	U	U	H
Matra	electrical and instrument engineering	R	RL	M
Michelin	rubber and plastics	S	S	FH
Moët-Hennessy	food, drink, and tobacco	U	U	M
Moulinex	electrical and instrument engineering	S	S	F
Olida et Caby	food, drink, and tobacco	S	S	H
Ortiz Miko	food, drink, and tobacco	R	RC	M
Pechiney	mechanical engineering and metals	R	RC	M
Pernod Ricard	food, drink, and tobacco	R	RC	M
Perrier	food, drink, and tobacco	R	RC	FH
Peugeot	transportation equipment	D	D	M
Poclain	mechanical engineering and metals	D	D	M
Provoust	textiles and clothing	R	D	M
Renault	transportation equipment	S	S	FH
Rhône-Poulenc	chemicals and pharmaceuticals	R	RC	M
Roquette Frères	chemicals and pharmaceuticals	S	S	M
Sacilor	mechanical engineering and metals	S	S	M
Sagem	electrical and instrument engineering	R	RC	H
Saint Gobain	brick, pottery, glass, and cement	R	RL	M
Saint Louis Bouchon	food, drink, and tobacco	S	S	M
SAT	electrical and instrument engineering	R	RC	M
Schneider	mechanical engineering and metals	U	U	H
SEB	electrical and instrument engineering	R	RC	M

| Company | Largest sector of activity | Strategy | | Structure |
		'Dyas'	'Rumelt'	
Seita	food, drink, and tobacco	S	S	M
Sellier Leblanc	other	U	U	M
Snecma	transportation equipment	D	D	M
SNPE	chemicals and pharmaceuticals	R	RC	M
Socopa France	food, drink, and tobacco	R	D	M
Sodima Yoplait	food, drink, and tobacco	S	S	F
Sommer Alibert	rubber and plastics	R	RL	M
Télémécanique Electronique	electrical and instrument engineering	R	RC	M
Thomson	electrical and instrument engineering	R	RL	H
Total	petroleum	D	D	M
Usinor	mechanical engineering and metals	S	S	M
Valeo	mechanical engineering and metals	R	RC	M
Vallourec	mechanical engineering and metals	U	RL	M
Verrerie Cristallerie d'Arques	brick, pottery, glass, and cement	S	S	F

Main sector, strategy, and structure of large industrial firms, France, 1993

| | Largest sector of activity | Strategy | | Structure |
		'Dyas'	'Rumelt'	
Aérospatiale	transportation equipment	R	RC	H
Alcatel Alsthom	electrical and instrument engineering	R	RL	H
Arcadie	food, drink, and tobacco	D	D	FH
Bel	food, drink, and tobacco	S	S	M
Besnier	food, drink, and tobacco	D	D	M
BIC	rubber and plastics	R	RC	M
Bongrain	food, drink, and tobacco	S	S	M
BSN (Danone)	food, drink, and tobacco	R	RC	M

	Largest sector of activity	Strategy		Structure
		'Dyas'	'Rumelt'	
Bull	electrical and instrument engineering	S	S	M
Burelle	rubber and plastics	D	D	M
Carnaud/Metal Box (CMB)	mechanical engineering and metals	R	RC	M
CEA-Industrie	electrical and instrument engineering	R	RC	H
CGIP	mechanical engineering and metals	U	U	H
Charbonnages de France	mining and extraction	D	D	M
Chargeurs	textile and clothing	R	RC	M
Ciments Français	brick, pottery, glass, and cement	S	S	M
Cristallerie d'Arques	brick, pottery, glass, and cement	S	S	F
Dassault Aviation	transportation equipment	S	S	M
DMC	textile and clothing	R	RC	M
Doux	food, drink, and tobacco	S	S	M
EBF	mechanical engineering and metals	D	D	M
Elf Aquitaine	petroleum	R	D	H
EMC	chemicals and pharmaceuticals	R	D	M
Essilor	brick, pottery, glass, and cement	D	D	FH
Fimalac	mechanical engineering and metals	U	U	H
Financière Agache	food, drink, and tobacco	U	U	H
Framatome	electrical and instrument engineering	R	RC	M
Giat	transportation equipment	R	RC	M
Groupe Pierre Fabre	chemicals and pharmaceuticals	R	RC	M
Groupe de la Cité	printing, paper, publishing	R	RC	M
Guyomarc'h	food, drink, and tobacco	R	RC	M
IMETAL	mechanical engineering and metals	R	RL	M

	Largest sector of activity	Strategy		Structure
		'Dyas'	'Rumelt'	
L'Air liquide	chemicals and pharmaceuticals	D	D	M
L'Oréal	chemicals and pharmaceuticals	R	RC	M
Labinal	mechanical engineering and metals	R	RL	M
Lafarge-Coppée	brick, pottery, glass, and cement	R	RC	M
Legrand	electrical and instrument engineering	R	RC	FH
LVMH	food, drink, and tobacco	U	U	M
Matra-Hachette	electrical and instrument engineering	U	U	M
Michelin	rubber and plastics	S	S	M
Moulinex	electrical and instrument engineering	S	S	M
Ortiz-Miko	food, drink, and tobacco	R	RC	M
Pechiney	mechanical engineering and metals	R	RL	M
Pernod Ricard	food, drink, and tobacco	R	RC	M
PSA (Peugeot)	transportation equipment	S	S	M
Rémy-Cointreau	food, drink, and tobacco	R	RC	M
Renault	transportation equipment	S	S	FH
Rhône-Poulenc	chemicals and pharmaceuticals	R	RC	M
Sagem	electrical and instrument engineering	R	RC	M
Saint Gobain	brick, pottery, glass, and cement	R	RC	M
Saint-Louis	food, drink, and tobacco	R	RC	H
Schneider (Groupe)	electrical and instrument engineering	U	U	M
SEB	electrical and instrument engineering	R	RC	M
Seita	food, drink, and tobacco	R	D	M
Sextant Avionique	electrical and instrument engineering	R	RC	M
Snecma	transportation equipment	D	D	M

	Largest sector of activity	Strategy		Structure
		'Dyas'	'Rumelt'	
Socopa	food, drink, and tobacco	R	D	M
Sommer-Alibert	rubber and plastics	R	RC	M
Strafor-Facom	mechanical engineering and metals	U	U	M
Taittinger	other	U	U	FH
Technip	mechanical engineering and metals	S	S	FH
Thomson	electrical and instrument engineering	U	U	H
Total	petroleum	D	D	M
Usinor Sacilor	mechanical engineering and metals	S	S	M
Valeo	mechanical engineering and metals	R	RC	M
Vallourec	mechanical engineering and metals	D	D	M

Main sector, strategy, and structure of large industrial firms, Germany, 1983

	Largest sector of activity	Strategy		Structure
		'Thanheiser'	'Rumelt'	
Adidas	textiles and clothing	D	D	F
AEG	electrical and instrument engineering	U	RL	M
AGIV	mechanical engineering and metals	U	U	H
BASF	chemicals and pharmaceuticals	R	RC	M
Babcock	mechanical engineering and metals	D	D	M
Bayer	chemicals and pharmaceuticals	R	RC	M
Beiersdorf	chemicals and pharmaceuticals	R	RC	M
Benteler	mechanical engineering and metals	R	RC	M
Bertelsmann	printing, paper, publishing	R	RC	M

	Largest sector of activity	Strategy		Structure
		'Thanheiser'	'Rumelt'	
BMW	transportation equipment	S	S	F
Boehringer	chemicals and pharmaceuticals	D	D	M
Bosch	transportation equipment	U	RL	M
Bosch-Siemens	electrical and instrument engineering	R	RC	FH
Continental	rubber and plastics	R	RC	M
Daimler Benz	transportation equipment	S	S	FH
Degussa	chemicals and pharmaceuticals	D	DU	M
Diehl	electrical and instrument engineering	R	RC	M
FAG-Kugelfischer	mechanical engineering and metals	D	D	FH
Fichtel und Sachs	transportation equipment	R	RC	FH
Freudenberg	rubber and plastics	U	U	M
Friedrich Flick	transportation equipment	U	U	H
GHH/MAN	mechanical engineering and metals	U	U	H
Grundig	electrical and instrument engineering	S	S	FH
Heidelberger Zement	brick, pottery, glass, and cement	D	D	M
Henkel	chemicals and pharmaceuticals	R	RC	M
Hoechst	chemicals and pharmaceuticals	R	RC	M
Hoesch	mechanical engineering and metals	R	D	M
KHD	mechanical engineering and metals	R	RL	M
Klöckner Werke	mechanical engineering and metals	D	D	FH
Krupp	mechanical engineering and metals	U	U	M
Linde	chemicals and pharmaceuticals	U	U	M

	Largest sector of activity	Strategy		Structure
		'Thanheiser'	'Rumelt'	
Mannesmann	mechanical engineering and metals	U	RL	M
MBB	transportation equipment	R	RC	M
Melitta	electrical and instrument engineering	U	U	M
Merk	chemicals and pharmaceuticals	R	RC	M
Miele	electrical and instrument engineering	R	RC	FH
Mohnmeim	food, drink, and tobacco	S	S	M
Nixdorf	electrical and instrument engineering	S	S	F
Norddeutsche	chemicals and pharmaceuticals	S	S	FH
Oetker	food, drink, and tobacco	U	U	H
OMW	chemicals and pharmaceuticals	S	S	F
Porsche	transportation equipment	S	S	F
Preussag	mechanical engineering and metals	U	U	M
PWA	printing, paper, publishing	S	S	M
Ruetgers	chemicals and pharmaceuticals	R	RC	FH
Ruhrkohle	mining and extraction	D	D	FH
Saarbergwerke	mining and extraction	R	RC	FH
Salzgitter	mechanical engineering and metals	R	RL	M
Schering	chemicals and pharmaceuticals	R	RC	M
Siemens	electrical and instrument engineering	R	RL	M
Springer	printing, paper, publishing	D	D	M
Südzucker	food, drink, and tobacco	S	S	F
Tchibo	food, drink, and tobacco	U	U	FH
Thyssen	mechanical engineering and metals	U	U	M
Varta	electrical and instrument engineering	S	S	M

	Largest sector of activity	Strategy		Structure
		'Thanheiser'	'Rumelt'	
VIAG	other	U	U	H
Volkswagen	transportation equipment	D	DU	FH
Wacker	chemicals and pharmaceuticals	R	RC	FH
Zeiss	brick, pottery, glass, and cement	R	RC	H
ZF-Friedrichshafen	transportation equipment	R	RC	M

Main sector, strategy and structure of large industrial firms, Germany, 1993

	Largest sector of activity	Strategy		Structure
		'Thanheiser'	'Rumelt'	
AGIV	mechanical engineering and metals	U	U	H
Altana	chemicals and pharmaceuticals	R	RC	M
Bauer Verlag	printing, paper, publishing	S	S	M
BASF	chemicals and pharmaceuticals	R	RC	M
Bayer	chemicals and pharmaceuticals	R	RC	M
Bayernwerk	other	U	U	F/H
Beiersdorf	chemicals and pharmaceuticals	R	RC	M
Benckieser	chemicals and pharmaceuticals	U	U	M
Benteler	mechanical engineering and metals	R	RC	M
Bertelsmann	printing, paper, publishing	R	RC	M
BMW	transportation equipment	S	S	F
Boehringer Ingelheim	chemicals and pharmaceuticals	D	D	M
Bosch	transportation equipment	U	RL	M
Bosch-Siemens	electrical and instrument engineering	R	RC	M

	Largest sector of activity	Strategy		Structure
		'Thanheiser'	'Rumelt'	
Braun	chemicals and pharmaceuticals	R	RC	M
Bremer Vulkan	shipbuilding	U	RL	M
Continental	rubber and plastics	R	RC	M
Daimler Benz	transportation equipment	R	RL	M
Degussa	chemicals and pharmaceuticals	U	U	M
Deutsche Babcock	mechanical engineering and metals	R	RL	M
Diehl	transportation equipment	R	RL	M
FAG	mechanical engineering and metals	D	D	M
Freudenberg	rubber and plastics	U	U	M
GEA	mechanical engineering and metals	R	RL	M
Haindl	printing, paper, publishing	S	S	F/H
Heidelberger Zement	brick, pottery, glass, and cement	R	RC	M
Hella	electrical and instrument engineering	R	RC	F/H
Henkel	chemicals and pharmaceuticals	R	RC	H
Hoechst	chemicals and pharmaceuticals	R	RC	M
Holtzbrink	printing, paper, publishing	R	RC	M
KHD	mechanical engineering and metals	R	RL	M
Klöckner Werke	rubber and plastics	R	RL	M
Krupp	mechanical engineering and metals	U	U	M
Linde	chemicals and pharmaceuticals	U	U	M
MAN	transportation equipment	U	U	M
Mannesmann	mechanical engineering and metals	U	U	M
Merk	chemicals and pharmaceuticals	R	RC	M
Miele	electrical and instrument engineering	R	RC	F/H

	Largest sector of activity	Strategy		Structure
		'Thanheiser'	'Rumelt'	
Moksel	food, drink, and tobacco	R	D	F/H
Norddeutsche Affinerie	chemicals and pharmaceuticals	S	S	F/H
Oetcker	food, drink, and tobacco	U	U	H
OMW	chemicals and pharmaceuticals	S	S	F
Preussag	other	U	U	M
PWA	printing, paper, publishing	S	S	M
Röchling	electrical and instrument engineering	U	U	H
Ruhrkohle	mining and extraction	R	RL	F/H
RWE	electricity	U	U	H
Saarberg	mining and extraction	R	RL	F/H
Schering	chemicals and pharmaceuticals	D	D	M
Siemens	electrical and instrument engineering	R	RL	M
Springer	printing, paper, publishing	R	RC	M
Südzucker	food, drink, and tobacco	D	D	F/H
Tchibo	food, drink, and tobacco	U	U	H
Thyssen	mechanical engineering and metals	U	U	M
Varta	electrical and instrument engineering	S	S	M
VIAG	other	U	U	H
Voith	mechanical engineering and metals	U	U	M
Volkswagen	transportation equipment	S	S	M
Vorwerk	electrical and instrument engineering	U	RC	M
Wacker	chemicals and pharmaceuticals	R	RC	M
Wella	chemicals and pharmaceuticals	D	D	M
Zeiss	brick, pottery, glass, and cement	R	RC	H
ZF-Friedrichshafen	transportation equipment	R	RC	M

Main sector, strategy, and structure of large industrial firms, United Kingdom, 1983

	Largest sector of activity	Strategy		Structure
		'Channon'	'Rumelt'	
ABF	food, drink, and tobacco	R	RC	H
Allied Lyons	food, drink, and tobacco	R	RC	M
AMEC	mechanical engineering and metals	U	U	M
Babcock International	mechanical engineering and metals	R	U	M
Bass	food, drink, and tobacco	R	RL	M
BAT Industries	food, drink, and tobacco	U	U	M
BICC	electrical and instrument engineering	U	U	M
British Leyland	transportation equipment	S	S	M
Blue Circle Industries	brick, pottery, glass, and cement	D	DU	M
Bowater	printing, paper, publishing	R	D	M
British Aerospace	transportation equipment	R	RC	M
British Petroleum	petroleum	D	D	M
British Shipbuilders	shipbuilding	D	D	M
British Steel	mechanical engineering and metals	D	D	F
Brooke Bond Group	food, drink, and tobacco	R	RC	M
BTR	electrical and instrument engineering	U	U	M
Burmah Castrol	chemicals and pharmaceuticals	R	RL	M
Cadbury Schweppes	food, drink, and tobacco	R	RC	M
Coats Patons	textiles and clothing	R	RC	M
Consolidated Gold Fields	brick, pottery, glass, and cement	R	RL	H
Courtaulds	textiles and clothing	R	U	M
Dalgety	food, drink, and tobacco	R	RL	M
Delta	mechanical engineering and metals	R	RC	M
Distillers Co.	food, drink, and tobacco	R	RC	M

	Largest sector of activity	Strategy		Structure
		'Channon'	'Rumelt'	
DRG	printing, paper, publishing	R	RC	M
Dunlop Holdings	chemicals and pharmaceuticals	R	RL	M
GEC	electrical and instrument engineering	R	RL	M
GKN	transportation equipment	R	RL	M
Glaxo	chemicals and pharmaceuticals	R	D	M
Grand Metropolitan	food, drink, and tobacco	R	RC	M
Guinness	food, drink, and tobacco	D	DU	FH
Hanson	other	U	U	M
Hawker Siddeley Group	electrical and instrument engineering	R	RL	M
Hillsdown Holdings	food, drink, and tobacco	R	RC	M
ICI	chemicals and pharmaceuticals	R	RC	M
ICL	electrical and instrument engineering	S	S	F
IMI	mechanical engineering and metals	R	RL	M
Imperial Group	food, drink, and tobacco	R	RC	M
John Brown	mechanical engineering and metals	R	U	M
Johnson Matthey	mechanical engineering and metals	R	D	M
Lucas Industries	transportation equipment	R	RC	M
Metal Box / Caradon	mechanical engineering and metals	D	DU	M
Northern Engineering	mechanical engineering and metals	R	RL	M
Northern Foods	food, drink, and tobacco	R	RC	M
Pearson	printing, paper, publishing	U	U	M
Pilkington	brick, pottery, glass, and cement	D	D	M
Plessey	electrical and instrument engineering	R	RL	M

	Largest sector of activity	Strategy		Structure
		'Channon'	'Rumelt'	
Racal Electronics	electrical and instrument engineering	R	RC	M
Rank Hovis McDougall	food, drink, and tobacco	R	RC	M
Rank Organisation	electrical and instrument engineering	U	U	H
Reckitt & Coleman	chemicals and pharmaceuticals	R	RC	M
Redland	brick, pottery, glass, and cement	U	U	M
Reed International	printing, paper, publishing	R	D	M
RMC Group	brick, pottery, glass, and cement	D	D	M
Rolls Royce	transportation equipment	S	S	F
Rowntree Mackintosh	food, drink, and tobacco	D	D	M
Scottish & Newcastle	food, drink, and tobacco	D	D	M
Shell	petroleum	D	RL	M
SmithKline Beecham	chemicals and pharmaceuticals	R	RL	M
Standard Telephones	electrical and instrument engineering	R	RC	M
Tarmac	brick, pottery, glass, and cement	R	RC	M
Tate & Lyle	food, drink, and tobacco	R	RC	M
The BOC Group	chemicals and pharmaceuticals	R	RL	M
The RTZ Corporation	mining and extraction	R	RL	M
Thorn EMI	electrical and instrument engineering	R	RL	M
TI Group	mechanical engineering and metals	R	U	M
Trafalgar House	mechanical engineering and metals	D	DU	M
Ultramar	chemicals and pharmaceuticals	S	S	M

	Largest sector of activity	Strategy		Structure
		'Channon'	'Rumelt'	
Unigate	food, drink, and tobacco	R	RC	M
Unilever	food, drink, and tobacco	R	RC	M
United Biscuits	food, drink, and tobacco	R	RC	M
Vickers	transportation equipment	R	U	M
Wellcome	chemicals and pharmaceuticals	S	S	M
Western United Investment	food, drink, and tobacco	R	D	H
Whitbread	food, drink, and tobacco	R	RL	M

Main sector, strategy, and structure of large industrial firms, United Kingdom, 1993

	Largest sector of activity	Strategy		Structure
		'Channon'	'Rumelt'	
ABF	food, drink, and tobacco	R	RC	H
Allied Lyons	food, drink, and tobacco	R	RC	M
AMEC	mechanical engineering and metals	U	U	M
Arjo Wiggins Appleton	paper, printing, publishing	R	D	M
BAT Industries	food, drink, and tobacco	U	U	M
BBA Group	transportation equipment	U	U	M
BICC	electrical and instrument engineering	R	RL	M
Blue Circle Industries	brick, pottery, glass, and cement	U	U	M
Bowater	paper, printing, publishing	R	RC	M
BPB Industries	brick, pottery, glass, and cement	D	D	M
British Aerospace	transportation equipment	R	RL	M
British Nuclear Fuels	other	R	RC	M
British Petroleum	petroleum	D	D	M
British Steel	mechanical engineering and metals	D	D	M
BTR	transportation equipment	U	U	M
Burmah Castrol	chemicals and pharmaceuticals	R	RL	M

	Largest sector of activity	Strategy		Structure
		'Channon'	'Rumelt'	
Cadbury Schweppes	food, drink, and tobacco	R	RC	M
Carlton Communications	other	R	RC	M
Charter	mechanical engineering and metals	U	U	H
Coats Viyella	textiles and clothing	R	RC	M
Cookson Group	chemicals and pharmaceuticals	R	RL	M
Courtaulds	chemicals and pharmaceuticals	R	RC	M
Dairy Crest	food, drink, and tobacco	S	S	F
English China Clays	brick, pottery, glass, and cement	R	U	M
Fisons	electrical and instrument engineering	R	RL	M
GEC	electrical and instrument engineering	R	RL	M
GKN	transportation equipment	R	RL	H
Glaxo	chemicals and pharmaceuticals	S	S	M
Glynwed International	mechanical engineering and metals	R	RL	M
Grand Metropolitan	food, drink, and tobacco	R	RC	M
Guinness	food, drink, and tobacco	R	RC	H
Hanson	food, drink, and tobacco	U	U	M
Harrison & Crosfield	food, drink, and tobacco	U	U	M
Hillsdown Holdings	food, drink, and tobacco	R	RC	M
ICI	chemicals and pharmaceuticals	R	RC	M
IMI	mechanical engineering and metals	R	RL	M
Johnson Matthey	mechanical engineering and metals	R	RL	M
Lucas Industries	transportation equipment	R	RC	M

| | Largest sector of activity | Strategy | | Structure |
		'Channon'	'Rumelt'	
Metal Box / Caradon	mechanical engineering and metals	U	U	H
Northern Foods	food, drink, and tobacco	R	RC	M
Pearson	printing, paper, publishing	U	U	M
Pilkington	brick, pottery, glass, and cement	D	D	M
Racal Electronics	electrical and instrument engineering	R	RC	M
Reckitt & Coleman	chemicals and pharmaceuticals	R	RL	M
Redland	brick, pottery, glass, and cement	R	RC	M
Reed International	printing, paper, publishing	R	RC	M
RMC Group	brick, pottery, glass, and cement	R	RC	M
Rolls Royce	transportation equipment	R	RC	M
Scottish & Newcastle	food, drink, and tobacco	R	D	M
Shell	petroleum	D	D	M
Siebe	electrical and instrument engineering	U	U	M
Smith & Nephew	chemicals and pharmaceuticals	D	D	M
SmithKline Beecham	chemicals and pharmaceuticals	R	RC	H
T&N	mechanical engineering and metals	R	RL	M
Tate & Lyle	food, drink, and tobacco	R	RC	M
The BOC Group	chemicals and pharmaceuticals	R	RC	M
The RTZ Corporation	mining and extraction	D	D	M
Thorn EMI	electrical and instrument engineering	R	RC	M
TI Group	mechanical engineering and metals	U	U	M
Tomkins	food, drink, and tobacco	U	U	M
Trafalgar House	mechanical engineering and metals	U	U	M

	Largest sector of activity	Strategy		Structure
		'Channon'	'Rumelt'	
Unigate	food, drink, and tobacco	U	U	M
Unilever	food, drink, and tobacco	R	RC	M
United Biscuits	food, drink, and tobacco	R	RC	M
Wellcome	chemicals and pharmaceuticals	S	S	M
Williams Holdings	other	U	U	M
Zeneca Group	chemicals and pharmaceuticals	R	RC	M

Appendix II: Methodology

This appendix provides more details regarding our methodology, particularly the selection of firms, sources of data, and the classification of firms to strategic and structural categories.

Selecting the firms

The criteria we used to identify the samples of firms used in this study followed exactly those employed by the original Harvard European studies (Channon, 1973; Dyas and Thanheiser, 1976). Just as Harvard, we have compared countries at ten-year time intervals and included non-public companies. The 1983 and 1993 comparison points reflect the timing of our field research, conducted in 1994 and 1995. As we were concerned with national institutional effects we focused on the domestically owned firms among the largest 100 industrial companies in terms of sales in each of the two time periods: the Harvard studies likewise distinguished clearly between 'domestic' and 'foreign' firms, and concentrated their trend analyses on the domestic ones (Dyas and Thanheiser, 1976: 64–6).

Drawing on the annual lists published in the *Times 1000*, *L'Expansion*, and the *Schmacke Directory*, inclusion of a firm in this study was contingent on three basic criteria. First, the company had to be an 'ultimate parent' with no other firm owning more than 50 per cent of voting shares. To take one of the more complex examples, in the case of Bernard Arnault's empire (Illustration 6.1), LVMH was included as well as Financière Agache, being not majority-owned (indeed, it was separately quoted). Next, the firm had to be among the Top 100 *industrial* firms in terms of turnover in the respective country (France, Germany, United Kingdom) in 1983 or 1993. We include only, therefore, companies for the year in which they actually figured in the Top 100, while Harvard traced back the population of largest firms in 1970 through 1960 and 1950. Although Channon's (1973: 66) cross-checking with the largest United Kingdom firms in 1953 suggests that the discrepancy is likely to be small, Harvard's retrospective measure, because capturing growing firms over the previous two decades, may have exaggerated the trend to diversified business among the wider population. We follow Harvard, however, in excluding utilities and construction firms, as well as firms for which trade and services accounted for more than 50 per cent of turnover. Formerly non-industrial firms (in the sense of the Harvard studies) such as the RWE and the Bayernwerk which had diversified outside their core area such that industrial activities exceeded 50 per cent of their turnover are, of course, included: RWE and Bayernwerk are assigned to the 'other' category in Table 1.1's analysis of industry distributions. Third, companies had to be 'domestic' in the sense that their home base was in the respective country. In the interest of consistency, Shell and Unilever, both of which were treated as British companies by Channon (1973), were included in the samples for the United Kingdom in 1983 and 1993. Also included, for similar reasons, was Alcatel Alsthom, which was registered in the Netherlands to avoid renationalization, but whose headquarter functions and senior executives remained in Paris. American companies or other national companies were excluded from the respective list of top domestic firms. Because of internationalization, our populations of domestic firms are smaller than the original Harvard group's, which were 79, 78, and 84 respectively for France, Germany, and the

United Kingdom (Dyas and Thanheiser, 1976: 289; Channon, 1973: 64). The falling proportion of domestic firms in national Top 100s is in itself an index of growing international integration.

Data collection and data sources

In view of the large number of firms to be classified and the 'desire to collect data for each individual concern' (Channon, 1973: 17), we followed the Harvard scholars in relying primarily on published materials. We thus drew on a wide range of sources from annual reports and other 'official' company documentation (for example, press releases and in-house publications) to reports in the business press (extensive searches of the main daily and business newspapers in the three countries were carried out), and books and teaching case studies. Other data sources included official governmental publications (such as *'Der Bundesanzeiger'* in Germany) and national and international business directories (such as *Dafsa, The Directory of Multinationals, Dunn & Bradstreet, Liens Financiers, Qui Décide, Wer ist Wer, Who's Who* (British and French editions) and *The World Directory of Multinational Enterprises*).

We supplemented this information by interviewing senior managers in a sub-set of firms. In the overwhelming majority of cases we relied on just one informant per firm. These informants included chief executives and owner-managers, but were more often directors of finance, planning, or personnel, or their direct reports. The nature of these managers' positions generally gave them a good understanding of their firms as wholes, but we were anyway able to cross-check and fill in with published data. Interviews were almost all tape-recorded. In France managers in twenty-eight firms were interviewed; in Germany and the United Kingdom twenty-five each, equivalent proportions to the original Harvard studies. We believe interviewing in just a sub-set of firms did not introduce significant biases in classification (Channon, 1973, changed one of his diversification classifications and none of his organizational classifications after interviewing), and certainly increased our understanding of strategic and structural categories in practice.

Categories

It was important for us to ensure consistency with the previous Harvard studies both over time and across countries. However, the definitions of strategy and structure are quite sparse in the original studies and vary in detailed wording as well (for instance, compare Channon, 1973: 13–15 with Dyas and Thanheiser, 1976: 25). In order to elucidate the underlying reasoning used in operationalizing these definitions, we therefore paid a good deal of attention to the Harvard group's accompanying conceptual and theoretical arguments and, especially, to the more-detailed case studies which they provided in the original theses (Channon, 1973; Dyas, 1972; Thanheiser, 1972). Based on these, we developed standardized templates on which relevant company information was entered to provide the basis for independent classification by two researchers. This practice of having two researchers classify each firm independently departs from Harvard's original individual judgement method, but was designed to control for any subjectivity. Any disagreements between the two researchers were resolved in discussion with a third researcher (Dr Francesco Curto). The level of initial agreement on strategy classifications was 93.4 per cent, which is comparable to other studies using this method (for example, Hoskisson et al., 1993). The level of initial agreement for the classifications of structure was 97.3 per cent. This high level of agreement on structure is attributable to the prevalence of multidivisional firms and, among holding companies, the very clear evidence for incomplete administrative control in the substantial asset values of their minority shareholdings (see below).

It is worth pausing to consider the extent to which these categories may be valid outside the country of their origin, the United States. Taylor (1985: 42) warns that comparative political science has been distorted by attempts to impose alien categories of American social science on very different kinds of social practices around the world: 'The not surprising result is a theory of political development which places the Atlantic-type polity at the summit of human achievement'. We recognize the danger, but think it small for European big business. The concepts of diversification and divisions are now widely used in the European business press and company annual reports. In France and Germany the very same words are often used, though also equivalents such as *branche* or *Sparte* for division. Business and executive education in Western Europe is dominated by American concepts. American consulting, accounting, investment, and computing firms have been active in Europe for many decades. In our interviews we tended to avoid using the more formal categories developed by Harvard, probing rather for the business activities underneath them. Our company informants rarely had any difficulty in recognizing our interests. Diversification and divisionalization are meaningful and significant categories for European big business.

Strategy measurement and classification

Diversification can be measured in many ways, with numerical methods based on product counts and Standard Industrial Classifications jostling with the categorical methods of Harvard (Hall and St John, 1994). Consistent and reliable SIC and product data were not consistently available over our time period in Europe. It is in part for lack of choice, therefore, as well as for the sake of longitudinal consistency that we have continued to rely on the Harvard categories originally used in the European studies of Channon (1973) and Dyas and Thanheiser (1976). These any way remain the most widely used diversification classification methods in strategy research (Dess et al., 1995). The four basic categories are the single business, dominant business, related business, and unrelated business strategies introduced in Chapter 5 (Figure 5.1). It is important, however, to note slight variations in the operationalization of these categories among both the European Harvard researchers and researchers in the United States (Rumelt, 1974; Markides, 1995).

The strategic categories used by the European Harvard studies (Channon, 1973; Dyas, 1972; Thanheiser 1972) are firmly based on the classification scheme developed by Wrigley (1970). However, the European studies introduced a number of refinements and modifications. First, and here we must note a difference to the Rumeltian approach discussed below, vertical integration was explicitly considered as a related strategy (Channon, 1973: 12). Second, no single core skill was required for a company to be classified as related. Rather 'a domino pattern with different skills along the chain, linking the different activities' was considered sufficient (Dyas, 1972: 121). The skills linking the individual businesses thereby had to be 'specific to the business concerned' (Dyas, 1972: 117). More general managerial skills 'such as the ability to get financing for new ventures', however, were not considered concrete enough to constitute a link between businesses for purposes of classification (Dyas, 1972: 117). In this sense, 'corporate relatedness' (Grant, 1988) or 'dominant logics' (Prahalad and Bettis, 1986) were excluded.

Each of the European researchers added further minor modifications. Thus Channon (1973) used a 70 per cent cut-off point to differentiate between related and unrelated diversification, whilst Thanheiser (1972: IV, 11) introduced a 5 per cent cut-off point (cf. Dyas and Thanheiser, 1976: 151). Dyas (1972: 125) intentionally did not indicate a specific cut off point. He states that, it 'will be noted that no exact definition has been given as to what percentage of a company's activities had to be unrelated for a company to be placed in this category'. If a company outside the dominant and single categories had less than 5 per cent of sales in an unrelated area Dyas considered it as related (Dyas 1972: 129). Above that level he used the 'intention and current direction of management's thinking' to arrive at a classification (Dyas 1972: 125). However, a proportion of unrelated businesses above 30 per cent (if not transitory) would be considered sufficient to warrant classification as unrelated, regardless of intent (Dyas, 1972).

Likewise, Rumelt (1974: 12) developed a classification scheme which was 'similar in spirit and broad outline to Wrigley's, but differed in a number of important respects'. One of the innovations offered by Rumelt (1974: 11–24, 29) is the introduction of three ratios to guide the classification process: these are the specialization ratio (SR), the related ratio (RR), and the vertical ratio (VR). The *specialization* ratio captures the proportion of turnover 'attributable to a firm's largest discrete product-market activity' (Rumelt 1974: 11). The *related ratio* is defined 'as the proportion of a firm's revenues attributable to its largest group of related businesses' (Rumelt 1974: 16). Again, relatedness was defined in terms of technological, scientific, and/or market relatedness. Reflecting the intent of the strategic category approach to capture managerially relevant phenomena the *vertical ratio* is introduced to identify those vertically integrated firms where 'much of the management task ... has to do with coordinating the elements in the processing chain' (Rumelt 1974: 20). Accordingly, the vertical ratio is defined as 'the proportion of the firm's revenues that arise from all by-products, intermediate products, and end products of a vertically integrated sequence of processing activities' (Rumelt 1974: 23). Firms in which such vertically related activities accounted for 70 per cent or more of turnover where included under the dominant business category. This treatment of vertical integration differs from the practice of the European researchers who included such firms under the related business category.

To allow for a more differentiated analysis Rumelt (1974) also subdivided some of Wrigley's (1970) original four categories. In the present study the related-constrained and related-linked sub-categories of strategy were used in the analysis of financial performance. In order to distinguish between these two categories the Rumeltian scheme identifies *constrained* and *linked* patterns of related diversification. In a pure constrained pattern individual businesses are related to virtually all other businesses taken one at a time (Rumelt, 1974: 19). A linked pattern resembles the 'domino pattern' identified by the European researchers mentioned above (Dyas, 1972: 121). Here individual business need only be linked to at least one other business to constitute a linked pattern. Related firms are assigned to one of the sub-categories—related-constrained or related-linked— depending on 'the group of businesses (constrained or linked) that, in terms of revenues' is the largest. Note that if the company has businesses that are unrelated to the rest (obviously below 30 per cent) these are *not* included in the analysis. As we see in Chapter 5, these sub-categories of related diversification are associated with different levels of performance.

All firms were classified according to both the respective national method and the Rumeltian method: Appendix I provides a full list.

The classification of organizational structures

Just as with strategy, we followed the Harvard studies in defining our categories of organizational structure (Channon, 1973; Dyas, 1972; Thanheiser, 1972). The broad characteristics of these structures—the functional, functional-holding, holding, and multidivisional forms—are discussed in Chapter 6. This appendix offers details on how the structure classification was operationalized in the present study.

Due to its central position in Harvard's classification scheme, the multidivisional organization was used as the basic reference point. This practice is similar to the approach taken by Hill (1988) and Markides and Williamson (1996). Seen from this perspective, the functional, functional-holding, and holding forms can be seen as organizational types in which essential characteristics of a multidivisional are missing. Important characteristics of the multidivisional that might be missing include the decentralization of operations, the ability to allocate resources across businesses, and the capacity to exert control. Following the European group (Channon, 1973: 217), we did not insist on the formal criteria of Williamson (1975), especially in regard to the élite staffs and formal strategic planning on which he placed emphasis. Holding companies often came with distinct national characteristics: i.e. cascades of participations in France, horizontal unrelated participations in Germany, and more fully owned but unintegrated related subsidiaries in the United Kingdom.

Structural classification was guided by four main criteria, drawn from the definitions, discussions, and actual classification practices of the original Harvard studies. As a general rule we focused on the overall pattern of the data to arrive at a classification: with the one exception noted below no single criterion was sufficient on its own to support a particular classification. It is important to see that structural classification does not rely simply on organizational charts.

The first set of criteria referred to the roles and position of top management itself. Here the operational centralization of sales and manufacturing tasks, in the form of a main board sales or production director, was taken as a strong indicator of either a functional or functional-holding form. The next set related to the basic ability of top management, and the corporate centre more generally, to exert the full and systematic control associated with a multidivisional organization. Here we used formal indicators associated with the extent of minority share holdings held by the focal firm. This was the only criterion which on its own precluded classification as a multidivisional. A firm was considered not to be a multidivisional if companies in which the focal organization controlled 50 per cent or less of voting shares accounted for the equivalent of 30 per cent of turnover or fixed assets (this cut-off point is not specified in the original Harvard studies, but is consistent with that used in measuring diversification). With such ownership patterns the focal company shares control of a very significant part of its business with other owners and thus cannot function in the systematic fashion of a multidivisional organization. The shift from a holding to a divisional structure under such circumstances would typically require large expenditures on equity, boardroom change, alterations in legal status, and consolidation of subsidiary companies. The third set of criteria related to the relative power of top management, reflected, for instance, in the ability fully to control the appointment of subsidiary and divisional heads. This, for instance, was not the case at German energy company RWE, where external political factors affected appointments of sub-unit heads, or at the French conglomerate Matra Hachette, where a large shareholder had operational responsibility for one of the major businesses. Finally, there were criteria dealing with the formal aspects of organizational structure, including the organizational chart, but also the existence of corporate-wide procedures and systems, common systems of accounting and control, and efforts to integrate overlapping businesses into coherent and discrete units.

Appendix I classifies each company by structure.

PERFORMANCE

Studies of strategy, structure, and performance in Europe typically confine themselves to public companies—as we see in Chapter 4, not necessarily typical of their economies (Bühner, 1987; Cable and Dirrheimer, 1983). A particular feature of our populations—domestically-owned Top 100 industrial firms in each country—is that they include many private, non-quoted companies. As a consequence, we have been unable to rely simply on the large standard databases for our performance figures.

The United Kingdom was the easiest case, providing computerized performance data on the overwhelming majority of companies through Datastream. The few gaps were filled directly from annual reports, on a consistent basis. In France, all data were obtained direct from annual reports, existing databases proving too patchy and inconsistent for reliable use, especially for the earlier period. Many of the older annual reports were sourced directly from the archives of Crédit Lyonnais. In Germany, again data came directly from annual reports, and also from the *Bundesanzeiger* and the *Wegweiser durch deutsche Unternehmen*.

Full performance analyses, using various financial performance measures, are available in Mayer (1999).

References

Albert, M. (1991). *Capitalisme contre capitalisme*. Paris: Editions Du Seuil.

Aldrich, H. (1988). 'Paradigm Warriors: Donaldson versus the Critics in Organization Theory'. *Organization Studies*, 9: 20–5.

Alford, B. W. W. (1994). 'Chandlerism: the New Orthodoxy of US and European Corporate Development'. *Journal of European Economic History*, 23/3: 631–43.

Armour, H. O. and Teece, D. J. (1978). 'Organisational Structure and Economic Performance: A Test of the Multidivisional Hypothesis'. *Bell Journal of Economics*, 9: 106–22.

Barham, K. and Heimer, C. (1998). *ABB: The Dancing Giant*. London: Pitman Publishing.

Bartlett, C. and Ghoshal, S. (1993). 'Beyond the M-Form: Towards a Managerial Theory of the Firm', *Strategic Management Journal* (Special Issue), 14: 23–46.

Batsch, L. (1993). *La Croissance des groupes industriels*. Paris: Economica.

Bauer, M. and Bertin-Mourot, B. (1996). *Vers un modele européen de dirigeants? Comparison Allemagne/France/Grand-Bretagne*. Paris: CNRS/Boyden.

Bauer, M., Bertin-Mourot, B., and Thobois, P. (1995). *Les No. 1 des 200 plus grandes entreprises en France et en Grande-Bretagne*. Paris: CNRS/Boyden.

Bauman, Z. (1991). *Modernity and Ambivalence*. Cambridge: Polity Press.

Baumol, W. J. (1962). 'On the Theory of the Expansion of the Firm'. *American Economic Review*, 52: 1078–87.

Becht, M. and Boehmer, E. (1998). 'Transparency of Ownership and Control in Germany', *European corporate governance network*, http://www.ecgn.ulb.ac.be.

Bergh, D. and Holbein, G. (1997). 'Assessment and Redirection of Longitudinal Analysis: Demonstration With a Study of Diversification and Divestiture Relationship'. *Strategic Management Journal*, 18/7: 557–71.

Berghahn, V. R. (1987). *The Americanization of West German Industry, 1945–1973*. Leamington Spa: Berg.

Berglöf, E. (1990). 'Capital Structure as a Mechanism for Control', in M. Aoki, B. Gustafsson, and O. E. Williamson (eds.), *The Firm as a Nexus of Treaties*. London: Sage, 237–62.

Berle, A. A. and Means, G. C. (1932). *The Modern Corporation and Private Property*. New York: Macmillan.

Bettis, R. (1991). 'Strategic Management and the Straight-Jacket: an Editorial Essay'. *Organization Science*, 2/3: 315–19.

Bhagat, S., Shleifer, A., and Vishny, R. (1990). 'Hostile Takeovers in the 1980s: the Return to Corporate Specialization'. *Brookings Papers: Microeconomics*, 1–84.

Braverman, H. (1974). *Labor and Monopoly Capital: the Degradation of Work in the Twentieth Century*. New York: Monthly Review Press.

Broadberry, S. N. (1997). *The Productivity Race: British Manufacturing in International Perspective, 1850–1990*. Cambridge: Cambridge University Press.

Brummer, A. and Cowe, R. (1994). *Hanson: the Rise and Rise of Britain's Most Buccaneering Businessman*. London: Fourth Estate.

Bühner, R. (1985). 'Internal Organisation and Return: an Empirical Analysis of Large Diversified German Corporations', in J. Schwalbach (ed.), *Industry Structure and Peformance*. Berlin: Edition Sigma, 197–222.

——(1987). 'Assessing International Diversification of West German Corporations'. *Strategic Management Journal*, 8: 25–37.

——(1992). *Management Holding: Unternehmensstruktur der Zukunft*. Landsberg am Lech: Verlage Moderne Industrie.

Burrell, G. and Morgan, G. (1979). *Sociological Paradigms and Organizational Analysis*. London: Heinemann.

Cable, J. and Dirrheimer, M. J. (1983). 'Hierarchies and Markets: an Empirical Test of the Multidivisional Hypothesis in West Germany'. *International Journal of Industrial Organization*, 1: 43–62.

Calori, R., Lubatkin, M., Very, P., and Veiga, J. (1997). 'Modelling the Origins of Nationally-Bound Administrative Heritages: a Historical Institutional Analysis of French and British Firms'. *Organization Science*, 8/6: 681–96.

Callas, M. B. and Smircich, L. (1999). 'Past Postmodernism? Reflections and Tentative Discussions'. *Academy of Management Review*, 24/4: 649–71.

Canals, J. (1996). *Economic Performance and Bank-Industry Relationships*. Paper presented at the EMOT workshop. Berlin.

Capon, N., Christodolou, C., Farley, J. U., and Hubert, J. (1987). 'A Comparative Analysis of the Strategy and Structure of United States and Australian Corporations'. *Journal of International Business Studies*, 18: 51–84.

Carroll, P. N. and Noble, D. W. (1977). *The Free and the Unfree: a New History of the United States*. Harmondsworth, Middlesex: Penguin.

Cassis, Y. (1997). *Big Business: the European Experience in the Twentieth Century*. Oxford: Oxford University Press.

Castells, M. (1996). *The Rise of the Network Society, i. The Information Age: Economy, Society, and Culture*. Oxford: Blackwell.

Chandler, A. D. jun. (1962). *Strategy and Structure: Chapters in the History of the Industrial Enterprise*. Cambridge, Mass.: The MIT Press.

——(1977). *The Visible Hand: Managerial Revolution in American Business*. Cambridge, Mass.: The MIT Press.

——(1982). 'The M-Form: Industrial Groups, American Style'. *European Economic Review*, 18/3–23.

——(1984). 'The Emergence of Managerial Capitalism', *Business History Review*, 58: 473–503.

——(1990). *Scale and Scope, The Dynamics of Industrial Capitalism*. Cambridge, Mass.: Harvard University Press.

——(1991). 'The Function of the HQ Unit in the Multibusiness Firm'. *Strategic Management Journal*, 12: 31–50.

——(1992). Corporate Strategy, Structure and Control Methods in the United States during the 20th Century'. *Industrial and Corporate Change*, 1: 263–84.

——(1996). 'Corporate Strategy, Structure and Control Methods in the United States During the Twentieth Century', in G. Dosi and F. Malerba (eds.), *Organization and Strategy in the Evolution of the Enterprise*. Basingstoke: Macmillan, 223–45.

——(1997). 'The United States: Engines of Economic Growth in Capital-Intensive and Knowledge-intensive Industries, in A. D. Chandler, F. Amatori, and T. Hikino (eds.), *Big Business and the Wealth of Nations*. Cambridge: Cambridge University Press, 63–101.

——Amatori, F. and Hikino, T. (1997). 'Introduction', in A. D. Chandler jun., F. Amatori, and T. Hikino (eds.), *Big Business and the Wealth of Nations*. Cambridge: Cambridge University Press.

——and Hikino, T. (1997). 'The Large Industrial Enterprise and the Dynamics of Modern Economic Growth', in A. D. Chandler jun., F. Amatori, and T. Hikino (eds.), *Big Business and the Wealth of Nations*. Cambridge: Cambridge University Press, 24–57.

Chang, S. J. and Choi, U. (1988). 'Strategy, Structure and Performance of Korean Business Groups: a Transaction Cost Approach'. *Strategic Management Journal*, 10/2: 141–58.

Channon, D. F. (1973). *The Strategy and Structure of British Enterprise*. London: The Macmillan Press.

Chia, R. (1995). 'From Modern to Postmodern Organizational Analysis'. *Organization Studies*, 16/4: 580–605.

——(1997). 'Essai: Thirty Years On: from Organizational Structures to the Organization of Thought'. *Organization Studies*, 18/4: 685–708.

Child, J. (1972). 'Organizational Structure, Environment and Performance: the Role of Strategic Choice'. *Sociology*, 6: 1–22.

——(1981). 'Culture, Contingency and Capitalism in the Cross National Study of Organizations', in L. L. Cummings and B. M. Staw (eds.), *Research in Organizational Behavior*. Greenwhich, Conn.: JAI Press, 303–56.

——(1982). 'Divisionalization and Size—a Comment on the Donaldson-Grinyer Debate'. *Organization Studies*, 3/4: 351–3.

Clegg, S. (1990). *Modern Organization: Organization Studies in the Postmodern World*. London: Sage.

Coase, R. H. (1937). 'The Nature of the Firm'. *Economica*, NS 4: 13–16, November, 386–405. Reprinted in B. E. Supple (ed.), (1992). *The Rise of Big Business*. Aldershot: Edward Elgar, 111–30.

Coffee, J. C. jun. (1996). 'Institutional Investors in Transitional Economies', in R. Frydman, C. W. Gray, and A. Rapaczynski (eds.), *Corporate Governance in Central Europe and Russia, i. Banks, Funds, and Foreign Investors*. Budapest: Central European University Press, 111–86.

Couret, A. and Martin, D. (1991). *Les Sociétés holdings*. Paris: Presses Universitaires de France.

Daems, H. (1978). *The Holding Company and Corporate Control*. Martinus Nijhoff: Leiden.

Davies, S., Matraves, C., Petts, D., and Röller, L.-H. (1999). *The Corporate Structure of UK and German Manufacturing Firms: Changes in Response to the SEM*. London: Anglo-German Foundation.

Davis, G. F., Tinsley, C. H., and Diekmann, K. A. (1994). 'The Decline and Fall of the Conglomerate Firm in the 1980s: the Deinstitutionalization of an Organizational Form'. *American Sociological Review*, 59: 547–70.

Dess, G. A., Gupta, G., Hennart, J. F., and Hill, C. W. L. (1995). 'Conducting and Integrating Strategy Research at the International, Corporate, and Business Levels: Issues and Directions'. *Journal of Management*, 21/3: 357–93.

DiMaggio, P. and Powell, W. W. (1983). 'The Iron Cage Revisited: Institutional Isomorphism and Collective Rationality in Organizational Fields'. *American Sociological Review*, 48: 147–60.

Dittus, P. and Prowse, S. (1996). 'Corporate Control in Central Europe and Russia:

Should Banks Own Shares?', in R. Frydman, C. W. Gray, and T. Rybczynsiki (eds.), *Corporate Governance in Central Europe and Russia, i. Banks, Funds and Foreign Investors.* Budapest: Central European University Press, 20–67.

Djelic, M.-L. (1998). *Exporting the American Model: the Postwar Transformation of European Business.* Oxford: Oxford University Press.

Donaldson, L. (1982). 'Divisionalization and Size—a Theoretical and Empirical Critique'. *Organization Studies,* 3/4: 321–37.

——(1995). *American Anti-Management Theories of Organizations: a Critique of Paradigm Proliferation,* Cambridge: Cambridge University Press.

——(1996). *For Positivist Organization Theory.* London: Sage.

Dosi, G. and Kogut, B. (1993). 'National Specificities and the Context of Change: the Coevolution of Organization and Technology', in B. Kogut (ed.), *Country Competitiveness: Technology and the Organization of Work.* New York: Oxford University Press, 249–62.

Dosi, G., Teece, D. J., and Winter, S. (1992). 'Towards a Theory of Corporate Coherence: Preliminary Remarks', in G. Dosi, R. Gianetti, and P. A. Tonnelli (eds.), *Technology and Enterprise in a Historical Perspective.* Oxford: Clarendon, 185–211.

Doyle, P. (1990). 'Britain's Left and Right-Handed Companies: the Corporate Philosophies of Britain's Chief Executives'. *MBA Review,* March/5–9.

Drucker, P. (1946). *The Concept of the Corporation.* London: John Day.

Dyas, G. P. (1972). 'Strategy and Structure of French Enterprise', unpublished doctoral dissertation, Cambridge, Mass.: Harvard Business School.

——and Thanheiser, H. (1976). *The Emerging European Enterprise.* London: Macmillan.

Eberwein, W. and Tholen, J. (1993). *Euro-Manager or Splendid Isolation? International Management. An Anglo-German Comparison.* Berlin: de Gruyter.

Edwards, C. D. (1955). 'Conglomerate Bigness as a Source of Power'. *National Bureau Committee for Economic Research, Business Concentration and Price Policy.* Princeton: Princeton University Press, 331–60.

Edwards, J. and Fischer, K. (1994). *Banks, Finance and Investment in Germany.* Cambridge: Cambridge University Press.

Espeland, W. N. and Hirsch, P. (1990). 'Ownership Changes, Accounting Practice the Redefinition of the Corporation'. *Accounting, Organizations and Society,* 15/1–2: 77–96.

Ferguson, C. H. (1990). 'Computers and the Coming of the US Keiretsu'. *Harvard Business Review,* July–August, 55–70.

Fligstein, N. (1985). 'The Spread of the Multidivisional Form Among Large Firms'. *American Sociological Review,* 50: 377–91.

——(1987). 'The Intraorganizational Power Struggle: Rise of Finance Personnel to Top Leadership in Large Corporations'. *American Sociological Review,* 52: 44–58.

——(1990). *The Transformation of Corporate Control.* Cambridge, Mass.: Harvard University Press.

——and Brantley, P. (1992). 'Bank control, owner control or organizational dynamics: who controls the modern corporation?' *American Journal of Sociology,* 98/2: 280–307.

Franks, J. and Mayer, C. (1990). 'Capital Markets and Corporate Control: a Study of France, Germany and the UK'. *Economic Policy,* 10: 189–231.

——and ——(1998). '*Ownership and Control of German Corporations.*' Working Paper, Said Business School, University of Oxford.

Freeland, R. F. (1996). 'The Myth of the M-Form? Governance, Consent and Organizational Change'. *American Journal of Sociology,* 102: 483–526.

Fruin, M. (1992). *The Japanese Enterprise System: Competitive Strategies and Cooperative Structures.* Oxford: Clarendon Press.

Fukao, M. (1995). *Financial Integration, Corporate Governance, and the Performance of Multinational Companies.* Washington, DC: The Brookings Institution.

Galbraith, J. K. (1967). *The New Industrial State.* Boston: Houghton Mifflin.

Gall, L. (1995). *The Deutsche Bank, 1870–1995*, London: Weidenfeld & Nicolson.

Gerlach, M. (1992). 'The Japanese Corporate Network: a Blockmodel Analysis', *Administrative Science Quarterly*, 37: 105–26.

Ghoshal, S. and Bartlett, C. (1995). 'Changing the Role of Top Management: from Structure to Process'. *Harvard Business Review*, Jan.–Feb.: 86–96.

—— and ——(1998). *The Individualized Corporation.* London: Heinemann.

Giddens, A. (1979). *Central Problems in Social Theory*, London: Macmillan.

Godellier, E. (1995). *De la stratégie locale à la stratégie globale: La formation d'une identité de groupe chez Usinor*, Paris: Doctoral Thesis, Ecole des Hautes Etudes en Sciences Sociales.

Gordon, R. A. and Howell, J. E. (1959). *Higher Education for Business.* New York: Columbia University Press.

Gospel, H. (1992). *Markets, Firms and the Management of Labour in Modern Britain.* Cambridge: Cambridge University Press.

Granovetter, M. (1985). 'Economic Action and Social Structure: the Problem of Embeddedness'. *American Journal of Sociology*, 91/3: 481–510.

——(1995). 'Coase Revisited: Business Groups in the Modern Economy'. *Industrial and Corporate Change*, 4/1: 93–130.

Grant, R. M. (1988). 'On Dominant Logic, Relatedness and the Link between Diversity and Performance'. *Strategic Management Journal*, 9/6: 639–42.

——and Jammine, A. P. (1988). 'Performance Differences between the Wrigley-Rumelt Strategic Categories'. *Strategic Management Journal*, 9/4: 333–46.

——, ——, and Thomas, H. (1988). 'Diversity, Diversification, and Profitability Among British Manufacturing Companies, 1972–84'. *Academy of Management Review*, 31/4: 771–801.

Gray, J. (1998). *False Dawn: the Delusions of Global Capitalism.* London: Granta.

Guillén, M. F. (1994). *Models of Management: Work, Authority and Organization in a Comparative Perspective.* Chicago: University of Chicago Press.

Hadlock, C. J. and Lumer, G. B. (1997). 'Compensation, Turnover and Top Management Incentives: Historical Evidence'. *The Journal of Business*, 70/2: 153–87.

Hahn, D. (1994). *Planungs und Kontrollrechnung.* Wiesbaden: Gabler.

Halal, W. E. (1993). 'The Transition from Hierarchy to . . . What?', in W. E. Halal, A. Geranmayeh, and J. Pourdehnda (eds.), *Internal Markets: Bringing the Power of Free Enterprise Inside Your Organization.* New York: John Wiley, 27–51.

Hall, E. H. and St John, C. H. (1994). 'A Methodological Note on Diversity Measurement', *Strategic Management Journal*, 15: 153–68.

Hamilton, R. T. and Shergill, G. S. (1993). *The Logic of New Zealand Business: Strategy, Structure and Performance.* Auckland: Oxford University Press.

Hampden-Turner, C. and Trompenaars, F. (1993). *The Seven Cultures of Capitalism.* London: Piatkus.

Hamilton, G. C. and Biggart, N. W. (1988). 'Market, Cultures and Authority: a Congarative Analysis of Management and Organisation in the Far East'. *American Journal of Sociology*, 94 Supplement: 52–94.

Hamilton, G. G. and Feenstra, R. C. (1995). 'Varieties of Hierarchies and Markets: an Introduction'. *Industrial and Corporate Change*, 4/1: 51–91.

Handy, C. (1992). 'Balancing Corporate Power: a New Federalist Paper'. *Harvard Business Review*, 59–72.

Hannah, L. (1977). *Concentration in Modern Industry: Theory, Measurement, and the UK Experience*, London: Macmillan.

——(1991). 'Scale and Scope: Towards a European Invisible Hand?'. *Business History*, 33: 297–309.

——(1998). 'Survival and Size Mobility Among the World's Largest Industrial Corporations, 1912–1995'. *American Economic Review*, 88/2: 62–5.

Hatfield, D. E., Liebeskind, J. P., and Opler, T. C. (1996). 'The Effects of Corporate Restructuring on Aggregate Industry Specialisation'. *Strategic Management Journal*, 17/1: 55–72.

Hayes, R. H. and Abernathy, W. (1980). 'Managing Our Way to Economic Decline'. *Harvard Business Review*, July–August, 67–85.

Hayward, M. L. and Hambrick, D. C. (1997). 'Explaining the Premium Paid for Large Acquisitions: Evidence of CEO Hubris'. *Administrative Science Quarterly*, 42/1: 103–27.

Hedlund, G. (1994). 'A Model of Knowledge Management and the N-Form Corporation'. *Strategic Management Journal*, 15: 73–90.

Hickson, D. J., Hinings, C. R., McMillan, C. J., and Schwitter, J. P. (1974). 'The Culture-Free Context of Organization Structure, A Tri-National Comparison'. *Sociology*, 8: 59–80.

Hill, C. W. (1988). 'Internal Capital Market Controls and Financial Performance in Multidivisional Firms', *Journal of Industrial Economics*, 37/1: 67–82.

Hofstede, G. (1980). *Culture's Consequences*. Newbury Park, CA: Sage.

——(1991). *Cultures and Organizations*. London: McGraw Hill.

Holland, S. (1976). *The Socialist Challenge*. London: Quartet.

Hollingsworth, J. R., Schmitter, P. C., and Streeck, W. (eds.) (1994). *Governing Capitalist Economies: Performance and Control of Economic Sectors*. Oxford: Oxford University Press.

Hollingsworth, J. R. and Boyer, R. (1997). 'The Coordination of Economic Actors and Social Systems of Production', in J. R. Hollingsworth and R. Boyer (eds.), *Contemporary Capitalism: the Embeddedness of Institutions*. Cambridge: Cambridge University Press, 1–54.

Hoskisson, R. E. and Hitt, M. A. (1994*). Downscoping—How to Tame the Diversified Firm*. New York: Oxford University Press.

Hoskisson, R. E., Hill, C.W. L., and Kim, H. (1993). 'The Multidivisional Structure: Organisational Fossil or Source of Value'. *Journal of Management*, 19: 269–98.

Hoskisson, R. E. and Johnson, R. A. (1992). 'Corporate Restructuring and Strategic Change: the Effect on Diversification Strategy and R&D Intensity'. *Strategic Management Journal*, 13: 625–34.

Hu, Y.-S. (1992). 'Global or Stateless Corporations are National Firms with International Subsidiaries'. *California Management Review*, 34/2: 107–26.

Jelinek, M. A. (1979). *Institutionalizing Innovation: a Study of Organizational Learning Systems*. New York: Praeger.

John, R. R. (1997). 'Elaborations, Revisions, Dissents: Alfred D Chandler Jr.'s The Visible Hand after Twenty Years'. *Business History Review*, 71/2: 151–200.

Jones, G. (1997). 'Global Perspectives and British Paradoxes'. *Business History Review*, 71/2: 291–8.

Jong, H. W. de (1997). 'The Corporate Triangle: the Structure and Performance of Corporate Systems in a Global Economy', in W. Lazonick (ed.), *The Corporate Triangle: the Structure and Performance of Corporate Systems in a Global Economy.* Oxford: Blackwell, 34–61.

Kadushin, C. (1995). 'Friendship Amongst the French Financial Elite'. *American Sociological Review*, 60: 202–21.

Kay, N. M. (1997). *Pattern in Corporate Evolution.* Oxford: Oxford University Press.

Kerdellant, C. (1992). *Les Nouveaux Condottières.* Paris: Calman-Levy.

Kerr, C., Dunlop, J. T., Harbison, F. H., and Myers, C. A. (1960). *Industrialism and Industrial Man.* Boston, Mass.: Harvard University Press.

Khanna, T. and Palepu, K. (1999). 'Policy Shocks, Market Intermediaries, and Corporate Strategy: the Evolution of Business Groups in Chile and India', *Journal of Economics and Management Strategy*, 8/2: 271–310.

Kilduff, M. and Mehra, A. (1997). 'Postmodernism and Organizational Research', *Academy of Management Review*, 22/2: 453–81.

Kipping, M. (1999). 'American Management Consulting Companies in Western Europe, 1920 to 1990: Products, Reputation, and Relationships'. *Business History Review*, 73: 190–220.

Kocka, J. (1999). *Industrial Culture and Bourgeois Society: Business Labor and Bureaucracy in Modern Germany.* New York: Bergham Books.

Kogut, B. (1992). 'National Organizing Principles of Work and the Erstwhile Dominance of the American Multinational Corporation'. *Industrial and Corporate Change*, 1: 285–325.

——and Parkinson, D. (1993). 'The Diffusion of American Organizing Principles to Europe', in B. Kogut (ed.), *Country Competitiveness: Technology and the Organization of Work.* New York: Oxford University Press.

—— and ——(1998). 'Adoption of the Multidivisional Structure: Analyzing History from the Start'. *Industrial and Corporate Change*, 7: 249–73.

Kono, T. (1984). *Strategy and Structure of Japanese Enterprises.* London: Macmillan.

Kuisel, R. F. (1993). *Seducing the French: the Dilemma of Americanization.* London: University of California Press.

Lane, C. (1989). *Management and Labour in Europe.* Aldershot: Edward Elgar.

——(1991). 'Industrial Reorganization in Europe: Patterns of Convergence and Divergence in Germany, France and Britain'. *Work, Employment and Society*, 5/4: 515–39.

——(1995). *Industry and Society in Europe: Stability and Change in Britain, Germany and France.* Aldershot, Hants: Edward Elgar.

Lawrence, P. and Lorsch, J. W. (1967). *Organization and Environment: Managing Differentiation and Integration.* Boston, Mass.: Harvard Business School.

Lazonick, W. (1991). *Business Organisation and the Myth of the Market Economy.* Cambridge: Cambridge University Press.

Lichtenberg, F. R. (1992). 'Industrial De-Diversification and Its Consquences for Productivity'. *Journal of Economic Behavior and Organization*, 18: 427–38.

Liedtke, R. (1993). *Wem gehört die Republik?* Frankfurt am Main: Eichborn.

Littler, C. (1982). *The Development of the Labour Process in Capitalist Societies.* London: Heinemann.

Locke, R. R. (1989). *Management and Higher Education Since 1940: the Influence of America and Japan on West Germany, Great Britain and France.* Cambridge: Cambridge University Press.

Locke, R. R. (1996). *The Collapse of the American Management Mystique*. Oxford University Press.

Luffman, G. A. and Reed, R. (1982). 'Diversification in British Industry in the 1970s'. *Strategic Management Journal*, 3: 303–14.

Lyotard, J.-F. (1984). *The Postmodern Condition: a Report on Knowledge*. Manchester: Manchester University Press.

McArthur, J. and Scott, B. (1969). *Industrial Planning in France*. Boston, Mass.: Harvard Business School.

McCraw, T. K. (1988). 'Introduction: the Intellectual Odyssey of Alfred D. Chandler, Jr.', in T. K. McCraw (ed.), *The Essential Alfred Chandler*. Boston, Mass.: Harvard Business School Press, 1–21.

Mahoney, J. T. (1992). 'The Adoption of the Multidivisional Form of Organization: a Contingency Model'. *Journal of Management Studies*, 29/1: 49–72.

McKenna, C. D. (1997). 'The American Challenge: McKinsey & Company's Role in the Transfer of Decentralization to Europe, 1957–1975'. *Academy of Management Best Paper Proceedings*, 226–31.

Markides, C. C. (1995). *Diversification, Refocusing, and Economic Performance*. Cambridge, Mass.: The MIT Press.

——and Williamson, P. J. (1996). 'Corporate Diversification and Organizational Structure: a Resource Based View'. *Academy of Management Journal*, 39/2: 340–67.

Marris, R. (1964). *The Economic Theory of Managerial Capitalism*. London: Macmillan.

Mayer, C. (1994).The Assessment: Money and Banking: Theory and Evidence. *Oxford Review of Economic Policy*, 10/4: 1–13.

Mayer, M. (1999). 'Large Industrial Firms in Western Europe: Strategy, Structure and Performance in Social Context'. Unpublished Ph.D., University of Warwick.

——and Whittington, R. (1996). 'The Survival of the European Holding Company: Institutional Choice and Contingency', in R. Whitley and P. H. Kristensen (eds.), *The Changing European Firm*, London: Routledge, 87–112.

—— and ——(1999). 'Strategy, Structure and "Systemness": National Institutions and Corporate Change in France, Germany and the UK, 1950–1993'. *Organization Studies*, 20/6: 933–60.

Meyer, J. W. and Rowan, B. (1977). Institutionalized Organizations: Formal Structure as Myth and Ceremony. *American Journal of Sociology*, 83: 340–63.

Miles, R. E. and Snow, C. (1992). 'Causes of Failure in Network Organizations'. *California Management Review*, 34/4: 53–72.

——, ——, Mathews, J., Miles, G., and Coleman, H. J. (1997). 'Organizing in the Knowledge Age: Anticipating Cellular Forms'. *Academy of Management Executive*, 11/4: 7–24.

Mintzberg, H. (1979). *The Structuring of Organizations*. Englewood Cliffs, NJ: Prentice Hall.

Mitchell, B. R. (1976). *European Historical Statistics*. London: Macmillan.

Montgomery, C. A. (1994). 'Corporate Diversification'. *Journal of Economic Perspectives* 8/3: 163–78.

Morin, F. and Dupuy, C. (1993). *Le Coeur financier européen*. Paris: Economica.

Mork, R., Shleifer, A., and Vishny, R. (1990). 'Do Managerial Objectives Drive Bad Acquisitions?'. *Journal of Finance*, 45/1: 31–48.

Mouzelis, N. (1995). *Sociological Theory: What Went Wrong?* London: Routledge.

Mowery, D. C. (1992). Finance and Corporate Evolution in Five Industrial Economies, 1900–1950. *Industrial and Corporate Change*, 1/1: 1–36.

Nibler, M. (1998). 'Bank Control and Corporate Performance in Germany: the Evidence'. Unpublished Ph.D., University of Cambridge.

Nouzille, V. (1998). *L'Acrobate: Jean-Luc Lagardère, ou, les armes du pouvoir*, Paris: Seuil.

Odagiri, H. (1992). *Growth Through Competition; Competition Through Growth: Strategic Management and the Economy in Japan*. London: Oxford University Press.

Ouchi, W. G. (1980). 'Markets, Bureaucracies and Clans'. *Administrative Science Quarterly*, 25: 129–41.

Palmer, D. A., Devereaux Jennings, P., Zhou, X. (1993). 'Late Adoption of the Multidivisional Form by Large U.S. Corporations: Institutional, Political, and Economic Accounts'. *Administrative Science Quarterly*, 38: 100–31.

——, Friedland, R., Devereaux Jennings, P., and Powers, M. (1987). 'The Economics and Politics of Structure: the Multidivisional Form and the Large U.S. Corporation'. *Administrative Science Quarterly*, 32: 25–48.

Parks, S. J. (1985). *Reconstructing Marxian Economics*. New York: Praeger.

Parsons, T. (1964). 'Evolutionary Universals in Society'. *American Sociological Review*, 29: 339–57.

——(1966). *Sociological Theory and Modern Society*. New York: Free Press.

Pascale, R. T. (1990). *Managing on the Edge*. New York: Simon & Schuster.

Pavan, R. J. (1976). 'Strategy and Structure: the Italian Experience'. *Journal of Economics and Business*, 28: 254–60.

Penrose, E. (1959). *The Theory of Growth of the Firm*, New York: John Wiley & Sons.

Peters, T. J. and Waterman, R. H. jun. (1982). *In Search of Excellence: Lessons From America's Best-run Companies*. New York: Harper & Row.

Pettigrew, A. and Fenton, E. (2000). *The Innovating Organization*, London/Thousand Oaks: Sage.

Pfeffer, J. (1997). *New Directions in Organization Theory*. New York: Oxford University Press.

Pierson, F. C. et al. (1959). *The Education of American Businessmen*. New York: McGraw Hill.

Piore, M. J. and Sabel, C. F. (1984). *The Second Industrial Divide*. New York: Basic Books.

Prahalad, C. K. and Bettis, R. (1986). 'The Dominant Logic: a New Linkage between Diversity and Performance'. *Strategic Management Journal*, 7: 485–501.

—— and Hamel, G. (1990). 'The Core Competence of the Corporation'. *Harvard Business Review*, 68/3: 79–91.

Prowse, S. (1995). 'Corporate Governance in International Perspective: a Survey of Corporate Control Mechanisms Amongst Large Firms in the US, UK, Japan and Germany'. *Financial Markets, Institutions and Instruments*, 4/1: 1–63.

Pugh, D. S. and Hinings, C. R. (1976). *Organizational Structure: Extensions and Replications: the Aston Programme II*. Farnborough, Hants: Saxon House.

Reed, M. (1986). *Redirections in Organizational Analysis*. London: Tavistock.

Robins, J. and Wiersema, M. F. (1995). 'A Resource-Based Approach to the Multibusiness Firm: Empirical Analysis of Portfolio Interrelationships and Corporate Financial Performance'. *Strategic Management Journal*, 16: 277–99.

Roll, R. (1986). 'The Hubris Hypothesis of Corporate Takeovers', *Journal of Business*, 59/2: 197–216.

Romanelli, E. and Tushman, M. L. (1994). 'Organizational Transformation as Punctuated Equilibrium: an Empirical Test'. *Academy of Management Journal*, 37/5: 1,141–56.

Rondi, L., Sembenelli, A., and Ragazzi, E. (1996). 'Determinants of Diversification Patterns', in S. Davies and R. Lyons (eds.), *Structure, Strategy and Competitive Mechanisms*. Oxford: Clarendon Press.

Rostow, W. W. (1960). *Stages of Economic Growth: a Non-Communist Manifesto*. Cambridge: Cambridge University Press.

Roy, W. G. (1997). *Socializing Capital: the Rise of the Large Industrial Corporation in America*. Princeton, NJ: Princeton University Press.

Ruigrok, W. and Tulder, R. van (1995). *The Logic of International Restructuring*. London: Routledge.

Ruigrok, W., Achtenhagen, L., Wagner, M., and Rüegg-Stürm, J. (2000). 'ABB: Beyond the Global Matrix—Towards the Network Multidivisional Organization', in A. Pettigrew and E. Fenton (eds.). *The Innovating Organization*, London/Thousand Oaks: Sage.

Rumelt, R. P. (1974). *Strategy, Structure and Economic Performance*. Cambridge, Mass.: Harvard University Press.

——(1982). 'Diversification Strategy and Profitability'. *Strategic Management Journal*, 3: 359–69.

——, Schendel, D., and Teece, D. (1994). 'Fundamental Issues in Strategy', in R. Rumelt, D. Schendel, and D. Teece (eds.), *Fundamental Issues in Strategy*. Boston: Harvard Business School Press.

Sako, M. (1992). *Prices, Quality and Trust: Interfirm Relations in Britain and Japan*. London: Cambridge University Press.

Schleifer, A. and Vishny, R. W. (1996). 'Large Shareholders and Corporate Control'. *Journal of Political Economy*, 94: 461–88.

Schmidt, V. A. (1996). *From State to Market? The Transformation of French Business and Government*. Cambridge: Cambridge University Press.

Schmitz, R. (1989). 'Zur Erfolgsrelevanz der interne Organisation börsennotierter Industrieaktiengesellschaften', in H. Albach, *Organisation*, Wiesbaden: Gabler.

Scott, B. R. (1973). 'The Industrial State: Old Myths and New Realities'. *Harvard Business Review*, March–April, 135–48.

Scott, J. (1997). *Corporate Business and Capitalist Classes*. Oxford: Oxford University Press.

Servan Schreiber, J.-J. (1969). *The American Challenge*. New York: Avon Books.

Servan Schreiber, J.-L. (1993). *Le Métier de patron*. Paris: Fayard.

Shaw, C. (1995). 'Engineers in the Boardroom: Britain and France Compared', in Y. Cassis (ed.), *Management and Business in Britain and France*. Oxford: Oxford University Press, 159–70.

Shenhav, Y. (1999). *Manufacturing Rationality*. Oxford: Oxford University Press.

Shutt, J. and Whittington, R. (1987). 'Fragmentation Strategies and the Rise of Small Units: Cases from the North West'. *Regional Studies*, 21/1: 13–23.

Sorge, A. (1991). 'Strategic Fit and the Societal Effect: Interpreting Cross-National Comparisons of Technology, Organization and Human Resources'. *Organization Studies*, 12/2: 161–90.

Spender, J. C. (1992). 'Business Policy and Strategy: an Occasion for Despair, a Retreat to Disciplinary Specialization, or for New Excitement?' *Academy of Management, Best Papers, Proceedings*, 1992, 42–6.

——and Grant, R. M. (1996). 'Knowledge and the Firm: Overview'. *Strategic Management Journal*, 17: 5–9.

Stearns, L. B. and Allan, K. D. (1996). 'Economic Behavior in Institutional Environments: the Corporate Merger Wave of the 1980s'. *American Sociological Review*, 61: 699–718.

Stewart, R. (1994). *Managing in Britain and Germany*. Basingstoke: Macmillan.

Strange, S. (1988). *States and Markets*. London: Pinter Publishers.

Supple, B. (1992). *The Rise of Big Business*. Aldershot: Elgar.

Suzuki, Y. (1991). *Japanese Management Structures, 1920–80*. Basingstoke: Macmillan.

Swords-Isherwood, N. (1980). 'British Management Compared', in K. Pavitt (ed.), *Technological Innovation and British Economic Performance*. London: Macmillan, 88–99.

Taylor, C. (1985). *Philosophy and the Human Sciences: Philosophical Papers 2*. Cambridge: Cambridge University Press.

Teece, D. J. (1993). 'The Dynamics of Industrial Capitalism: Perspectives on Scale and Scope'. *Journal of Economic Literature*, 31: 199–225.

——, Pisano, G., and Shuen, A. (1997). 'Dynamic Capabilities and Strategic Managment'. *Strategic Management Journal*, 18/7: 509–33.

Thanheiser, H. (1972). 'The Strategy and Structure of German Enterprise'. Unpublished doctoral dissertation, Harvard Business School.

Tichy, N. M. and Sherman, S. (1993). *Control Your Own Destiny or Someone Else Will: How General Electric is Revolutionising the Art of Management*. New York: Doubleday.

Toulmin, S. (1990). *Cosmopolis: the Hidden Agenda of Modernity*. Chicago: Chicago University Press.

UNCTAD (1996). *Companies without Borders: Transnational Corporations in the 1990s*. London: Thompson Business Press.

Volberda, H. (1998). *Building the Flexible Firm: How to Remain Competitive*. Oxford: Oxford University Press.

Weber, M. (1947). *The Theory of Social and Economic Organization*, New York: Free Press.

Wernerfelt, B. (1984). 'A Resource Based View of the Firm'. *Strategic Management Journal*, 5: 171–80.

Whitley, R. (1991). 'The Social Construction of Business Systems in East Asia'. *Organization Studies*, 12/1: 47–54.

—— (1992). *European Business Systems. Firms and Markets in their National Contexts*. London: Sage.

—— (1994). 'Dominant Form of Economic Organization in Market Economies'. *Organization Studies*, 15: 153–82.

—— (1996). 'The Social Construction of Economic Actors: Institutions and Types of Firm in Europe and other Market Economies', in R. Whitley and P. H. Kristensen (eds.), *The Changing European Firm: Limits to Convergence*. London: Routledge, 39–67.

—— (1999). *Divergent Capitalisms*. Oxford: Oxford University Press.

Whittington, R. (2000). 'Corporate Structure: from Policy to Practice', in A. Pettigrew, H. Thomas, and R. Whittington (eds.), *The Handbook of Strategy and Management*. London: Sage.

—— and Mayer, M. (1997). 'Beyond or Behind the M-Form? The Structures of European Business', in H. Thomas, D. O'Neal, and M. Ghertman (eds.), *Strategy, Structure and Style*. Chichester: John Wiley.

——, ——, and Curto, F. (1999). 'Chandlerism in Post-War Europe: Strategic and Structural Change in France, Germany and the UK, 1950–1993'. *Industrial and Corporate Change*, 8/3: 519–50.

——, Pettigrew, A., Peck, S., Fenton, E., and Conyon, M. (1999). 'Change and Complementarities in the New Competitive Landscape: a European Panel Study, 1992–1996'. *Organization Science*, 10/5: 583–600.

Wiener, M. (1981). *English Culture and the Decline of the Industrial Spirit, 1850–1980*. Cambridge: Cambridge University Press.

Williams, J. R., Paez, B. L., and Sanders, L. (1988). 'Conglomerates Revisited'. *Strategic Management Journal*, 9: 403–14.

Williamson, O. E. (1970). *Corporate Control and Business Behaviour: an Inquiry into the Effects of Organization Form on Enterprise Behaviour*. Englewood Cliffs, NJ: Prentice Hall.

——(1971). 'Managerial Discretion, Organization Form and the Multidivisional Hypothesis', in R. Marris and A. Wood (eds.), *The Corporate Economy*. London: Macmillan, 343–86.

——(1975). *Markets and Hierarchies: Analysis and Antitrust Implications*. New York: Collier Macmillan.

——and Bhargava, N. (1972). 'Assessing and Classifying the Internal Structure and Control Apparatus of the Modern Corporation', in K. Cowling (ed.), *Market Structure and Corporate Behaviour*. London: Gray Mills.

Windolf, P. and Beyer, J. (1995). 'Kooperativer Kapitalismus'. *Kölner Zeitschrift fuer Soziologie und Sozialpsychologie*, 47/1: 1–36.

Wood, S. and. Kelly, J. (1982). 'Taylorism, Responsible Autonomy and Management Strategy', in S. Wood (ed.), *The Degradation of Work?* London: Hutchinson, 74–89.

Woodward, J. (1965). *Industrial Organization: Theory and Practice*. London: Oxford University Press.

Woronoff, D. (1994). *Histoire de l'industrie en France*. Paris: Seuil.

Wrigley, L. (1970). 'Divisional Autonomy and Diversification'. Unpublished Ph.D. dissertation. Harvard Business School.

Zysman, J. (1983). *Governments, Markets and Growth*. Oxford: Martin Robertson.

——(1994). 'How Instititions Create Historically Rooted Trajectories of Growth'. *Industrial and Corporate Change*, 3: 243–83.

Index